A White-Collar Profession

▲

Best wishes in your career!

Jim Howard

A White-Collar Profession

**AFRICAN
AMERICAN
CERTIFIED
PUBLIC
ACCOUNTANTS
SINCE 1921**

Theresa A.
Hammond

The University of North Carolina Press
Chapel Hill and London

© 2002 The University of North Carolina Press
All rights reserved
Manufactured in the United States of America

Designed by Heidi Perov
Set in Minion and MetaPlus
by Keystone Typesetting, Inc.

The paper in this book meets the guidelines for permanence
and durability of the Committee on Production Guidelines for
Book Longevity of the Council on Library Resources.

Portions of this book have been reprinted with permission from
the *Proceedings* of the council meetings and annual meetings of
the American Institute of Certified Public Accountants, Inc.,
copyright 1941, 1942, 1965, and 1969.

Library of Congress Cataloging-in-Publication Data
Hammond, Theresa A.
A white-collar profession: African American certified public
accountants since 1921 / Theresa A. Hammond.
p. cm.
Includes bibliographical references and index.
ISBN 0-8078-2708-8 (cloth: alk. paper)
ISBN 0-8078-5377-1 (pbk.: alk. paper)
1. Accounting—United States—History—20th century.
2. African American accountants—Biography. I. Title.
HF5616.U5.H27 2002
331.6′396073—dc21 2001057010

cloth   06   05   04   03   02   5   4   3   2   1
paper   06   05   04   03   02   5   4   3   2   1

In grateful memory of

Richard Austin, CPA
Charles Beckett, CPA
Lincoln Harrison, CPA
Theodore Jones, CPA
Theodora Rutherford, CPA
Elmer Whiting, CPA

Contents

▲

Illustrations, Figures, and Table

▲

Acknowledgments

▲

This book would not have been possible without the generosity of pioneering African American CPAs who sat down and talked about their experiences with a total stranger. Several of them are now deceased, and this book is dedicated to their memory: Richard H. Austin, Michigan CPA 1941; Charles A. Beckett, Illinois CPA 1941; Lincoln J. Harrison, Louisiana CPA 1946; Theodore A. Jones, Illinois CPA 1940; Theodora F. Rutherford, West Virginia CPA 1960; and Elmer J. Whiting Jr., Ohio CPA 1950.

Talmadge Tillman Jr. met me at the airport, introduced me to everyone I interviewed in Los Angeles, and knew where to find every relevant document or article. He is a researcher's dream, and he became a dear friend. Bert Mitchell, who wrote a pioneering study of black CPAs in 1968, has been a source of encouragement and knowledge since I met him in 1989, while I was working on my dissertation.

Denise Streeter identified the first 100 African American CPAs in a study for the National Association of Black Accountants in 1990. She shared her findings with me and paved the way for this work. Sian Hunter at the University of North Carolina Press has been a wonderful supporter and adviser throughout this process. My sister Ruth E. Hammond used her writing expertise to improve every chapter. Boston College and Ernst & Young provided financial support, while my colleagues at Boston College provided moral support and were unfailingly helpful despite my nontraditional choice of research field. Paul Breines, Andy Buni, Maureen Chancey, Jeff Cohen, Gil Manzon, Jack Neuhauser, Kevin Newmark, Ron Pawliczek, Andrea Roberts, Ken Schwartz, Greg Trompeter, and Diane Vaughan all earned my gratitude.

Other people who provided comments and encouragement include Jane Ashley, Ida Robinson Backmon and her students at North Carolina A&T State University, Edder Bennett, Elizabeth Chambliss, Michael Clement, Christine Cooper, Pamela Davis, Cindy Desch, Carol Donelan, Anne Fleche, Finley Graves, Chris Hall, Pat Hammond, Jim Hayes, Mary Iber, Gregory Johnson,

Cheryl Lehman, Paul Miranti, Dan Mont, Richard Newman, Lucius Outlaw, Glenn Perkins, Gary Previts, Shannon Spahr, Arlene Stein, David Thomas, Cynthia Williams Turner, Paula Wald, Juliet Walker, David Wilkins, and the Reading Group on the Professions at Harvard Law School.

My research assistants, Juan Concepcion, Anna Diaz, Monique McNeil, Andrea Orr, and Jackie Taylor, went beyond the call of duty to track down obscure articles and to compile data. The librarians at Boston College have been exceptionally helpful, especially the interlibrary loan staff. At other libraries it seems that I was always asking questions until five minutes before closing, yet the librarians at the American Institute of CPAs, Atlanta University, Boston University, Columbia University, Howard University, the University of Illinois, Jackson State University, the New York Public Library's Schomburg Center for Research in Black Culture, the Auburn Avenue Research Library on African-American Culture and History, and North Carolina A&T State University were consistently patient.

Finally, two basketball players made me feel like this was a team project. Since 1991, when I conducted my first interview for the book, my BC colleague Betty Bagnani has shared my excitement. We must have walked a thousand miles while discussing what to do with the material I was gathering. I could slip a copy of my latest chapter under her door at 10 P.M., and invariably she would have comments by 10 A.M. the next day. Cal Bouchard joined the team near the end of the project, but she beat Betty's turnaround time, providing faxed comments from training camp within hours. She meticulously edited the footnotes and bibliography and remained cheerful and enthusiastic throughout a phenomenally tedious job. I don't know what I would do without either one of them.

I made every effort to honestly represent the experiences of the African Americans who shared their stories with me. We shared the same objective: as Theodora Rutherford put it, she was happy to participate "for the cause." The contributions of many, many people made this book possible, but any remaining errors, omissions, and misinterpretations are my own.

A White-Collar Profession

▲

1

The Whitest Profession

When Theodora Fonteneau Rutherford graduated summa cum laude from Howard University in 1923, she dreamed of becoming a certified public accountant (CPA). Her favorite accounting professor had encouraged the talented nineteen-year-old to strive for the pinnacle of the accounting profession, providing her with questions from prior CPA examinations to help her prepare. She earned a scholarship to Columbia University's graduate school of business, and she hoped that New York would provide opportunities that had been unavailable in the southern states in which she had been raised. Although she was bright, well-educated, hardworking, and determined, Rutherford was prevented from achieving her goal for the next thirty-seven years. When she finally became a CPA in 1960, she was one of only a few dozen African American CPAs in the entire country.

This book chronicles the stories of several of the pioneering African American men and women who managed to surmount the obstacles to becoming a CPA and whose history has been all but ignored. Their experiences paralleled those of African Americans who pursued other professions in the twentieth century. Segregated educational institutions posed challenges to acquiring the requisite expertise; white employers, whether hospitals, law firms, or CPA firms, were reluctant to hire African Americans; clientele were limited to the economically disadvantaged African American community; and professional societies held meetings in segregated hotels or excluded African Americans outright. The stories of these individuals provide a new and important perspective on the history of the professions, the perspective of those who fought to join elite occupations in which they were not welcome.

In the 1920s, African Americans were excluded from most professions. Exclusion—whether based on educational achievement or on race—is a tradi-

African American Representation in Three Professions, 1930, 1960, 1997

Year	Lawyers	Doctors	CPAs
1930	0.8%	2.5%	0.03%
1960	1.0	2.0	0.1
1997	2.7	4.2	Between 0.75 and 0.99

Sources: U.S. Bureau of the Census, *Fifteenth U.S. Census, 1930*, "Occupational Characteristics," table 13, *Eighteenth U.S. Census, 1960*, "Occupational Characteristics," table 3, and *Statistical Abstract of the United States, 1998*, 417–19; *History of Black Accountancy*, 8–15; Edwards, *History of Public Accounting*, 346–47; Bert Mitchell and Virginia Flintall, "The Status of the Black CPA: Twenty-Year Update," *JoA* 170, no. 2 (1990): 59–69; *Report on Minority Accounting Graduates, Enrollment, and Public Accounting Professionals*, 1997, AICPA Library; Julia Lawlor, "Blacks Counted Out of Accounting, Study Says," *USA Today*, 9 August 1990, B1; *Report on the Status of Blacks*.

tional method by which professions enhance their prestige. From their professional beginnings, both law and medicine found that limiting their ranks to the most powerful group in society—wealthy white males—reinforced their own power. CPAs adopted this strategy in the late nineteenth and early twentieth centuries, emulating the exclusivity of the more established professions.[1]

The dearth of African Americans among CPAs is not only a result of exclusion from well-paying professional positions but also the consequence of African Americans' exclusion from the financial sector. CPAs share the defining elements of other professions: a specified area of expertise, a government-granted monopoly over this expertise, and strict rules of entry and conduct. But unlike the quintessential professions of law and medicine, the work of a CPA is completely dependent upon the business activities that drive the American economy. This unique position is one cause of CPAs' status as the least diverse of the major professions.

Differences in the development of the professions help explain the variations in underrepresentation.[2] African American doctors and lawyers were denied participation in majority-white institutions for most of the twentieth century, but they were leaders in meeting the medical and legal needs of the African American community. In contrast, centuries of restricted economic opportunities resulted in few African American–owned businesses large enough to require the services of a CPA. Consequently, until the 1960s, only under exceptional circumstances could African American CPAs earn a livelihood within the black community. This difference also meant that while African American medical and law schools have a long history, black colleges rarely offered programs in accountancy.

THE HISTORY OF THE CPA PROFESSION AND
THE DEVELOPMENT OF THE EXPERIENCE REQUIREMENT

Barriers to the professions also differed at the entry level. Entrance to the medical and legal professions primarily depended on obtaining the appropriate education and passing state-supervised examinations. Becoming a CPA not only required passing the certified public accountancy examination but also serving an apprenticeship, called an experience requirement, by working for a licensed CPA. For most of the twentieth century, virtually no whites would hire and train an African American to become a CPA, justifying this by claiming that clients would not tolerate an African American's involvement in their financial affairs. The experience requirement constituted an extremely effective barrier; by 1965 there were only one hundred African American CPAs—one in *one thousand* CPAs.

Certified public accountancy developed in the United States later than most professions. The first laws creating CPAs were passed in New York in 1896. Accountants and bookkeepers had existed in the United States since the country's inception, but public accounting did not begin to expand until the early twentieth century. Accountants and bookkeepers keep track of a company's or an individual's records, whereas CPAs are authorized to provide audits—external reviews of an organization's accounting records—certifying that these records comply with accounting regulations. This authority made CPAs the most elite members of the accounting field. While the term "accountants" encompasses a variety of roles, including working within corporations, the government, and small businesses, CPA firms operate like law firms—CPAs work for themselves or in partnerships and provide services to clients.

Public accounting rose in importance along with industrialization and the concentration of capital. As companies became larger, they sold stock to raise capital rather than being controlled by small groups of manager-owners. The stock market created "absentee owners," people who held stock in a corporation but were not involved in its management. These stockholders required assurance that companies were meeting expectations, and the public accountants' audits attested to the reliability of the company's income statement and balance sheet. The goal of these audits was to strengthen investor confidence, enabling companies to raise the capital needed for the mammoth corporations that emerged in the decades after the Civil War.

Variation among public accountants and questions regarding their reliability led to efforts to organize the profession in order to enhance its credibility. The primary model for these efforts was the British system of chartered accountancy. In England, prospective chartered accountants were required to serve a five-year apprenticeship in order to earn the authority to attest to corporate financial statements. In the late nineteenth and early twentieth centuries, many English chartered accountants came to the United States to take advantage of the emerging need for their services. Together with their United States counterparts in public accounting, they sought to forge a professional credentialing process.

Disagreements immediately arose over whether the British model should be emulated. Several United States–born public accountants objected to the apprenticeship model, which restricted professional entry to the wealthy few who could afford to pay for the apprenticeship. Those who preferred the British model, however, stressed the prestige associated with such a plan. By confining entry to the upper and middle classes, the profession would enhance its legitimacy and promote a status comparable to those professions already established in the United States, especially medicine and law. Early debates about the profession's direction pitted eastern Anglo-Saxon Protestant elites, who favored restrictive entry, against midwestern, often Catholic, first- and second-generation Americans from continental Europe and Ireland. The latter group favored educational and testing requirements, which they perceived as more democratic and more consistent with American ideals.[3] Not unexpectedly, given their exclusion from mainstream society, African Americans were completely ignored in the debate.

Because of the intense regional and social differences, efforts to create national criteria failed. Instead, each state developed its own laws governing the profession. Most states, including New York, compromised, requiring both the passage of an examination and an apprenticeship with a CPA. This apprenticeship, which differed from the British system in that the employee was paid for his or her work, varied by state: some required only one year and others required as many as three.[4]

Even without the complete adoption of the British five-year apprenticeship system, the experience requirement had an exclusionary effect because it created a nearly impenetrable barrier to African Americans who desired to become CPAs. By the end of the twentieth century, there were 400,000 CPAs in the United States, less than 1 percent of whom were African American.

Although the profession garners relatively little media attention, it does wield substantial power over the nation's most consequential financial transactions. In addition to involvement in tax regulations and business management, CPAs have the exclusive authority to audit the income statements of all publicly traded corporations. Today a handful of firms dominate the industry: PricewaterhouseCoopers, Arthur Andersen, KPMG, Deloitte & Touche, and Ernst & Young. These firms audit over 95 percent of the Fortune 500, earning 1998 revenues in excess of $40 billion.[5] But none of these firms employed African Americans until the 1960s.

THOSE WHO MADE IT

African Americans who managed to become CPAs prior to the 1960s had exceptional characteristics. All of them personified talent, persistence, and resilience. These pioneers were remarkably accomplished students with outstanding educational backgrounds, exceeding those of many of their white counterparts. Some moved hundreds of miles to achieve their educational goals, to obtain employment with an African American, or simply to find a state that allowed African Americans to take the CPA examination. Some spent years seeking employment in the field. A few of the earliest CPAs came from the most elite African American families in the nation. A handful appeared to be white. All these characteristics reduced the difficulties they faced; nevertheless, intense challenges remained.

Because finding employment with a white-owned CPA firm was nearly impossible, African Americans helped each other. Arthur J. Wilson became a CPA in Chicago in 1923, before the State of Illinois passed legislation requiring an apprenticeship with a CPA. Wilson then provided experience to others, so that by 1945 half of all the African American CPAs in the country worked in Chicago. Chicago CPAs provided services to some of the largest black-owned businesses in the country. Men and women in other African American business centers—Atlanta, Detroit, and New York—similarly blazed a trail that others could follow. Those who wished to become CPAs often had no alternative but to move to meet the experience requirement by working for one of these pioneers.

Moving typically meant moving north. Business education was severely restricted in the South, and barriers to employment were insurmountable. Many African Americans, excluded from the business programs of their state universities prior to the civil rights movement, went to northern schools in order to major in accounting. Until the 1960s, there was only one school in the

South that offered substantial business education to African Americans, Atlanta University. Interviews with dozens of African American CPAs from all regions of the country revealed that many of them received early encouragement from one influential man, Jesse B. Blayton Sr., an accounting professor at Atlanta University who became Georgia's first African American CPA in 1928.

Moving north did not solve every problem, however. All those who earned their CPAs prior to the 1960s exemplified perseverance. Some applied for dozens of jobs before finding a crack in the system, even in ostensibly liberal cities such as New York and Los Angeles. Many reluctantly turned to teaching, a field open to African Americans as long as schools were segregated.

Obtaining a CPA license did not mark the end of the struggle. African American CPAs usually had to eke out a living within the black business community, since it was almost impossible to attract white clients. Many had to retain full-time jobs while conducting their professional practice at night and on weekends—despite the fact that their white contemporaries found certified public accountancy to be a lucrative profession. In addition, for decades African American CPAs were excluded from many CPA professional associations and meetings and thus were denied opportunities to make business contacts and remain current with professional developments. For example, Dr. Lincoln Harrison, who earned his CPA in Louisiana in 1946, was not admitted to the Louisiana Society of Certified Public Accountants until 1970.

The Civil Rights Act of 1964, which forbade employment discrimination on the basis of race, brought an end to the most intransigent barriers to African Americans' becoming CPAs. In the late 1960s, the major CPA firms began recruiting at black colleges and the American Institute of CPAs initiated programs to encourage African Americans to major in accounting. President Lyndon B. Johnson's War on Poverty provided much-needed funds to urban community organizations, which in turn required the services of CPAs. This finally provided sufficient clientele in the African American community to enable many African American CPAs to earn a living within the field. The expansion of civil rights organizations also led to more demand for black CPAs. When the State of Alabama charged Martin Luther King Jr. with tax evasion, he hired Atlanta CPA Jesse Blayton to help clear him.

Following the civil rights movement, there was a surge in African American participation in the profession. In 1961, for the first time, a major firm hired an African American accounting graduate. During the mid-1960s a handful more were hired. The biggest change came at the end of the decade, when the American Institute of CPAs called for efforts to integrate the profession. For a short period, the major public accounting firms, which had previously refused to hire African Americans, began actively recruiting at black colleges. In 1968, the major firms in New York employed only eighteen African American accounting professionals. By 1970, there were more than 100 African Americans in the same offices.

That surge sputtered in the 1980s. Proactive efforts to expand opportunity shrank as affirmative action plans came under siege from the Reagan administration. The representation of African American professionals in major CPA firms declined by over 25 percent. In the century's last decade, participation leveled off as some firms recognized that the slide was disadvantageous to preserving their clients, who themselves were becoming increasingly diverse. As in earlier periods, African American CPAs played the key role in ensuring that opportunity did not completely disappear. Through the expansion of programs at historically black colleges, activism on the part of African American CPAs, and the growing National Association of Black Accountants, African American leadership persevered as the profession entered a new century.

2

The Firsters

Chauncey L. Christian must have been nervous when he sat down to take the Kentucky certified public accountancy examination in 1926. The test was notoriously difficult—only a small fraction of those who took it passed. Christian himself had failed one of the four parts of the examination on his previous attempt. He had studied accounting through a correspondence course, which may have led him to wonder whether his preparation was adequate for an examination that only twelve Kentuckians would pass that year.[1] He shared these worries with the fifty other men who endured two days of grueling questions such as "Explain the relationship between a sinking fund and an allowance for depreciation."[2]

But Chauncey Christian had another worry, one not shared by his peers. He was afraid that the examination monitors would discover that he was an African American.

By the end of the 1930s, there were almost 27,000 certified public accountants in the United States. Eight were African American. These eight men overcame daunting odds against their entry into the profession. They became CPAs at a time when African Americans were actively excluded from business and financial pursuits. Like other members of the small group of African American professionals in the 1920s and 1930s, they were exceptionally intelligent, well-educated, and hardworking. Intelligence, education, and hard work were not sufficient, however, to gain access to this new profession intent on emulating the exclusivity of law and medicine. Being fair-skinned enough to pass for white, like Chauncey Christian, eliminated one barrier, but connections and luck also played major roles in separating African Americans who succeeded from those who were unable to become CPAs.

AFRICAN AMERICAN EDUCATION IN THE
EARLY DECADES OF THE TWENTIETH CENTURY

Education was essential to the success of those African Americans who joined the ranks of CPAs in the 1920s and 1930s. John W. Cromwell Jr., who became the first African American CPA in the United States in 1921, had a master's degree from Dartmouth College. Wilmer F. Lucas, who in 1929 became the first African American CPA in New York and the fifth in the nation, graduated from New York University's Graduate School of Business, one of the top two accounting programs in the country.[3]

These educational accomplishments stood in stark contrast to the typical educational experience of African Americans in the first decades of the twentieth century. When John Cromwell finished his undergraduate degree in 1906, only 1 in 3,600 African Americans was a college graduate. College attendance was not common for any group of Americans, but whites were five times more likely to go to college than were African Americans. In the 1920s, the African American illiteracy rate, at about 20 percent, was ten times that of native-born whites.[4]

Deprivation of education had been a central principle of slavery; it had been against the law to educate enslaved persons. After the Civil War, the denial of education, particularly education in math and commerce, facilitated the exploitation of the newly freed Americans. African Americans were exploited both by the sharecropping system, under which they farmed land owned by whites and paid "rent" in crops, and by landlord-owned company stores, where black agricultural workers bought supplies at inflated prices. Not uncommonly, these systems left former slaves so deeply indebted to their landlords that they were prevented from seeking other employment, and their lack of financial knowledge left them at the mercy of the landowners. For example, one man who had previously been enslaved was persuaded to sign a ten-year work contract by his former owner. A decade later, believing that his contract had been fulfilled, he attempted to leave. But he was told that he owed $165 to the company store and was required to remain several more years to work off the debt.[5]

Immediately after the Civil War, hundreds of African Americans, sometimes in conjunction with northern missionaries, developed schools to eradicate the illiteracy and innumeracy that had been forced upon those who were enslaved. Former slaves of all ages flocked to these schools determined to learn skills previously denied to them.

As education became more widely available, both white and African American communities debated the proper role of African American education. The main issue was whether the new schools should be modeled on white education or whether they should emphasize only the industrial and domestic pursuits to which most African American employment was confined. The classics curricula at elite African American colleges such as Howard University in Washington and Fisk University in Nashville were often sneered at by those who considered Latin and Greek to be beyond the grasp of the descendants of enslaved people.[6] Some people, including many African American leaders, complained that such education was useless since there were no employment opportunities for classically trained African Americans. W. E. B. Du Bois, the leading proponent of classical higher education for African Americans, disagreed. A graduate of Fisk University and the first African American to earn a Ph.D. from Harvard University, he was convinced that the "Talented Tenth" of the black population should be well educated in order to raise the economic and social status of the entire African American community. Booker T. Washington, the president of Tuskegee Normal and Industrial Institute in Alabama, was the leading black proponent of industrial education. He believed that African Americans should receive practical training that would lead to dependable employment, and that future progress toward equality would depend upon the willingness of African Americans to prove themselves within the existing system.

In the early decades of the twentieth century, philanthropic support was primarily directed toward meeting Washington's goals. The Rosenwald Fund, a northern foundation that provided substantial support for many of the first black high schools in the South, pushed industrial education partly to make its propositions palatable to the white southern power structure. Most southern communities had no public high schools that African Americans could attend—school board members often argued that such education was unnecessary for a group destined to work in agricultural and domestic pursuits. In southern states, fewer than 4 percent of African Americans between fifteen and nineteen years of age were enrolled in high school in the first decade of the twentieth century. In 1915, Atlanta's high-school-aged population was 42 percent African American and New Orleans's high-school-aged population was 26 percent African American. Each had four white public high schools, but despite having the largest African American populations in the United States, neither had a black public high school.[7] During this same period, John Cromwell, the first African American CPA, not only finished high school but also graduated with honors from Dartmouth *and* earned a master's degree.

Southern resistance to educating African Americans could be intractable. When, in 1931, representatives of the Rosenwald Fund encouraged the New Orleans Parish School Board to approve a black high school, they offered a design emphasizing auto mechanics, bricklaying, gardening, barbering, and dressmaking. They also explicitly promised that the curriculum would not include accounting and bookkeeping because training in those fields might enable African Americans to compete for jobs reserved for whites.[8] African American leaders protested the notion of a high school designed to reinforce their economic subordination, and the New Orleans Parish School Board saw no need to provide training for jobs that African Americans were already filling. Despite the Rosenwald Fund's offer of significant financial support, the school board refused to build a black high school.

African American colleges faced similar obstacles. Because philanthropists found industrial education for African Americans appealing, the two best-endowed African American colleges in the early decades of the twentieth century were Booker T. Washington's Tuskegee Institute and his alma mater, Hampton Institute in Virginia. A few colleges with less funding, including Howard and Fisk, offered a liberal arts curriculum. Professional education, especially business education, was even more rare. A study of 4,778 graduates of 14 private African American colleges who graduated between 1868 and 1932 identified only 25 accountants and bookkeepers, 0.5 percent of total graduates. In contrast, 47 percent of the graduates were educators, 11 percent members of the clergy, 10 percent medical professionals, and 3 percent lawyers.[9] Because schools, churches, and hospitals were segregated, educated African Americans had some opportunities as teachers, clergy, doctors, and nurses—as long as they stayed on the correct side of the color line. African Americans aspiring to other professions were often discouraged by college guidance counselors because these counselors knew that few job opportunities awaited. Many African American college graduates had to accept positions for which they were overqualified, in the hope that better opportunities would open up. Others offered to work for free in order to garner professional experience. Where local conditions allowed, many well-educated African Americans worked as post office clerks or railroad porters because these jobs often paid better than the meager professional work that was available.[10]

THEODORA RUTHERFORD: CREDENTIALS BUT NO OPPORTUNITIES

For an African American coming of age in the 1920s or 1930s, the best available education rarely opened the doors of opportunity. One example is Theodora Fonteneau Rutherford, who wanted to become a CPA when she graduated from college in 1923. She was born in 1904 in the small southern town of Jeanerette, Louisiana, where her father owned an oyster restaurant and her mother was a teacher. As a child she saw how African American professionals were treated. An African American doctor in Jeanerette was run out of town by whites who were angry that he was providing health education to the African American community. As a result of the incident, Rutherford's mother decided that Jeanerette was too dangerous for her children, and she moved the family to Houston. She was so determined that her daughter get an education that she sent her to stay with another family to attend a private school when she was only five years old. Rutherford reports that "I knew before I could talk that I was going to college."[11]

When she finished high school at the age of fifteen, Rutherford considered Howard University and Oberlin College, a white Quaker school with an abolitionist history and the strongest record among majority-white colleges for graduating African American students. By 1898, Oberlin had 128 African American graduates. At the time, the University of Kansas held the second best record, with only sixteen black graduates.[12] However, Oberlin had a uniform, and Rutherford's mother did not want her to attend a school that required a uniform. So, in 1919 she entered Howard University. In a 1992 interview, she was amused by the thought that Oberlin's uniform had influenced her choice of college over seventy years earlier.

It was at Howard University that Rutherford decided to become a CPA. Her accounting professor, Orlando C. Thornton, convinced her that she should pursue the most respected credential in the accounting profession. He himself had wanted to become a CPA but was denied the opportunity to take the examination because he was African American.[13] Professor Thornton was Howard's only accounting instructor, and as such, he taught all five of the courses offered: elementary accounting, advanced accounting, cost accounting, accounting systems, and auditing. The description of Thornton's auditing class in the 1920 Howard University catalog states, "The work in auditing will be supplemented by many problems selected from among those given at C.P.A. examinations."[14] Thornton's interest in inspiring his students to set high goals is clear. At the time this catalog was published, there was not one single African American CPA in the country. According to available records, Professor Thornton himself never became a CPA.[15]

In 1923, at the age of nineteen, Theodora Rutherford graduated summa cum laude. She had the best scholastic record of those who graduated from Howard's School of Commerce and Finance.[16] Howard University's yearbook, *The Bison*, which featured the short stories and poetry of Rutherford's soon-to-be-famous classmate Zora Neale Hurston, highlighted the university scholarship that had been awarded to Theodora Velma Fonteneau (later Rutherford) in accounting.[17]

Rutherford's father died soon after she graduated from college, and her family's resources were limited, so Professor Thornton helped his outstanding student earn graduate school scholarships to Columbia University in New York and to Harvard University.[18] As an African American woman, Rutherford believed that if she chose Harvard, she would not be able to find suitable employment in Boston. She needed a job to pay her expenses, so she chose to go to Columbia because New York City, though its population was only 3 percent African American in the early 1920s, had a reputation for less employment discrimination.[19] In 1924, she became the first African American to earn a master's degree in accounting at Columbia.[20]

Earning her master's degree was not easy. As the only African American woman in the school, Rutherford felt scrutinized and isolated. She made friends with two white students, and the three studied together until she discovered that when they excused themselves at lunchtime, they ate in whites-only restaurants. She decided that if they were not willing to find a place where they could eat together, she would not help them with their studies.

To help pay for her expenses, Rutherford found a part-time job addressing envelopes. She appreciated the kindness of her supervisor, a white man, who supported her educational efforts by giving her short addresses so she could earn money quickly under her piece rate. Nevertheless, she encountered financial difficulties when her mother became ill and could not continue her support.

> For six weeks I lived on Campbell's soup, cereal, and milk. [My mother] was paying my room rent, so usually I only had to pay for food. I must have been a fool or something because anybody else would have quit. . . . For six whole weeks that's all I ate. Then I ended up sharing a room with two young women I had gone to Howard with. . . . As soon as my mom went back to work, she sent me some money. I went to a rotisserie on Sev-

enth Avenue. . . . Well, I bought a whole chicken, and I went next door and bought a whole chocolate cake. And I went home and gorged. My stomach wasn't used to that kind of food. I can't stand to look at a chocolate cake now. I'll always like chicken, and I've always liked Campbell's soup. I've often thought I should tell Campbell's soup about that experience. That's all I ate for six weeks, and I still like it.[21]

Rutherford survived the varied ordeals of graduate school, and in 1924, at the age of twenty, she seemed to be on target for becoming a CPA. She had everything going for her—the brilliance that led her to her summa cum laude graduation from Howard University when she was only nineteen; a graduate education at Columbia University; the determination that allowed her to live on soup for weeks to achieve her goal; the support of a mother whose primary interest was in her success; and the inspiration of an African American mentor, O. C. Thornton, who pushed his student to achieve what he had been denied. She lived in the North, in a city she had chosen for its employment opportunities. She was eager to earn the CPA and willing to make sacrifices to do so. Yet Theodora Fonteneau Rutherford did not become a CPA in the 1920s. Nor did she become a CPA in the 1930s. It was not until 1960 that she achieved certification. She had the education, talent, and determination, but an impenetrable barrier stood in her way, the experience requirement.

When she finished her master's degree, Theodora Rutherford knew that she would not be able to get a job working for a CPA firm in New York despite the fact that her educational credentials far exceeded those of most members of the profession. In the mid-1920s, only 36 percent of CPAs born in the United States had earned college degrees. The profession's main publication, the *Journal of Accountancy*, called for stricter educational standards but acknowledged that "some of the ablest and most successful" CPAs were not college graduates. Not one state in the early 1920s required *any* college education; some did not even require high school graduation.[22] Despite Rutherford's Columbia University graduate degree, the experience requirement prevented her from earning her CPA for the first half of the twentieth century because she could not find a job with a CPA firm. Although New York was known as a liberal city, the professions were not open to African Americans. This report from A. Philip Randolph's *The Messenger* indicates what conditions were like for African American New Yorkers even at the lower rungs of the accounting field in the 1920s: "Edward B. Ward, who was recently appointed head bookkeeper at the Chelsea Exchange Bank, 135th Street and Seventh Avenue, New York, N.Y., was forced to resign because the white clerks would not cooperate with him. He has returned to his former position as head bookkeeper at the Public National Bank [an African American–owned bank] where he was previously employed for nine years. *Another victory for liberalism in Gotham!*"[23] In New York's African American community in the 1920s, a position as head bookkeeper in a Harlem bank was an enviable one. Theodora Rutherford's goals were much higher. She wanted to become a CPA. Instead, like many well-educated African Americans at the time, she found a job teaching.

John W. Davis, president of West Virginia State College, asked her to join his faculty. President Davis kept track of the best-educated African Americans, and he found Rutherford through his contacts at Howard University. Rutherford regretfully told her mother that she was not going to return to Houston. Like many African Americans fortunate enough to have the option, she preferred to remain in the North: "I explained it this way later. In West Virginia, if somebody called me 'nigger,' I could slap them. In Louisiana if somebody called me 'nigger,' and I slapped them, they'd lynch me. And it wasn't any better in Texas. . . . My last year in Texas, my mother had an altercation with a streetcar conductor. There were a lot of empty seats, but they were all on the wrong side of the sign that said, 'colored.' And I just decided that I wasn't going to put myself through all that. I'm not always going to be looking at the 'colored' sign."[24] It was her understanding that there was a CPA working for West Virginia State, and she jumped at the chance to fulfill the experience requirement.

It turned out that there were no CPAs on the faculty. Rutherford was not able to meet West Virginia's apprenticeship requirement, and she was therefore not allowed to sit for the CPA examination. She never did get a position working for a CPA. When, decades later, West Virginia changed its requirements and allowed a graduate degree to substitute for the experience requirement, Rutherford took the examination with people less than half her age. In 1960, thirty-six years after earning her master's degree, she became the first African American CPA in West Virginia. Forty years after Professor O. C. Thornton was selecting CPA examination questions in order to prepare his students for the pinnacle of the profession, he received a phone call from his star student. Theodora Rutherford was calling to tell him that their dream had finally come true.

THE FIRST AFRICAN AMERICAN CPAS

Ironically, the fact that Theodora Rutherford chose liberal New York worked to her disadvantage when it came to entering certified public accountancy. The profession was young in the 1920s, and many states had not yet instituted an experience requirement. Unfortunately for Rutherford, New York had the oldest and most established CPA laws and the most stringent criteria for licensing. West Virginia, where Rutherford taught, also had an experience requirement. Not surprisingly, most of the African Americans who became CPAs in the 1920s did so in states that had not yet instituted the experience requirement.

In 1921, twenty-five years after the first CPA certificate was granted in the United States, John W. Cromwell Jr. became the first African American to earn a CPA. Cromwell was a member of one of the leading African American families in the United States. His father was a teacher, a political activist, an attorney, and chief examiner of the Money Order Department for the United States Post Office. He organized the *People's Advocate*, which became a leading African American newspaper in the District of Columbia.[25] Cromwell's older sister Otelia was also a trailblazer. At a time when most northern white schools did not admit African Americans, she became the first African American graduate of Smith College and went on to earn a Ph.D. in English at Yale University in 1926.[26]

John Cromwell Jr. himself was exceptional. He graduated from the exclusive college preparatory division of Howard University and attended Dartmouth College in New Hampshire. Dartmouth had graduated only 7 African Americans in the 130 years between its founding in 1769 and 1899.[27] Cromwell graduated as the best science student in the class of 1906 and was elected to the Phi Beta Kappa honor society. A year later he completed his master's degree. He spent one year working for General Electric in a position it reserved for Dartmouth's top science graduate, but he did not remain in industry with his classmates. Instead he returned to Washington, D.C., and became a mathematics teacher, working at the most prestigious high school for African Americans in the United States, Washington's Dunbar School. One of his students was Robert Weaver, who was later appointed secretary of housing and urban development by President Lyndon Johnson. Other Dunbar graduates include Edward Brooke, the first African American senator in the twentieth century; Benjamin Davis, the first African American general in the U.S. Army; Charles Drew, the doctor famous for improving blood transfusions; and most of the

The first African American CPA, John W. Cromwell Jr., New Hampshire, 1921.
Photo courtesy of Adelaide Cromwell.

African American middle class in Washington, D.C., in the first half of the twentieth century.[28]

Fifteen years passed between John Cromwell Jr.'s college graduation and the year he became a CPA. He was a teacher in Washington, D.C., yet he traveled to New Hampshire to take the CPA examination and earn his CPA. Apparently he, like Professor Thornton, was not allowed to sit for the CPA exam in the Washington area.[29] Virginia and Maryland, the logical states in which a Washington resident might have taken the examination, required experience. New Hampshire, which instituted its CPA legislation in 1921, did not. He took the examination the year New Hampshire, the state in which he had attended college, became one of the last three states in the country to enact CPA legislation.[30]

After earning his CPA, Cromwell continued to teach high school and began to practice accountancy in the District of Columbia. He worked almost exclusively within the black community, serving lawyers, churches, restaurants, and funeral homes and becoming the controller for Howard University in 1930.[31] Forty years after he earned his CPA, he was still the only African American CPA in the District of Columbia as well as the only African American to hold a certificate from New Hampshire.[32]

A NEW PROFESSION IN PURSUIT OF PRESTIGE

In the early 1920s, when Theodora Rutherford found it impossible to become a CPA in New York and John Cromwell had to travel 500 miles to take the examination in a state with new CPA legislation, leaders of the profession were working to consolidate and advance their prestige. While audits were not required for publicly traded companies until 1934, many companies voluntarily hired auditors in order to persuade investors and creditors of their financial soundness, and CPAs had an interest in persuading more companies to pursue this option. The *Journal of Accountancy* published numerous articles in the 1910s and 1920s reflecting this quest for legitimacy and respect and urging emulation of other professions, especially law and medicine.[33]

The profession's prestige was enhanced when the U.S. Treasury recommended exempting CPAs from armed combat in World War I and instead, like physicians, enrolling them in a volunteer reserve to utilize their expertise on behalf of the war effort.[34] Increased taxation during the war exacerbated the strain the draft placed on the supply of accountants; corporations sought accountants to help them calculate tax liabilities under the new laws; and the Internal Revenue Service required increased personnel to account for the increased revenues. Previous editorials in the *Journal of Accountancy* had argued that accountants were essential to war and should not be wasted in roles—specifically combat—that any man could fill.[35] These war developments enhanced the standing and legitimacy of accounting.

Contrary to the experiences of the earliest African American CPAs—and of those who *wanted* to become CPAs such as Theodora Rutherford and O. C. Thornton—the *Journal of Accountancy* described public accountancy as being open to talented and qualified new professionals. Simultaneously, the journal called for more homogeneity, lamenting the difficulty of ensuring the quality of geographically dispersed professionals. The journal also criticized the lax standards some states set for prospective CPAs. In 1926, when a new national professional organization was formed, several states were cited for their inferior standards, and the new Institute of Accountants did not automatically accept state CPA society membership as sufficient for membership in the national organization. The institute pleaded for more uniform rules, noting that those states with the newest CPA legislation had particularly weak requirements.[36] Although the journal did not mention him, John Cromwell Jr. might not have obtained certification without the so-called lax standards applied by New Hampshire when he got his CPA in 1921. Despite his outstand- . ing educational credentials, he would likely have found it impossible to meet the experience requirement of working for a CPA, which would have disqualified him from taking the exam in those states whose standards the journal extolled.

The *Journal of Accountancy* encouraged young men to enter the field, but clearly the image the new profession was striving for did not include African Americans. References to African Americans are absent from the journal's early years, but its occasional mention of female CPAs provides some insight by analogy. A few *Journal of Accountancy* articles did mention the possibility of women becoming CPAs but acknowledged that, because of gender bias, they would face extreme difficulty in finding employment.[37] An article in 1923 stated that while "[women's] ability in accountancy is unquestioned," auditing entailed late nights and traveling to various businesses to review their accounts, factors inimical to "heterogeneous personnel." In addition, "There is the utterly unwarranted objection, raised by some clients, when a woman appears as a representative of the accountant. . . . To such men it is not only a shock but almost an indication of disregard if a woman is sent to undertake the work of a practitioner."[38] The article went on to say that women were more successful at becoming CPAs in those states that did not yet have experience requirements, since it was so difficult for women to find CPAs willing to employ them and supervise their work.

African American accountants were not addressed in the *Journal of Accountancy* until 1933, but it is clear that in the 1920s African American men and women faced conditions worse than those of white women. Jobs that required travel and odd hours were more comfortable to "homogeneous"—all white male—groups. If clients considered it a sign of disregard when a white woman was sent to review their accounting records, it is more than probable that public accounting firms also thought sending an African American woman or man would not fit their professional image—that is, if they even considered employing African Americans. In fact, when the issue arose in later decades, public accounting firms often attributed their unwillingness to hire African Americans to the fact that they did not want to cause discomfort to their clients.

"ACCOUNTING AS A FIELD FOR COLORED MEN"

In 1933, the *Journal of Accountancy* published an article entitled "Accounting as a Field for Colored Men," the only article on the issue to appear in an accounting publication before the 1960s.[39] The circumstances surrounding publication of this article are a mystery because the *Journal of Accountancy* has no records for this period. While women had been mentioned in the journal in relation to their role in the profession at large, this article did not anticipate any mainstreaming of African American CPAs. The article resulted from a study conducted while the African American author, I. Maximilian Martin, worked on his master's thesis in accounting at the University of Pennsylvania's Wharton School.[40] Through a survey of African American colleges, he found that there were seven black CPAs in the United States in the early 1930s. Most of their clients were small African American–owned businesses, but some reported having white clients as well. Consistent with other studies indicating an absence of professional education available to African Americans, Martin found that African American colleges offered little in the way of accounting education. Though twenty of the fifty-four colleges surveyed offered some accounting classes, only seven offered auditing, the main function of the CPA, and only three offered income tax classes.[41]

Martin found that the biggest barrier to participation in the field was the lack of opportunity to get training with CPAs. He reported that white firms declined to hire African American accountants because the firms were afraid that their clients would not accept them. Martin pointed out that as states increased restrictions on certifying CPAs by implementing experience requirements, entry to the profession would become even more difficult for African Americans. This exclusion from becoming a CPA, Martin pointed out, made it much more difficult for an African American to gain credibility as an accountant; the CPA credential conveyed knowledge, reliability, and prestige. Martin concluded that the public accounting profession was the "most difficult one for colored men to enter," but he saw some signs for hope in other areas of accounting. He noted that some state governments were beginning to hire African Americans as accountants, that teaching accounting was a viable option, and that growth in African American businesses should lead to an increase in opportunities. The article reflected an underlying assumption that certified public accountancy would remain racially stratified: he did not even suggest that white CPAs—the *Journal of Accountancy's* readership—hire African Americans.

Martin noted that three of the African American CPAs he found in his survey had received their training from white professionals. The article does not mention any names, but one of these was Wilmer F. Lucas, the first African American CPA in New York State. Of the five African American CPAs of the 1920s, only Lucas was certified in a state that required experience working for a CPA.[42] A 1922 graduate of New York University's Graduate School of Business, he became a CPA in 1929.

Lucas met his experience requirement by working for Daniel Levy & Company in Manhattan. Lucas's son reports that "Father said he was always indebted to the Jewish people for giving him an opportunity."[43] Perhaps the discrimination Jews faced made them more likely to sympathize with the experiences of African Americans and to help them find employment. Anti-Semitism among leading CPAs was evident in an incident contemporaneous with Lucas's efforts to become a CPA. In 1927, national officers of Beta Alpha Psi, the honors fraternity for accounting majors, revoked Boston University's chapter ostensibly because of nonpayment of dues, but actually because there were too many "Hebrew" members in the chapter.[44]

In 1937, Lucas started his own CPA firm on Harlem's 125th Street, Lucas & Tucker, which provided experience to other prospective African American CPAs. Lucas's employees referred to him as General Lucas, a title he earned in his highly decorated army career.[45]

AFRICAN AMERICANS IN BUSINESS

Once Wilmer Lucas met the stringent New York State requirements for becoming a CPA, he maintained a full-time job as an accountant for the State of

New York in addition to his CPA practice. John Cromwell faced a similar situation: he continued to teach high school for years after becoming a CPA.[46] In a period when white CPA firms were experiencing tremendous growth and expansion, the few African Americans who were CPAs could not piece together enough business to support themselves.[47] Unlike African American doctors, teachers, and clergy, who could find African American patients, students, and congregations (though they earned lower salaries than those of whites in the same fields), African American CPAs' opportunities were restricted by the absence of clients for their firms. African American businesses large enough to require services beyond bookkeeping were quite rare.

Slavery and its vestiges had limited African American involvement in commerce and severely constrained the opportunity to amass sufficient capital to open businesses. The clientele of white businesses often included both African Americans and whites, whereas that of black-owned businesses was usually confined to African Americans. While some notable African American banks and insurance companies were founded in the decades after the Civil War, most black businesses were extensions of roles performed under slavery, including personal services such as catering, shining shoes, cutting hair, and providing funeral services.[48]

White-owned businesses typically had better access to suppliers and other necessary business connections; they sometimes used their clout to prevent suppliers from servicing black-owned businesses. Many African American customers preferred patronizing the better-stocked, lower-priced white-owned businesses rather than black-owned businesses, which did not enjoy the same connections.[49]

The largest African American businesses were in banking and insurance because white-owned banks and insurance companies were often unwilling to serve the needs of African American clients. African American banks often got started because African Americans found it virtually impossible to get credit from white-owned institutions and because many African Americans did not trust whites to safeguard and return their money. These larger black businesses also faced problems. The few black banks that existed in the first decades of the twentieth century, for example, often had difficulty persuading the standard check-clearing channels to honor checks drawn on their banks.[50]

At least two of the first eight African American CPAs benefited from their employment in sizable African American–owned businesses. When Chauncey Christian earned his CPA in Kentucky in 1926, he was working in Louisville as a bookkeeper and stenographer. Most of his work was for a construction firm owned by Samuel Plato, one of the first African American contractors and architects. Plato designed churches and houses and was the first African American to win a contract to build U.S. post offices: he built thirty-seven between 1925 and 1941.[51]

When Christian considered becoming a CPA, Plato encouraged him to study for the examination through a correspondence course. Although Christian did not have to work for a CPA to meet his experience requirement, Kentucky did not allow African Americans to sit for the CPA examination. Christian was of mixed lineage, but as in all southern states, even a small percentage of African American heritage resulted in a person's being classified as "Negro" and thus excluded from mainstream opportunities. Christian followed the advice of a friend who urged him to submit his application to take the CPA examination in Kentucky on the last possible day so that the state examiners would not have time to do the background check that would reveal his racial classification. The examiners did not notice anything unusual, and he was able to take the examination without interruption. If the state had conducted the background check, it would have discovered that Christian had attended and taught at African American schools. Out of fifty applicants, he was one of only seven people who passed the examination. His employer was elated with Christian's rare accomplishment.[52] Later, the two became partners in Plato's firm.

In the 1940s, Christian moved his family to New York where he became the "Show Business Accountant," working for the Moe Gale Theatrical Agency as controller. The Jewish-owned agency served clients such as Lucky Millander, Sarah Vaughan, Ella Fitzgerald, Lester Young, the Ink Spots, and Erskine Hawkins. These African American entertainers were among the largest African American "businesses" in the country. Christian's professional practice, while lucrative, was mainly confined to the African American community but included some white businessmen as well as white performers such as Robert Merrill and Jane Pickens.[53]

JESSE B. BLAYTON: THE DEAN OF NEGRO ACCOUNTANTS

The best-known of the African American CPAs of the 1920s, Jesse B. Blayton, also saw his opportunities shaped by the African American business community. Blayton earned his CPA in Georgia in 1928 and, because he encouraged so many others to join the profession, he became known as the "Dean of

Negro Accountants."[54] Due to his prominence, he was commonly mistaken for being the first African American CPA in the United States;[55] in the 1970s, when *Jet* published obituaries for both John Cromwell and Jesse Blayton, each man was identified as having been the first black CPA.[56]

Though Blayton's accomplishment was often confused with that of John Cromwell, the two came from starkly dissimilar backgrounds. In contrast to the Cromwell family's prominence, Blayton was born in 1897 in Oklahoma Territory to an illiterate father and a mother whose education had ended in the fourth grade. His father was a shaman turned Baptist preacher (Blayton's paternal grandfather was a Creek Indian), and his mother was, despite her own limited education, a schoolteacher.

Realizing that lack of schooling had stunted his family's opportunities, Blayton was determined to get a good education. He attended federally supported Native American elementary and high schools and then entered Langston University, an African American college in Oklahoma, where he studied science. His education was interrupted by World War I, when he volunteered for the army. Fortuitously, one of his officers suggested that he study accounting:

> I didn't really quite understand what it was, but somehow it had a nice sound to it. I told my mother about it, and she said, "What is accounting?"
>
> I said, "Well, it's something like being cashier in a bank."
>
> She said, "Lord God, my son's lost his mind!"
>
> She was almost right. In those days there were no Negro CPAs, no Negro accountants of any kind, and I had never heard of a business run by Negroes. . . . There was nothing in my experience or the experience of anyone I knew to indicate that I could succeed in accounting or banking or business. There was absolutely nothing I could look forward to, but I went ahead anyway. I just decided that since I was an American, too, I ought to have the same chance as everybody else.[57]

After the war, Blayton spent the early 1920s in Chicago studying accounting at the Walton School of Commerce and then moved to Atlanta, which had the largest African American population in the United States.

Like Chauncey Christian, Blayton got his start in a black-owned business: he became an accountant and auditor for the Standard Life Insurance Company. Heman Perry, the president of Standard Life, was a well-connected businessman whose interests extended beyond insurance to include real estate

Jesse B. Blayton (Georgia CPA 1928), the "Dean of Negro Accountants."
Photo courtesy of Atlanta University Center, Robert W. Woodruff Library;
photographer: Griffith J. Davis.

and banking. African American leaders including Booker T. Washington and W. E. B. Du Bois supported Perry's efforts to expand black business ownership. Blayton and other well-educated African Americans worked for Perry; Blayton said that Standard Life's "official staff . . . read like a . . . social register of Negroes at the time."[58] Perry eventually encountered financial difficulties, and Blayton and two of his colleagues ultimately bought out Citizen's Trust, the bank that Perry had founded to finance his other businesses. Blayton's prominence in Atlanta's business world rose as he expanded his business enterprises to include a bottling company, a savings and loan, a radio station, and a nightclub.[59]

In addition to his business pursuits, Blayton was a member of the most common profession for African Americans: he was a teacher. In the mid-twenties he became a professor at Morehouse College, part of the Atlanta University complex, under whose auspices faculty member W. E. B. Du Bois had conducted turn-of-the-century studies of African American college graduates and African American businesses. With the encouragement of Du Bois and other Atlanta University colleagues, Blayton established a Department of Economics and Business Administration and vastly expanded the school's course offerings in business. In 1928, before the state instituted an experience requirement, Blayton became the first African American CPA in Georgia. In 1930, he was named the Carnegie Foundation Chair in Accountancy at Atlanta University, and in that role he inspired and helped many of his students to become CPAs.[60] His prominence was enhanced in 1936 when he was asked to meet with Secretary of Labor Frances Perkins to discuss President Franklin Roosevelt's New Deal programs from an African American perspective.[61] Clippings from the *Atlanta Daily World*, the only African American daily newspaper in the country at the time, show that he was in demand as an authoritative and popular speaker on business issues.[62]

As part of that desire to inspire others, in 1939 Blayton authored a bulletin for the Colored Division of the National Youth Administration, a New Deal program, describing the untapped opportunities that African Americans could pursue in accounting.[63] Acknowledging that African American accountants would not be able to find employment in mainstream businesses, he suggested that they needed to convince small African American organizations such as farms, fraternal orders, funeral homes, and churches that good record keeping was both crucial and cost-effective.

Blayton also recommended approaching some large businesses. He noted that most large African American insurance companies depended upon white accountants to keep their records. Blayton suggested that black business executives often believed that regulators were better persuaded by and had more confidence in white CPAs than in African American CPAs and therefore feared that they would be at a disadvantage if they used African American CPAs to audit their records. Blayton pointed out, however, that all the accountants for the largest black insurance company in the country were African American and that it had no problems with regulators. He was convinced that a larger problem was the scarcity of African American accountants; he believed that these insurance companies would prefer to hire African American CPAs if they were available.

Blayton's recommendations notwithstanding, African Americans who desired to become CPAs in the 1920s and 1930s faced hurdles beyond those of acquiring education and attracting African American clients. The few African Americans who became CPAs in those decades faced an inhospitable environment. By 1939, only 8 out of the 27,000 CPAs in the country were African American. Even with his tremendous family advantages and exceptional educational background, John Cromwell Jr. had to take the CPA examination in New Hampshire, a northern state that had recently started granting CPAs and had not yet adopted an experience requirement. In order to prevent being excluded, Chauncey Christian had to let the examiners assume he was white. Under her mother's guidance and with the help of a concerned professor, Theodora Rutherford got the best accounting education available in the United States in the 1920s. Nevertheless she still was excluded from the profession.

The few African Americans who became CPAs in the 1920s and 1930s were often forced to work in other fields, such as teaching, in order to earn a living. Because the first several African American CPAs were scattered around the country, they dealt with obstacles as isolated individuals. Soon, however, a critical mass of African American CPAs developed in Chicago, the center of black business in the early decades of the twentieth century. If you were African American, this meant that Chicago was the best place in the country to become a CPA.

3

The Black Metropolis

When Hiram L. Pittman was discharged from army service after World War II, he headed for Chicago, convinced that it would offer more opportunities in accounting than would his hometown of Omaha. He had no idea how fortuitous a choice he had made. In no other city could he have met as many African American CPAs. Theodore A. Jones, Chicago's fourth black CPA, hired Pittman to help him with an audit. Charles A. Beckett, Chicago's fifth African American CPA, referred him to an accounting job in an African American hospital. Soon thereafter, Mary T. Washington, the first African American female CPA, invited him to join her firm and become her business partner. Of the fourteen African American CPAs in the country by the end of World War II, fully half were in Chicago.

In comparison to the rigid racial divisions in the southern states during the first half of the twentieth century, Chicago was supposed to be the promised land. Relatively speaking, it was. By the 1940s, the influx of southern African Americans seeking employment in Chicago had led to unprecedented black political and economic power, and this in turn led to unprecedented opportunities for African American CPAs. More than one-quarter of the first 100 African American CPAs, including the first two women, practiced in Chicago. Still, like their counterparts in other parts of the country, African Americans in Chicago were excluded from the mainstream of the profession.

THE GREAT MIGRATION

From World War I through World War II, hundreds of thousands of African Americans moved from southern states to Chicago in the hope of escaping domestic and agricultural work and finding well-paid employment in the manufacturing sector. Expanding war industries, combined with strict limitations on immigration resulting from World War I and the "Red Scare," opened opportunities for African Americans. Between the 1910 census and the 1950 census, Chicago's African American population increased elevenfold, growing from 44,000 to nearly half a million—from 2 percent of the city's population to 14 percent. The only U.S. city with a larger black population was New York.[1]

Life in Chicago was almost universally viewed as superior to life in the South. Chicago's abolitionist history had led to civil rights laws far in advance of the rest of the nation. By 1885 schools were de jure desegregated and African Americans had legal access to public accommodations and the ballot box. Laws mandating school attendance meant that, in early-twentieth-century Chicago, eighteen-year-old African Americans were almost as likely to have completed high school as were their white counterparts.[2]

In Chicago, African Americans wielded more power than in any other part of the country, mainly because they were not denied the right to vote. Chicago politicians courted these votes, and this led to significant, though not commensurate, African American power in city politics. In 1940, in the southern states of Alabama, Louisiana, Mississippi, and South Carolina, less than one-half of 1 percent of African Americans twenty-one years of age or older voted in the presidential election. In Chicago, the right to vote was unfettered by racial exclusions. In 1928, black voters in Chicago put an end to the quarter-century absence of African Americans in Congress when they elected Oscar De Priest to the U.S. House of Representatives. By 1944 there were at least fifteen African Americans with influential government jobs, including members of the city council and state senate and the head of the Chicago Housing Authority.[3]

Employment opportunities expanded along with political opportunities. In the 1930s and 1940s, African Americans had more access to jobs as lawyers, social workers, postal employees, teachers, firefighters, and police officers than in most other cities.[4] In 1941, the University of Chicago became the first majority-white university in the country to hire an African American, psychologist Allison Davis, as a teaching member of its faculty.[5]

Progress was not unlimited, however. While education and voting rights were progressive compared to other locales, housing and employment proved resistant to integration. Even in Chicago, well-educated African Americans' work opportunities were usually confined to the African American community. Chicago schools were segregated—not by law, but as a result of segregated neighborhoods—and the schools in the "Black Belt" did not typically meet the standards of the majority-white schools. Though rates of high school attendance between blacks and whites were similar, job opportunities upon graduation were not. Because of this discrimination, school counselors advised African American students to choose their curriculum in accordance with potential employment opportunities, and the recommended curriculum rarely included courses in business.[6]

Many employers claimed that they were not prejudiced, but they did not want to risk hiring African Americans for positions that dealt with the public out of fear of losing clients. Even though many acknowledged that *most* of their customers would not mind, they did not want to risk losing *any* customer; thus, white-collar employment was exceedingly difficult for African Americans to achieve well into World War II.

These barriers to white-collar employment, though they posed a challenge, were not as impermeable as they were in other parts of the country. Chicago was considered the "Black Business Capital of the World." Due to both the large African American population and also, ironically, due to racial segregation, black-owned businesses succeeded in Chicago as they did in no other city. During World War I, the unprecedented availability of high-wage jobs led to the development of the first sizable African American middle class in the country. African American–owned businesses existed because black Chicagoans with war industry jobs could afford to patronize them.[7] The existence of these businesses meant that there was more demand for African American CPAs in Chicago than anywhere else.

CHICAGO'S FIRSTERS: ARTHUR WILSON AND MARY WASHINGTON

In 1923, Arthur J. Wilson became the second African American CPA in the United States and the first in Illinois. Wilson was the cashier for the Binga State Bank, one of the two largest black-owned banks in the United States. Owner Jesse Binga took pride in providing opportunities to some of the best-educated African Americans in the city, including Arthur Wilson, a graduate of the University of Illinois.[8]

In the early 1920s, Wilson had passed the examination for a job with the Internal Revenue Service. However, the IRS would not hire African Americans. The State of Illinois had not yet instituted an experience requirement for CPAs, so Wilson took and passed the CPA examination and developed a small accounting practice in the evenings and on weekends while working for the Binga State Bank. After the bank failed during the early 1930s, Wilson went to work as an accountant for the State of Illinois.[9] He maintained his public accounting practice, but there were not enough small African American businesses requiring CPA services to provide Wilson with full-time work. Despite having been denied IRS experience, Wilson was an expert tax preparer, and he was able to help many small black business owners reduce their tax liabilities and increase their disposable income. Wilson's nephew, John E. Wilson, who later took over Wilson's CPA practice, reports that his uncle's tax expertise contributed to the expansion of the African American middle class in Chicago.[10]

In addition to his practice, Wilson used his position as a prominent member of the African American community to promote racial equality. In 1934, he and two other "race leaders" filed a complaint against a restaurant that refused to serve them. The National Association for the Advancement of Colored People (NAACP) successfully prosecuted the restaurant under the Illinois Civil Rights Act.[11] Refusing service to African Americans had been against the law in Illinois since 1885, though many restaurants continued to exclude customers based on race. Unlike in the South, however, African Americans who were refused service in Chicago had access to legal recourse.[12]

Because the State Board of Accountancy in Illinois adopted an experience requirement in 1927, four years after Wilson was certified, those who followed in his footsteps faced this additional hurdle. With Wilson providing the opportunity for experience, Mary T. Washington became the first African American female CPA in 1943. Born in 1906, she started her career as a bookkeeper for the Douglas National Bank and later worked for the Binga State Bank, where she was Arthur Wilson's assistant.[13] When the bank failed, she developed a close professional association with another black-owned business, the Fuller Products Company, which manufactured beauty products for the African American community.

The founder of Fuller Products, Samuel B. Fuller, was determined to spur the business careers of other African Americans.[14] With his encouragement, Mary Washington opened a CPA practice in the Fuller Products Company building. Fuller provided the foundation for her practice; every Monday morning for thirty-five years a $100 retainer check appeared on her desk. Her primary clients were black-owned businesses, but, unlike other African American CPAs, she also had many Jewish clients, perhaps partly because she was so light-skinned that she could easily have passed for white.[15]

NEW DEAL PROGRESS

While Arthur Wilson and Mary Washington were overcoming the odds in Chicago, the Roosevelt administration marked a turning point in African American opportunities. President Franklin Delano Roosevelt's New Deal programs and progressive judicial appointments raised hopes and instigated subtle, but permanent, changes in attitudes, as well as tangible economic benefits. Roosevelt was the first U.S. president to take a strong vocal stand against lynching, though he equivocated when it came to antilynching legislation because he feared jeopardizing southern Democrats' support for his New Deal programs. Despite this, during the 1930s African Americans began to have a major impact on the U.S. political scene. Following the demographic shift of African Americans to the North, where they could vote, both of the major parties had to acknowledge African American interests. In the 1936 presidential election, for the first time both the Republicans and the Democrats publicly courted the African American vote, which played a decisive role in national elections. Another political first occurred that year when the Democratic National Convention included two African American speakers.[16]

Although they were a long way from being uniformly supportive of civil rights, U.S. Supreme Court decisions in the 1930s gave African Americans hope for progress. By the end of 1940, the NAACP had celebrated seventeen victories before the U.S. Supreme Court. The whites-only primary in Texas had been upheld unanimously by the Court in 1935, but white primaries were outlawed in 1944 after a major NAACP campaign. The eight justices who voted to overturn the 1935 decision were all Roosevelt appointees.[17]

The president's wife, Eleanor Roosevelt, also advanced the inclusion of African Americans, and she won admiration in African American communities because of her leadership. She was a major supporter of the NAACP and advocated equal treatment of African Americans in New Deal programs, which, especially in the early years and particularly in the South, discriminated against African Americans in wages and hiring. She was outspoken in her support for antilynching legislation. In 1939, she took her best-known stand on behalf of civil rights: she resigned from the Daughters of the American Revolution after the organization refused to let the African American contralto Marian Anderson perform at Constitution Hall. According to a Gallup Poll, two-thirds of Americans agreed with her decision. Eleanor Roosevelt was so popular among African Americans that both Roosevelts are pictured in FDR's 1940 reelection advertisement in the NAACP's publication, *The Crisis.*[18]

During the same period, grassroots activism in African American communities, including Chicago, also inspired change. In 1929, African American Chicagoans garnered national attention with their "Spend Your Money Where You Can Work" campaign. They protested white-owned businesses in the "Black Belt" that depended on black patronage for their revenue yet refused to hire African American employees. The success of these campaigns resulted in their proliferation across the country.[19] The publicity also led to the recognition that this black patronage could be converted to support for black-owned businesses, which led to the opening of African American–owned insurance companies and to an emphasis on African Americans creating employment within the community.[20]

THEODORE JONES: MEMBER OF FDR'S "BLACK CABINET"

The fourth African American CPA in Chicago, Theodore Jones, benefited both from the concentration of African American business and from the political changes of the 1930s and 1940s. As a high school student in 1920s Chicago, Jones worked for a drugstore after school. He met a white accountant who came in for an hour a week to update the drugstore's financial records, and Jones noticed that the accountant earned more in that one hour than did the store's full-time employees in an entire week. Jones decided to become an accountant.

Despite the family's poverty, in 1929 his mother encouraged him to enter the University of Illinois in Urbana. In virtually all of his classes, Jones was the only African American. There were few housing options for African Americans in Urbana. Like most black students, Jones joined a fraternity, where many of his housemates were from southern states that did not allow African Americans to attend their major universities.[21] An excellent student, Jones reports that he generally felt he was treated fairly in his accounting classes, with one notable exception. One of his instructors refused to call on him when he raised his hand—a common approach among faculty who resented the presence of African Americans in their classrooms.[22] Jones decided to make a game of it. While following class discussion, he would pretend to be staring outside the window. Only then would the instructor call on him, and Jones would provide the correct answer. Soon the instructor would call on him when he raised his hand.

Jones's family was unable to send him much money, but he worked his way through school and graduated in 1933, in the depths of the Great Depression. White students were able to seek employment through the University of Illinois placement office, but African American students were unable to locate jobs through this system. At the university, Jones had learned about the prestige associated with certified public accountancy, and he resolved to become a CPA. However, he did not even consider applying for a job in a white-owned firm because he was certain of rejection. When he graduated with his degree in business, the best job he could get was as a part-time grocery clerk.

Soon thereafter, Jones landed a job as a caseworker with the Chicago Bureau of Public Welfare. Demand for social workers had increased with the onset of the depression.[23] However, Jones had not lost his desire to be a CPA, and changes brought about by the Roosevelt administration provided an opportunity to pursue his dream. In 1935, Congress adopted the Social Security Bill, which greatly increased the payroll reporting requirements of small businesses. Jones walked the black business districts soliciting payroll businesses, at $10, $15, or the occasional $25 a month. He opened a little office with no heat, and worked on his own. Arthur Wilson advised him on starting an accounting firm, as did some of his former professors from the University of Illinois. Since Jones was only making $100 a month as a caseworker, it did not take him long to replace that income with his small payroll accounting fees. He continued to live with his mother, who encouraged him to develop this new career.

Jones passed the CPA examination, and a former professor from the University of Illinois, Hiram T. Scovill, supervised his work and signed off on his experience requirement, making him, in 1940, Illinois's third African American CPA. His connections with the University of Illinois, a leading school in the field of accountancy, also led Jones to become the first African American member of the American Institute of Accountants (AIA), the leading professional organization for CPAs. Scovill and Paul Green, another University of Illinois professor, sponsored Jones's admission to the institute, and in 1942 he became a member. Jones says he "held the distinction" of being the only member of the institute who had been elected in convention. Ordinarily the admissions committee of the institute made decisions on admitting new members, but since Jones was apparently the first African American to apply for membership,[24] his nomination was referred to the full convention, where he was elected to membership by a majority.[25]

This unprecedented action took place despite continual claims by the AIA that "it should be possible for every eligible and desirable accountant of either sex to obtain admission to the national body of professional accountants."[26] Aside from the 1933 *Journal of Accountancy* article discussed in chapter 2, there is no mention of African American CPAs in published institute literature prior to the 1960s. Even the histories of various major CPA firms and state societies written in recent decades ignore the experiences of African Americans in the profession, though they often mention the earliest entry of women.[27] While African American CPAs were largely invisible to the mainstream of the profession, some documents concurrent with the time of Jones's admission to the institute illuminate the attitudes toward African Americans held by the leaders of the profession.

At a meeting of the institute in May of 1942, T. Edward Ross, former vice president of the AIA and co-founder of one of the largest and most prestigious firms in the country, gave his report as secretary of the history committee. He included a "joke" in his report: "I am in somewhat the position of the lady who telephoned to the golf club. She asked the colored locker man who answered the 'phone if her husband was there. He said, 'No ma'm, he ain't here.' She said, 'How do you know? I haven't given you my name.' He said, 'It don't make no difference, lady, there ain't never nobody's husband here.'" The minutes indicate that the story was followed by laughter.[28]

The institute's main publication, the *Journal of Accountancy*, also used African Americans as a source of humor. In 1940, it published an address by Victor Stempf, an institute officer who would become its president a few years later, before the Maryland Association of Certified Public Accountants. The speech chastised certain members of the profession for their "vulgar display of so-called advertising." He continued, "Here in Baltimore, even your houseman would probably say: 'He shua do recommen' hisself highly!'"[29]

The minutes of the fifty-fourth annual meeting of the AIA, held in 1941 in Detroit, include a "joke" from Edwin Wagner, an institute member from St. Louis. Wagner invited the institute to have its next meeting in St. Louis, and he prefaced his invitation with the following:

Perhaps some of you younger men will remember back in the days of prohibition when a great many of the prohibition officers were strewn along the highways to capture moonshiners, and so forth. Down in Kentucky on one highway one morning a truck was seen going along. An enforcement officer came up and stopped the truck. He asked, "What have you got in that truck?"

"Oh, nothing but some fertilizer and a nigger."

He drove on for another ten miles, and again was accosted by an enforcement officer.

"What have you in the truck?"

"Nothing but fertilizer and a nigger."

After going a short distance, another officer stopped him and asked the same question.

"Nothing but fertilizer and a nigger."

After he left, the nigger raised up and said, "Please, sir, boss, the next time we stop I wish you would introduce me first."[30]

Both the nonchalance of the speakers and the laughter that the minutes indicate followed these "jokes" point to the prevailing culture in the institute. Apparently the leading CPAs took for granted that African Americans they might encounter would fill subservient roles such as doormen and locker-room attendants and that it was perfectly acceptable to use racist terms and stereotypes.[31] The fact that Theodore Jones applied for membership may have taken them by surprise.

While struggling for acknowledgment within the mainstream of the profession, Jones was also developing his accounting practice within the African American business community. Supreme Liberty Life Insurance Company, one of the largest black-owned businesses in the country and the largest in Chicago, became his major client.[32] Impressed with some work Jones had done as Supreme Liberty's CPA, the firm's president, Earl Dickerson, invited him to join the company as its chief accountant.

Jones worked closely with Dickerson, who was also a leading civil rights activist and a prominent attorney, and this association led to major changes in both men's lives concurrent with changes in wartime Washington, D.C. In reaction to pressure from civil rights groups to desegregate jobs in the defense industry during World War II, President Roosevelt created the Federal Committee on Fair Employment Practices (FEPC) and named Earl Dickerson as one of two black members on the five-member committee. Dickerson asked

Jones to work for the committee in Washington, and Jones became part of the growing—and unprecedented—number of African Americans working for the Roosevelt administration and known informally as the "Black Cabinet."[33]

Jones was responsible for making logistical arrangements for hearings on discriminatory conditions around the country. Although the FEPC had no enforcement mechanisms, these hearings provided public airing of biased practices and shamed some industries into becoming more equitable. Dickerson's life was often threatened as he traveled in the South to hold these hearings, but despite the threats, he never failed to appear.[34]

During World War II, many of the major white accounting firms dealt with the "manpower" shortage by hiring white women to fill the jobs left by men called into service, and Jones's firm followed a parallel course.[35] Jones hired Elvera Taylor as a staff member, and she managed the firm while he was in Washington. In 1949, Taylor became only the second African American female CPA. Meanwhile, the largest and most prestigious accounting firm in Chicago at the time, Arthur Andersen, refused to hire women to handle the employee shortage during World War II because "it wasn't generally accepted" and "the executives would have raised their eyebrows." Instead, they required overtime and persuaded retirees to return temporarily.[36] If Chicago's major accounting firm would not hire white women because it would mar the image of the firm, it is doubtful that African American applicants would have been welcome. People like Jones and Taylor did not bother to apply for these jobs.

While Taylor was running his accounting firm, Jones entered another political battle. Not content with the fact that Jones had become the first African American member of the AIA, Robert Weaver, a leader of Roosevelt's "Black Cabinet," suggested that Jones apply for membership in the Illinois State Society of CPAs.[37] Weaver believed that the Illinois State Society would be more resistant than the national organization, and that Jones, as an employee of the FEPC, should apply in order to break the racial barriers. With Jones's Washington connections and high profile, the two men thought it was a case that would pressure the society to admit an African American.

And the society did feel pressure. After filing his application, Jones received a phone call saying that the society was willing to extend membership provided Jones did not attend any of its social functions. Fifty years later, in his elegant apartment overlooking Lake Michigan and decorated with pictures featuring his meetings with various U.S. presidents and senators, he recalled the phone call with incredulity: "Can you imagine that? That's what they said; they actually said that to me." The caller said that the members would not like having him at their dinners or dances but that he could come to their professional presentations. This is despite the fact that the *Journal of Accountancy* had long extolled the importance of social connections as critical to the smooth functioning of the profession,[38] and despite the fact that the society, perhaps because it was one of the oldest and best established, was praised by the *Journal of Accountancy* as "one of the most active and constructive of state organizations."[39] Jones would not accept the restriction, and he declined to join the state society on its members' terms. Back in Illinois after his work in Washington, he became active in the NAACP, and he believes that this activism worried the Illinois State Society enough to grant him full membership in 1948.

It was not unusual for professional organizations to exclude African Americans in the 1940s. Both legal and medical professional organizations excluded African Americans; the Chicago Bar Association was the largest professional association in the city, and it admitted only one very light-skinned African American in 1945 while rejecting others' membership applications. African Americans were not welcome in the American Medical Association and the American Bar Association until the 1950s.[40] Allison Davis, the prominent African American psychologist who became the first teaching professor at a white university in 1941, was not allowed to join the University of Chicago's faculty club until 1948.[41] White professionals protested that these organizations were merely social clubs, but African Americans recognized that the professional organizations led to expanded business opportunities as well as social prestige.[42]

CHARLES BECKETT: "I HAPPEN TO BE A CERTIFIED PUBLIC ACCOUNTANT"

Jones's contemporary, Charles Beckett, became a CPA in Illinois in 1941. He reports that he did not bother applying for membership in the Illinois State Society of CPAs when he passed the examination in 1941 because "they'd have thrown [his application] out of the window." Beckett came to Chicago after graduating from Morehouse College, where Jesse Blayton had been one of his professors, and Atlanta University, where he earned a master's degree in economics. He majored in accounting as an undergraduate because he fell in love with it and found it very simple. During the depression he moved to Chicago to work for the *Chicago Defender*, one of the largest African American newspapers in the country.[43] The *Defender* had played a major role in the Great

Migration; black train porters distributed it during their travels, and it was full of encouragement for southerners to move north. Beckett worked in the circulation department for a short time before becoming the business manager. He had wanted to become a CPA since his days as a student of Blayton's, and he took the examination when he got to Chicago. Like the majority of first-time examinees, he failed the exam and realized that he needed more training.[44]

Beckett enrolled at Northwestern University, where Mary Washington had studied, taking accounting and business law classes, as well as a review course for the CPA examination. In the latter course, the professor told Beckett he was doing him a favor by tolerating his presence in the classroom but required him to sit separately from the other students. Beckett was single-minded in his pursuit of the CPA, so he didn't complain. He shrugged off this and other offenses. He said, "They treated me all right. But I never needed to rely on them for my social involvement. I completed courses, studied my lessons pretty well, and I'd make an 'A' out of the course. That was all I was interested in."[45]

Not all of Beckett's professors were hostile. When he graduated, one of them arranged a part-time job with a small white-owned accounting firm so Beckett could meet the experience requirement. Beckett knew that virtually all the white-owned firms in Chicago refused to hire African American accountants at the time and felt fortunate to have the opportunity.

Beckett went on to establish his own CPA practice, initially providing services at no charge in order to demonstrate his value to the small businesses, such as grocery stores, that were his clients. In this practice, he followed Jesse Blayton's advice that African American accountants serve as "missionaries" to the black business community and convince it of the value of a CPA's services.[46] He continued to work exclusively in the African American community throughout his career, usually maintaining other employment outside of his practice. In 1943, John H. Johnson—publisher of *Negro Digest* and later *Ebony*, which soon made him the wealthiest black person in the country—hired Beckett, whom he described as a "brilliant young Black CPA." Beckett continued to work for Johnson until Beckett retired, despite the fact that Johnson's bankers pressured him to hire a major white public accounting firm.[47]

In contrast to his work for the wealthy John H. Johnson, Beckett's main interest was in expanding opportunities for the economically disadvantaged. When he worked for a small credit union, he began organizing groups of tenants to form cooperatives and buy apartment buildings. He helped hundreds of African Americans in Chicago become homeowners. He named a housing development after his friend and business associate, Paul G. Stewart, who had become Chicago's second African American CPA in 1937 but who passed away shortly thereafter.

Beckett's assistant for over thirty years, Jean Chambliss, says she used to ask him why he entered a profession that was so closed. He responded that he never wanted to take the easy way out. When she learned, in 1992, that Beckett had been only the tenth African American CPA in the country, she said, "I never realized that thirty years ago [he] was one of twenty CPAs. And people would . . . meet [him and] say, 'Well, what do you do?'. . . And he would always say, 'I happen to be a certified public accountant.' . . . I'd wonder why he always says *I happen to be* a certified public accountant. [Now] I see why: because that was quite a happening. . . . I knew there weren't many, but I didn't know that he was in such an exclusive fraternity."[48]

Despite the fact that it was easier for an African American to become a CPA in Chicago than in any other city, it was nonetheless a lofty achievement that elicited admiration. The fact that accountants were well respected is indicated by the 1940 edition of *Who's Who in Colored America*, which profiles several people in accounting-related professions, including Jesse Blayton.[49] A survey of African American college students in the 1940s ranked accounting as a very highly regarded field.[50] Members of the professions were at the "top" of Chicago's African American society in the 1940s; those who were the first to break into a new field were lauded in the black press as "Race Heroes." Only about 2 percent of Chicago's African Americans had attended college by the mid-1940s, and with his master's degree and CPA, Beckett had achieved a pinnacle among Chicago African Americans.[51]

The early group of African American CPAs in Chicago, including Beckett, Arthur Wilson, Theodore Jones, and Mary Washington, helped other African Americans earn their CPAs. In addition to Elvera Taylor, Jones provided experience to William Anderson, who became a CPA in 1953, and Edmond N. Fambro, who became a CPA in 1962. Beckett provided the requisite experience to Benjamin H. Crockett, who had earned a master's degree in mathematics from the University of Chicago in 1937 and who became a CPA in 1953.[52]

HIRAM PITTMAN JOINS MARY WASHINGTON'S FIRM

Another reason Illinois was more hospitable—or simply less hostile—to African Americans' becoming CPAs is that, unlike other states, Illinois allowed applicants to take the examination *before* meeting the experience requirement. Someone who passed the exam would not be automatically licensed, but he or she could use the examination passage as an additional attraction to potential employers. In 1949, the *Chicago Defender* ran a squib and picture announcing that Hiram Langford Pittman had passed the CPA examination. Mary Washington, the first African American female CPA, saw the notice and sent Pittman a congratulatory telegram. In order to meet him, she attended the banquet honoring those who had passed the examination. He went to work for her a few days later.

Hiram Pittman had grown up in Omaha, Nebraska, and was one of a handful of African American students in his high school class during the depression. His mother had been a teacher, and she insisted that he attend college in order to expand his economic opportunities. In the late 1930s, he was one of two African American freshmen at the University of Nebraska, a school with 6,000 students.

Pittman graduated in January 1942, just one month after the bombing of Pearl Harbor, and immediately was drafted into the U.S. Army. He had been in the Reserve Officers' Training Corps in college, so he entered the army as a staff sergeant. With three accounting courses under his belt, he responded to a notice stating that anyone with an accounting background could get a pay increase and a job at post headquarters in Fort Leonard Wood, Missouri. Pittman worked for Jerome P. Cahill, a white CPA from Minneapolis. Cahill was the first CPA Pittman had ever met, and Pittman became an expert in accounting for the post exchanges, service clubs, and guesthouses for which Cahill was responsible. Pittman eventually moved on to officers' candidate school, but his experience with Cahill convinced him that he wanted to become a CPA. As with Theodore Jones's observation of the drugstore accountant, Pittman saw that the distinction would lead to increased earnings.[53]

After his discharge, Pittman moved to Chicago where he met Theodore Jones, who invited him to work on one of his audit clients. There he met Jones's employee Elvera Taylor, and the two studied together for the CPA examination. Through the audit he worked on with Jones, he learned about Charles Beckett, and Beckett recommended that he apply for a job as an accountant at Provident Hospital, one of the first hospitals in the country to provide training to African American nurses and interns.[54]

After making $47.50 a week at Provident, Pittman left and doubled his income by teaching accounting and business law to African American returning veterans at the Cortez W. Peters Business School. Pittman was working for the business school and doing some accounting for clients on the side when he passed the CPA examination and was approached by Mary Washington and offered a job. Pittman was thrilled by the opportunity. Not only could he meet his experience requirement, but he soon doubled his income again to $13,000 a year. Samuel Fuller subsidized Mary Washington's first full-time hire by paying half his salary for his first six months.

Pittman believes that the best, most challenging piece of work he did as a CPA was a project that worried him so much that he developed ulcers. The U.S. Treasury Department had determined that Fuller Products was buying too much specially made alcohol and other restricted ingredients given the volume of hair products it was producing. Pittman investigated and could not account for about 10 percent of the volume of those special ingredients. Initially he thought that the containers were miscalibrated, but upon observing factory production, Pittman discovered that when a pint of water was mixed with a pint of alcohol, the two pints did not combine to make a quart. Because of the way the alcohol molecules combined with those of the water, mixing the two resulted in lost volume. Finally, Pittman had solved the frustrating problem of the "lost" alcohol.[55]

Pittman became Washington's partner in 1952, and the two hired several part-time employees to help with the expanding work. Their clients included Parker House Sausage, the two largest real estate firms on Chicago's south side, savings and loans, insurance companies, and social service agencies. "Miss Washington," as she was known by her employees, was meticulous and exacting. She developed the accounting systems for her clients, and her employees maintained them. As a relatively large black firm in the 1940s and 1950s, Washington and Pittman provided both tax and audit services, though, ironically, sometimes the black businesses upon which they relied for income grew too large and turned to more well-known, white-owned CPA firms for their audits. These businesses were often required to do so by their banks, which insisted on attestation by more familiar firms.[56]

Despite this, Washington & Pittman became a thriving and lucrative business, and its employees often worked sixteen-hour days. During tax season, Washington would make dinner for everyone while they worked late nights in her basement. Two of her former employees reported that an African American CPA at that time might be justifiably concerned about training other CPAs who might ultimately "steal" the limited business available in the African American community. Apparently Washington had no such fears and was generous and enthusiastic in encouraging others. Washington also provided

Mary Washington (Illinois CPA 1943) and other Illinois CPAs at one of her annual Christmas parties, circa 1950. *Standing, left to right*: Steven Marchman (1944); Cary Lewis (1950); Arthur Wilson (1923), the first African American CPA in Illinois; Isaac Little (1950); and Hiram Pittman (1949). Photo courtesy of Hiram Pittman.

an important focal point for all the black CPAs in Chicago: each year she hosted a memorable Christmas party.[57]

Because of the concentration of African American CPAs in Chicago, Jesse Blayton, the "Dean of Negro Accountants" and professor at Atlanta University, visited the city in 1952 and met with the local group of CPAs, which included not only Washington and Pittman but also Elvera Taylor, Theodore Jones, Arthur Wilson, Charles Beckett, G. Steven Marchman III, Cary B. Lewis Jr., Isaac Y. Little, and Frederick C. Ford.[58] The latter three men all began their careers in Washington's firm, earning CPAs in the early 1950s. Lewis went on to become an accounting professor; Little became an accountant for the Chicago Housing Authority; and Ford became the first African American to work for a major downtown real estate firm.

Like all of Washington's proteges, Hiram Pittman enjoyed his work with the firm. But he resented the racial exclusion in the accounting profession. He had heard how Theodore Jones had been asked not to attend social events when he tried to join the Illinois Society of CPAs. A few years later, Washington became the first African American woman to join the AIA, and she planned to attend the institute's annual meeting in 1952. The meeting was held at the Shamrock Hotel in Houston, which catered to wealthy oil magnates and movie stars. However, from its ostentatious opening in 1949 until 1962, the Shamrock did not admit African American guests.[59] Just before the Houston meeting, an officer of the Illinois Society of CPAs visited Washington and Pittman's office to ask Washington not to attend the meeting. Some members of the Illinois State Society were worried about the embarrassment the organization would experience if it were discovered that the light-skinned Washington was African American. As a result of these two incidents, Pittman resolved not to join the society and ignored its later requests that he become a member.[60]

It was not unusual for professional societies to hold meetings in segregated hotels in 1952. Nevertheless, several organizations, including the Congress of Industrial Organizations, the Steel Workers Organizing Committee, and many church groups, had earlier recognized that hosting meetings in segregated cities caused discomfort to their African American members and therefore refused to meet in such venues.[61]

Despite slights and exclusion by the leading professional organizations, becoming a CPA was a great source of accomplishment and pride. The feelings of pioneering African American professionals are described by a character in a 1942 Bette Davis movie. The film included one of the first portrayals of an African American with professional ambitions.[62] In it, Northwestern University graduate Ernest Anderson's character wants to study law, and when he explains his interest to a character played by Olivia De Havilland, he points out, "A white boy, he can take most any kind of job and improve himself. . . . He can get to be a clerk or a manager. A colored boy can't do that. He can keep a job or he can lose a job, but he can't get any higher up. So, he's got to figure out something he can do that no one can take away. And that's why I want to be a lawyer."[63]

Arthur Wilson, Mary Washington, Theodore Jones, Charles Beckett, and those they had trained had all achieved something no one could take away. They had earned their CPAs.

4

Postwar CPAs: Overcoming Barriers

Outside of Chicago, African Americans seeking to become CPAs in the 1940s
and 1950s continued to face many of the same barriers that had existed in
previous decades. Because most CPA firms refused to hire African Americans, black candidates found it difficult to meet state experience requirements. They also faced educational exclusion, employment and housing segregation, and an absence of the black-owned businesses necessary to provide a
client base.

In the years between World War II and the major civil rights legislation of
the 1960s, there was some amelioration of the intense resistance to African
Americans entering the professions. The war and its aftermath produced
unprecedented, though guarded, optimism for African Americans seeking
employment equality. Hitler's virulent racism and the horrors of the Holo-
caust had repulsed the American public, and many whites began to join
African Americans in seeing the injustice of the Jim Crow South. Most Americans were dismayed by stories of atrocities committed against black veterans
and of German soldiers held as prisoners of war in the South who enjoyed
privileges—such as eating in restaurants—denied to African American soldiers. Returning veterans who had fought for freedom abroad challenged
their second-class status in this country, and several became plaintiffs in the
NAACP's campaign to end school segregation.[1]

This activism influenced President Franklin D. Roosevelt to sign Executive
Order 8802 in 1941, making it illegal for the federal government and federal
contractors to discriminate on the basis of race. In addition to opening up
jobs in war industries, this order also led to unprecedented federal employment of African American professionals. The GI Bill of Rights, which provided tuition payments for veterans, led to an enormous increase in African
American college attendance after both World War II and the Korean conflict.

The slow but positive change continued during the Harry S. Truman administration. Against his advisers' recommendations, Truman included unprecedented support for African Americans' civil rights in his 1948 presidential election campaign. That same year he made history by becoming the first U.S. president to address the NAACP's annual convention.[2] Truman's leadership, combined with African American activism, helped lead to an end to segregation in the military in 1948.

RICHARD AUSTIN: MICHIGAN'S SECRETARY OF STATE

The changes that took place during these times opened the door for Michigan's first African American CPA. Richard H. Austin was born in 1913 in Alabama. His father was an itinerant coal miner who died of work-related injuries when Austin was only eleven. His mother moved the family to Detroit, where she had relatives, in the hope that her three sons would gain employment in the rapidly expanding auto industry. While she cleaned and cooked for white families, her two older sons went to work for a Polish Jewish immigrant who owned a shoe repair shop. When the depression hit in 1929, sixteen-year-old Austin found his employer's business thriving: Detroit residents who could not afford new shoes turned to repairing the old ones. The expanded business led to the need for a bookkeeper. Impressed by Austin's hard work and excellent grades in school, the shopkeeper asked him to take the job.[3]

Austin was an outstanding student. In contrast to Alabama, where schools were strictly segregated by law, or Chicago, where they were de facto segregated by neighborhood, Austin was allowed to choose the high school he would attend in Detroit. He chose Cass Technical High School, a predominantly white school that was one of the best in Detroit, because he hoped that it would lead to a job in the skilled auto trades.[4] In addition to his busy work life and his position as captain of the track team, Austin earned the highest grade point average in his graduating class of 350 students.

Impressed by Austin, the principal at Cass recommended that he go into teaching, the field most open to African Americans. Although the principal offered to help Austin find a college scholarship, Austin had no intention of going to college. He wanted to join the skilled trades because he needed to support his mother and younger brother. The principal pointed out that despite being the best student in his class, Austin had no chance of entering the skilled trades in Detroit's auto industry. Whites controlled the auto-workers' unions, and in depression-era Detroit there were few opportunities for anyone to enter the industry, especially an African American.[5] Given this reality, Austin decided to continue his bookkeeping job while awaiting an opportunity to enter trade school.

Austin expanded his bookkeeping knowledge by reading books on the subject and by querying the businesspeople he encountered while working for the shoe-repair store. Soon he attracted a few small African American–owned businesses as bookkeeping clients. He spent some time at the College of the City of Detroit (now Wayne State University) on an athletic scholarship, but because his family needed his income, he returned to full-time work. Setting aside his determination to enter trade school, Austin decided to improve his skills in the field in which he had serendipitously found himself. He enrolled in night classes in accounting at the Detroit Institute of Technology.[6] At school and from the banks and creditors of the small businesses for which he was working, he learned of the high regard that CPAs enjoyed. Although he had never met an African American CPA, through friends he learned of the existence of black CPAs in Chicago, Atlanta, Washington, and New York. He decided he would become a CPA.

Even though Austin excelled in his accounting classes, several of his teachers told him they considered it unwise that he pursue the field, since he would be unable to find appropriate employment upon graduation. He knew that even the federal government, one of the few employers of African American professionals in the 1930s, would not hire African American auditors in the Internal Revenue Service. As a college senior in 1936, he bravely tried to get employment with one of the CPA firms in Detroit. Although he was again at the top of his class and had exceptional work experience, the firms said that their clients would object to an African American accountant appearing in their offices to review their accounts.

Fortunately, one of Austin's instructors, J. Lee Boothe, was willing to help. A former employee of the major accounting firm of Price Waterhouse, Boothe now had his own CPA firm. Austin had several of his own clients already, including the Jewish merchants who had given him his start and several African American–owned businesses. Austin turned these clients over to Boothe, who then supervised Austin's work. Boothe also allowed Austin to review tax work and do some audit work for his own clients, though Austin did not visit their offices. The arrangement worked very well; the two men gained even more African American clients, including a large cemetery, now that Austin was working for a CPA. Austin became the first African American CPA in Michigan in 1941 and only the eleventh in the nation. He was probably the only CPA in the country that had met his experience requirement by offering *his* clients to a CPA.

Like his Chicago counterpart, Mary Washington, Austin was determined to increase the number of African American CPAs. For twenty-five years, his was the only firm that provided experience to African American prospective CPAs in Michigan. He trained at least five other men who became CPAs in the ensuing decades.[7] Elmer J. Whiting Jr. of Cleveland spent his honeymoon in Detroit for the express purpose of meeting Richard Austin and learning more about the possibility of becoming a CPA.[8] Ernest H. Davenport, who was a student of Jesse Blayton in Atlanta in the 1930s, moved to Detroit after serving in World War II solely for the chance to work with Austin and soon became a partner in the firm.[9]

As a man with exceptional contacts in the white business community, including his professor, J. Lee Boothe, Austin had little trouble joining the Michigan Association of CPAs. In the early 1940s, African Americans in Detroit had considerable political power and the largest NAACP chapter in the country. Vicious antiblack riots and accompanying police brutality had embarrassed liberal white city leaders in 1943.[10] In 1944, Austin's acquaintances in the profession, whom he had met through his accounting instructors as well as through his business contacts, planned a strategy to get him admitted to the Michigan Association without resistance. Austin's understanding was that leaders of the Michigan Association knew that other states had been hostile to African American members, and they wanted to avoid any embarrassment associated with being discriminatory. The association granted him membership after visiting his offices to ensure that his practice was compatible with industry standards, a step Austin believed they would have performed for any small CPA firm.

Like Mary Washington, Austin planned to attend the American Institute of Accountants' annual meeting in Houston in 1952 with one of his partners. When they discovered that the hotel would not accommodate African Americans, they did not attend. Austin and his colleague subsequently recommended to their friends in the institute that it no longer hold meetings at segregated hotels.[11] Nevertheless, the institute held its 1957 meeting at the segregated Roosevelt Hotel in New Orleans.[12] As Ellis Marsalis Sr., grandfather of Wynton and Branford Marsalis and owner of a New Orleans hotel that catered to prominent African Americans from the 1940s through the 1980s, noted, "If you were a black entertainer, it was all right for you to sing and dance at the Roosevelt Hotel, but you couldn't sleep there, even if you were Ray Charles."[13]

Austin's prominence in Detroit's black community, his later involvement with the NAACP and the Urban League, and his fundraising for the civil rights efforts of Martin Luther King Jr. led to his entry into politics.[14] After being elected Wayne County auditor in 1966, Austin ran for mayor of Detroit in 1969, and in a race that garnered national attention, he narrowly missed becoming the city's first black mayor.[15] In 1971, he became the first African American in Michigan's history to be elected to statewide office. He served as secretary of state for over two decades.

HEADING NORTH

Detroit was similar to Chicago. Black businesses provided a client base for prospective CPAs, and African Americans had sufficient political power to blunt the blatant discrimination that existed in the South. In southern states such as Mississippi and South Carolina, resistance to African American business development was intense.[16] In southern cities, with the exception of Atlanta, there was simply no market for African American CPAs. Even in Atlanta, Jesse Blayton found his primary employment as a faculty member, not as a professional accountant. In his accounting practice, many of Blayton's clients were segregated colleges, not businesses.[17] In 1950, despite the fact that 70 percent of African Americans lived in the South, the twenty-six African Americans who had earned their CPAs included only six who had done so in southern states. These six lived in border states, were educated in the North, or went north to practice their careers.[18] During the 1940s and 1950s, many African Americans who became CPAs found that moving north was critical to their ability to succeed in their chosen field.

One barrier to earning a CPA in the South was the lack of educational opportunity. Public grade schools and high schools came nowhere near achieving the "separate but equal" standard the U.S. Supreme Court had set in *Plessy v. Ferguson* in 1896. There were enormous discrepancies in funding between white and black schools. Because the best-educated African Americans in the country largely were confined to the teaching profession, black schools had many outstanding teachers, but salary differentials could mean white teachers were paid more than twice as much as their African American counterparts.[19]

School buildings were dilapidated; African American students used books that had been cast off by the white schools; and often no provision was made for busing rural black students to school, even in areas with well-developed transportation systems for white students.[20]

These disadvantages severely limited the number of African American students who were able to prepare themselves for college. Those relatively fortunate few who did attend college faced additional barriers to becoming accountants. Very few black colleges offered accounting courses because of the dearth of both well-trained accounting faculty and opportunities for their graduates. The southern white colleges that had accounting programs refused to admit African American students. In fact, in southern states it was explicitly illegal to admit African Americans to white schools.[21]

THE NAACP'S ATTACK ON DISCRIMINATION IN HIGHER EDUCATION

In the early 1930s, under the leadership of Charles Hamilton Houston, a Harvard-educated lawyer and dean of the Howard University Law School, the NAACP developed a strategy for ending school segregation. It began with an attack on precisely those professional schools that were preventing southern African Americans from studying fields like accounting. There were several strategic advantages to challenging professional programs first.[22] It was clear that the complete absence of availability of programs in law, pharmacy, education, and business violated the "separate but equal" doctrine that ostensibly governed the segregated educational system in the South. In addition, whereas the parents of grade-school children were often threatened with the loss of their jobs (or worse) if they insisted on fighting to integrate the grade schools,[23] many applicants for graduate school were in the relatively safe environs of undergraduate black colleges.[24] The NAACP also deemed this strategy more promising because resistance was likely to be less intense since few African Americans would attend graduate school.[25]

Houston and his team, which included his former Howard law student Thurgood Marshall, knew that there was no such thing as "separate but equal" schools. But instead of attacking this fiction directly, they took a carefully planned route, backing the southern states into corners where they could not justify their discriminatory policies. One of the first cases they undertook sought to force the University of Maryland's law school to accept a well-qualified black student, Donald Murray. The University of Maryland Law School represented an excellent starting point both because it was in a border state, where resistance was unlikely to be as insurmountable as it would have been in the Deep South, and because it was a law school. The judges who decided the cases were themselves law school graduates who, Houston and Marshall believed, would see through the sham of "separate but equal." The NAACP also hoped that the judges would recognize that some states' practice of paying tuition to send students to northern law schools would not provide an equivalent legal education. A Baltimore student who attended the University of Wisconsin Law School would not learn the laws of Maryland.[26]

The team persisted despite the disadvantages they faced in the legal profession: as African Americans they were not admitted to the American Bar Association, nor were they allowed to use its libraries.[27] Nevertheless, the strategy paid off. In 1936, the Maryland Court of Appeals agreed with the lower court's requirement that Murray be admitted to the law school.

Because of the team's success, this case was not appealed to the U.S. Supreme Court, but the NAACP's next major graduate education case was.[28] Years of NAACP-led litigation and activism in the black community of Missouri accompanied Lloyd L. Gaines's application to the University of Missouri law school. Some white leaders and students supported the cause as well. Finally, in 1938, the U.S. Supreme Court demanded that either Gaines be allowed to enter the University of Missouri School of Law or that the state provide *equal* legal education for African Americans *within* the state.[29]

Southern states reacted to these NAACP victories with panic. Although several states discussed the possibility of creating some regional graduate and professional programs for African Americans, the main responses fell into two categories. Some states attempted to develop "separate but equal" graduate and professional school programs at the African American colleges already in existence. The other common approach was to introduce or expand out-of-state scholarships to those African American students who wanted to pursue programs not available in their states despite the dubious legality of these scholarships. Only one state, West Virginia, responded by dropping its barriers and admitting African American applicants.[30]

Many of the earliest African American CPAs attended northern universities under the out-of-state scholarship provisions that resulted from the NAACP's legal efforts. Though these programs were clearly an effort to circumvent the Supreme Court's ruling in the *Gaines* decision, they also made it possible for

African Americans to attend some of the best colleges in the country, schools they otherwise would have been unable to afford. The president of Morgan State College, a black college in Baltimore, taunted the president of the University of Maryland by stating that Maryland's African American citizens preferred taking advantage of the out-of-state scholarships because they provided a higher quality education than that available at the university.[31]

FREDERICK FORD: MISSOURI'S LOSS

The State of Missouri lost an outstanding leader after augmenting its out-of-state tuition program in response to the *Gaines* case. Frederick Ford's father was a postal clerk and his brothers owned four restaurants in Missouri. When Ford finished high school in St. Louis in 1944, he wanted to pursue a business degree. The University of Missouri did not admit African Americans, and Lincoln University for Negroes did not offer an accounting curriculum. So the state paid the $80-a-year tuition for Ford to attend the University of Illinois, where he met other African American refugees from the South who were interested in becoming CPAs.

Ford was the president of the student senate at Illinois;[32] his grades were in the top 10 percent of his class; and he was an officer in Beta Alpha Psi, the accounting honors fraternity.[33] Like his classmates, Ford wanted to become a CPA because he had learned that it was the "height of the profession." Although he had studied under the leading accounting academics of the time, he saw no possibility of working for a white-owned CPA firm. He applied for a graduate teaching fellowship, and, though other men with weaker credentials were given these fellowships to finance their graduate education, Ford was not. Nevertheless, he worked his way through a master's degree before looking for a job in 1949. A recruiter from a major oil company addressed the accounting honors fraternity and encouraged the students to apply for accounting jobs with his company. But when Ford appeared for his interview, he was told that the company needed engineers, not accountants. His interviewer at the University of Chicago was more direct. When Ford responded to an accounting position advertisement, he was told that the head of the department was unlikely to be willing to employ an African American.

A fellow student then introduced him to Mary Washington, the first African American female CPA. Ford joined her firm and became a CPA in 1952. In

1951, Ford became the first African American professional in a downtown Chicago real estate office when Ferdinand Kramer, the progressive leader of Draper & Kramer, recognized his talent. Ford went on to become the senior vice president of finance for the organization. In the late 1950s, Kramer again demonstrated that leaders could bring about change. He used his clout in the community to insist that the Chicago Real Estate Board admit one of his African American employees to membership, threatening otherwise that he would withdraw all members of his large and powerful firm. As Ford reports, "Miraculously, they began to admit Negroes."[34]

"ARE YOU A COMMUNIST?"

Like Frederick Ford, Bernadine Coles Gines also had to head north to earn an accounting degree. Her grandfather had given her a Smith Corona portable typewriter when she was a child in Charlottesville, Virginia, and she and her sister dreamed of working in an office when they grew up. She attended Virginia State College, a black college, where the head of the business administration department, George G. Singleton, encouraged her to become a CPA. The University of Virginia was only about a mile from her home, but it might as well have been a thousand miles because it did not admit African Americans. Virginia had established an out-of-state scholarship program in reaction to Maryland's being forced to accept African American graduate students in the Murray case.[35] In 1946, under this program, Gines headed to New York University, where her mentor, Singleton, had gone to school.[36]

Gines finished her M.B.A. at New York University at just about the time New York became the first state to require a four-year college education to sit for the CPA examination.[37] Despite the fact that she exceeded this requirement, Gines had intense difficulty finding a position with a CPA firm. As difficult as her job search was in New York, she knew that things would be even worse in Virginia, so she remained in the city after graduation. From her residence at the YWCA in Harlem, she sent many letters of application but did not get a single interview. She worked as a bookkeeper for an African American newspaper, the *New York Age*, and learned from staff members there that Lucas & Tucker, the only African American CPA firm in New York in the 1940s, did not hire women.[38] Most CPA firms at that time did not hire women, though New York and Illinois were ostensibly the two states that were most open to female practitioners. New York's and Illinois's state CPA societies had the highest numbers of women (all of whom were white) serving on committees in the early 1950s.[39]

Gines moved from Harlem to Queens, and suddenly, because her address no longer revealed her race, she was invited for several interviews. Nevertheless, when she appeared for interviews, she received no offers. A partner at the first firm with which she interviewed told her that he could not hire her as an accountant. Instead, he asked if she could help him find a maid for his wife.[40]

After two years of searching, Gines was interviewed by two young Jewish men who quickly overcame their surprise that she was African American. After all her frustration, Gines says, "Of course, I was in seventh heaven that someone was actually talking to me."

Before they offered her the job, however, they asked if she was a Communist. As Gines reports, "People had gotten the notion [in 1949] that all black people must be Communists."[41] The incipient cold war had had a dual effect. On one hand, it increased pressure on the United States to appear to be the "land of freedom and opportunity" it purported to be. On the other, because Communist organizations had long been prominent supporters of civil rights, many African Americans were suspected of being Communists.[42] Gines had to overcome this prejudice, too, before the young men agreed to hire her.

One of the partners notified his clients that he had hired an African American, and when one objected, he dropped the client. The other partner simply included her in client visits as he would have any other employee, and Gines does not recall any problems with the firm's predominantly Jewish clientele in the three years she worked there.

Her employers offered to hold her job for her after her son was born, but, exhausted by a five-and-a-half-day work week at only $45 per week, she decided to follow her father's advice and go into the civil service. After she left, she was gratified to learn that her position at the CPA firm was filled by another African American. While working in the sales tax division for the City of New York, she typically had no problem with those she was auditing—they knew she had the authority to order more audits of their sales to ensure that the businesses were submitting the appropriate amounts of sales tax to the city. On one audit, a woman she was auditing referred to Gines as a CPA when talking to one of her colleagues. The colleague said, "Oh no. She may work for the city, but she's not a CPA." Gines had found a substantial error in his calculation of sales tax, and she took satisfaction in telling him that not only was she a CPA but also his miscalculation was going to cost his client a lot of money.[43]

THE D.C. FOUR: A COORDINATED ATTACK

Because of President Roosevelt's Executive Order 8802 banning employment discrimination by federal agencies and in war industries, and due to the mushrooming of bureaucracy during the New Deal and World War II, the federal government became the major employer of African American professionals in the 1940s and 1950s.[44] While Bernadine Gines was working for the City of New York, four young men in Washington, D.C., Benjamin L. King Sr., Arthur M. Reynolds Sr., Carroll D. Lee, and Jerome R. Broadus, decided they wanted to become CPAs. In addition to the barriers faced by those in New York, Chicago, and Detroit, these men faced legal segregation and a dearth of African American business. Nonetheless, they helped each other overcome these obstacles.[45]

As a student at Dunbar High School in Washington, D.C., in the 1940s, Benjamin King helped his father, a contractor, by keeping his payroll accounts. From his high school guidance counselor, he learned that becoming a CPA was the most desirable achievement in the accounting profession. He had wanted to specialize in accounting, but Virginia State, the African American college he attended, offered only four accounting classes, so he majored in business. One of his professors said that there were only twelve black CPAs in the country, and King decided immediately that he wanted to be number thirteen. He asked the professor why there were so few, and the professor's explanation—that the experience requirement posed an almost insurmountable barrier—foreshadowed King's own experience in the field.

After college, King was drafted into the Korean War, and when he was discharged, he worked for the federal government as an auditor for the Army Audit Agency. Despite the progress of African American professionals within the federal government, King's work there was not without its unpleasant incidents. As an auditor, his job was to review charges by contractors who sold war supplies to the U.S. government. One of these contractors resented the fact that an African American had been sent to his office, and he required that King work at a card table in an unheated garage. King became ill and missed a week of work, but he insisted that no one else replace him on the job. When he returned to work, he "disallowed everything"—he gave the audit special scrutiny and required the contractor to justify fully all of his reimbursement requests.

Another time, King and three white men he was supervising stopped in the Washington suburb of Silver Spring to eat at a chain restaurant on their way back from an audit. The four men waited interminably for service. When one of King's employees, a young man from Boston, got up to see what the problem was, he was told that they would not be served as long as King was with the group. King suggested that the white men eat while he waited, but his colleague was so angry that he insisted they return to Washington and find a place where they could eat together.

While working for the Army Audit Agency, King used the GI Bill to study accounting at American University, one of the first integrated colleges in Washington, D.C.[46] There he studied with three other African American government accountants who were interested in becoming CPAs: Carroll Lee, an accountant for the Navy; Jerome Broadus, one of the first African American Internal Revenue Service agents; and Arthur Reynolds, who worked for the Air Force Auditor General. Like King, Broadus and Reynolds were also studying under the GI Bill.[47]

The GI Bill of Rights was passed before the end of World War II to pay for education for returning veterans. Some academic elitists—including the presidents of Harvard University and the University of Chicago—initially opposed the GI Bill because it changed the composition of student bodies. Many young men who otherwise would not have been able to afford college had their expenses covered by the GI Bill of Rights, both after World War II and after the Korean War. The fact that the government paid soldiers' tuition changed the market for a college education. Exclusive schools found that they could not maintain earlier prejudices against African Americans and Jews while competing for this desirable, tuition-paying group of students that was flooding the campuses.[48]

Described as "the most revolutionary and racially empowering legislation in the 20th Century," the GI Bill of Rights was the first social legislation that was applicable regardless of race, despite the fact that some southern Congressmen opposed its being applied to black colleges and opposed equal benefits for white and black veterans.[49] As expected, the GI Bill resulted in an enormous change in opportunities for black Americans—a quarter million African Americans used GI Bill funding for college. Like their white counterparts, African American GIs were interested in practical training. Many became attorneys, teachers, ministers, and even accountants, under its provisions. African American veterans often used the GI Bill to train for professions in which few or no African Americans were employed; changing times led many to hope that opportunities might open up while they were in school, and they wanted to be ready.[50]

Benjamin King's first accounting firm partner, Arthur Reynolds, was part of that new wave of professionally educated African Americans. Whereas King was introduced to accounting through his father's business, Reynolds's attraction to the field was indirect. While he was an undergraduate at Howard University, Chicago's Mary Washington came to campus to see her daughter, a student there. She drove up in a long Cadillac, and Reynolds immediately wondered, "What does she do?" She told him about her firm and her work for Fuller Products and other major black-owned companies. To Reynolds, who was working his way through school, she "exuded affluence." He decided then that he wanted to become a CPA, like Mary Washington.

However, Reynolds found it impossible to find work with a CPA. After several failed attempts, he offered to work without remuneration for a white Howard University professor who owned a CPA firm. The professor declined. Reynolds says, "[In 1955] nobody, and I mean *nobody*, would hire a black as an accountant."[51]

Carroll Lee, whose path would soon cross with those of King and Reynolds, moved to the District of Columbia from Philadelphia in the late 1940s in the hope of expanding his job opportunities beyond teaching or factory work. He had been warned that accounting was a difficult major. But after he found his first accounting class easy, he decided to pursue a CPA. Lee learned that he needed a year's experience to get a CPA in the District of Columbia, so he "went to every CPA firm in the District to get that one year's experience." Every interview Lee had was the same: the interviewers claimed that they personally harbored no prejudices but that their clients would not tolerate an African American reviewing their accounting records.

Reynolds and Lee knew that John Cromwell, the first African American CPA in the country who had earned his certificate in New Hampshire, had a firm in Washington, so they went to see him about employment. But Cromwell did not have enough business to sustain other employees, and he did not hire them.[52] The four men, King, Lee, Reynolds, and Broadus, became more inventive in their approach.

King asked the District of Columbia CPA Board how he could become a CPA when no firm would hire him, and the board suggested that he move to Detroit—five hundred miles from home—to work for Richard Austin. King had no interest in moving. In a training program at the Army Audit Agency, he learned that there were two ways he could avoid the experience requirement. Each state had different CPA laws, and because so many of its residents worked for the federal government, the State of Virginia accepted four years of government accounting in lieu of working for a CPA. Maryland had a different set of criteria. Those who had earned an undergraduate degree in accounting at the University of Maryland did not have to meet any experience requirement. The men could not take advantage of this provision, however, because African Americans were not admitted to the university's undergraduate programs. Despite the 1936 *Murray* ruling admitting African Americans to the University of Maryland Law School, the school did not cease excluding black undergraduates until after *Brown v. Board of Education* was decided in 1954.[53] Those who attended school elsewhere had to "take just about every known accounting course" to avoid the experience requirement.[54] Since three of the four men—all except Lee—were pursuing graduate degrees, they had no trouble meeting the extra educational requirement, and Lee enrolled in all the necessary courses. Having met the educational requirement and having avoided the experience requirement, the men now had to meet a state residency requirement. King moved to his uncle's house in Maryland, but Reynolds, Lee, and Broadus had more difficulty finding homes because there were few areas in Maryland where African Americans were welcome.[55]

After becoming the state's first African American CPA in 1957, King joined the Maryland State Society of CPAs. However, when he sat down to dinner at his first meeting, everyone else at the table got up and moved. He never went back to a state society event.[56] Carroll Lee also joined the society but found that no matter how many meetings he attended, he had few opportunities to make business connections. After all, he pointed out, these were the same men who had refused him employment.[57]

Arthur Reynolds became a CPA in 1958; Carroll Lee followed in 1961; and Jerome Broadus joined them in 1963. The four men formed two CPA firms, King & Reynolds and Lee & Broadus. They retained their government jobs; Reynolds attended law school; and they ran their CPA firms in their "spare time." John Cromwell had been right: at the time there was not enough well-paying business to support more full-time, African American–owned CPA firms.

Despite this lack of business, the two CPA firms managed to provide CPA experience for other young African Americans. After what they had endured, Reynolds reported, they had an open office for any capable, hardworking person who wanted to meet the experience requirement.[58] There were many, including Benjamin King's children, whom he "bribed" as teenagers by making them work in his office if they wanted to drive his Lincoln or Cadillac. They must have liked the work: all five of them became accountants.[59]

LOS ANGELES: THE "LAND OF OPPORTUNITY"

Many African American southerners moved to California in the 1940s and 1950s, hoping for better opportunities. Two of these men, Talmadge C. Tillman Jr. of North Carolina and William D. Collins of Louisiana, hoped to become CPAs.

While Talmadge Tillman was growing up in Charlotte, North Carolina, in the late 1930s, he enjoyed working with numbers. One day an insurance agent came to the house collecting premiums, and Tillman became fascinated with his record-keeping book. He decided to become a CPA. One of the town's leading businessmen, a family friend, warned him that no one would ever hire him. But Tillman's mother believed that the coming war would open opportunities for African Americans, and she encouraged her son to pursue his dream.

When he graduated from high school, Tillman headed to Morehouse College in Atlanta. He was happy there, but he wanted to take more business courses than were available at the school in the early 1940s. He also wanted to see various parts of the United States, so he transferred to Indiana University, partly because it seemed like an adventure to move to a new part of the country.

Tillman enjoyed and was challenged by the coursework at Indiana University, but he was appalled by the conditions for African Americans in Bloomington. He was surprised to find that in some ways it was no different from the South. Dining and swimming facilities at the university had only recently been desegregated, and he still had to sit in the balcony at those movie theaters in which he was permitted. Looking back on it, he says he would have preferred a southern city like Charlotte or New Orleans because at least in major southern cities there were leading African American families to admire and emulate.

World War II interrupted Tillman's education, but he managed to study accounting in the Navy, where singer Harry Belafonte was his bunkmate. In 1948, he entered Syracuse University, where he became the first black graduate of its M.B.A. program.[60] Upon graduation he worked as an assistant cashier at Howard University in Washington, D.C., for one year. Then, because "in those days for a black guy [to have] an M.B.A. was really something else!," he became the accounting department chair at Texas Southern University, a black college in Houston.

In Texas, Tillman soon realized he had no chance of gaining the experience necessary to become a CPA. In 1951, he decided to move to California, where he was certain he could find a firm that would hire him.

Immediately upon arrival in Los Angeles, Tillman registered his resume with the California CPA Society. Based on his credentials, an undergraduate degree from Indiana University and an M.B.A. from Syracuse University, a CPA telephoned him and offered him the job over the phone. "I went to his office the next morning, and when I arrived he was on the telephone. He told me to 'have a seat, boy.' After he hung up the telephone he stated, 'Boy, what can I do for you?' I told him I was Tillman and that he had given me a job and told me to come to work. He looked at me and had a fit. He replied, 'You are a Negro.' He placed his head on the desk and just shook it. He then said, 'You are a Negro, I cannot give you the job.' "[61]

Tillman bought a detailed map of Los Angeles. Using a phonebook, he mapped out all the CPA firms in the city, spending six weeks walking different neighborhoods and applying for jobs. He knew he was ahead of his time, but he was convinced that "somewhere out there someone was going to give me a job." At the end of the six weeks, his conviction proved to be true, and he accepted a position as an auditor with the Los Angeles branch of a Jewish CPA firm based in New York.

Tillman worked for the firm for almost a year. To his knowledge, the clients did not react negatively to his being an African American, and he got along well with his colleagues. He was very impressed by his main supervisor, Al Schwartz, and enjoyed learning about auditing from him.

During this period, the managing partner of the office had been serving in the Korean War. As Tillman describes it, "After he came back from fighting for democracy, he walked in the office and saw me and a [black] girl named Linda. . . . He told me, 'It doesn't look good to have Negroes in the office.' " Within days, both Tillman and Linda had been fired by mail. Tillman returned some work to the office, where his colleagues seemed shocked by the incident. Tillman recalls one of his immediate supervisors saying, "How could he do it at a time like now, when I've been depending on you?" But there was no questioning the decision.

Tillman took a CPA review course at the University of California–Los Angeles from Professor Harold Simons and ranked third in a class of fifty.[62] Because Tillman had only met part of the two-year experience requirement, Simons sent Tillman to interview with a CPA firm that had four open positions. The firm recruiters gave him a written test, which was an unusual, if not unheard of, approach when interviewing someone with an M.B.A. for an entry-level job in accounting. When Tillman passed the test, he asked if he would get one of the jobs, but he was told he would not. Tillman asked them why they had given him the test if they knew they were not going to hire him. He was told, "We wanted to see what a Negro could know about accounting."

Tillman did not report the incident to Simons. He was afraid that he might ruin things for another African American who was interested in becoming a CPA or that Simons might not send him out on any more interviews.

Tillman also took examinations to work as an accountant for Los Angeles County, for the Department of Water and Power, the State of California, and the civil service. His ranking on these tests consistently put him in the top 5 percent of applicants. But he was never offered a job.[63] Tillman entered teaching and later went back to graduate school, earning a Ph.D. at the University of Southern California in 1967. When he became a CPA in 1968, he was only the sixth African American to have earned both a CPA and a Ph.D. in accounting.[64]

Like Tillman, William Collins was a World War II veteran and part of the wave of African American southerners seeking new opportunities in California. Collins had earned an undergraduate degree in education at Tuskegee Institute in Alabama before the war. When he moved to California, however, he found, in a cruel irony, that he was not able to find a teaching position because the schools were *not* segregated and black teachers were rarely hired.[65]

Collins got a job at the post office, where many well-educated African Americans in this period found steady, relatively well-paying employment.[66] He worked the night shift while attending the University of Southern California, where he majored in accounting and was near the top of his class. As he neared graduation in 1954, he registered with the university's employment office for interviews with the major accounting firms.

Apparently it did not occur to the recruiters that Collins might be African American. Based on his academic record, he was interviewed by several major CPA firms including Arthur Young; Price Waterhouse; Peat, Marwick and Mitchell; and Ernst & Ernst. Most of the recruiters conducted the interviews without betraying their surprise, concluding with "We'll call you." But they never did call. Collins recalls the recruiter from one of the major firms interrupting the interview before Collins could sit down, saying, "Mr. Collins, [this interview] is just a waste of my time and yours, too. We do not hire Negroes. . . . Now we have not had Jews in our firm until recently, and we haven't had Orientals in our firm until recently, but we have not come around to having blacks on our staff, not even in the clerical field."

These setbacks did not diminish Collins's determination to earn his CPA. He believed that Los Angeles was "fertile ground" for an African American CPA and that he would be able to earn a good living. He took and passed the CPA examination in 1957. Despite the fact that many firms had trouble finding employees who could pass the examination, which had a lower success rate than did comparable examinations in medicine, law, and engineering, each time Collins applied for a position he was turned down.[67] After three years of looking for a position with a firm, while continuing to work for the post office and being rejected every time the recruiter discovered his race, Collins decided to save time by sending the following application letter:

> Having passed the CPA examination, I am now faced with the problem of the experience requirement of the California Accountancy Act before I can receive a certificate to practice in this state as a Certified Public Accountant.
>
> My profile is as follows: Passed the CPA examination in May of 1957. Graduate of the University of Southern California with a "B" average in June of 1954. Graduate of Tuskegee Institute, Alabama in June of 1943 and a major in education. Spent twenty-eight months in the army. Type with reasonable degree of accuracy and speed. I am without actual experience.
>
> For the past eleven years, I have been employed in the Los Angeles Post Office. I am available for full or part time employment. Salary is immaterial. As a matter of fact, I would consider employment without remuneration. The experience would be invaluable to me.
>
> I am a Negro, thirty-nine years of age, married, and have one child.
>
> If you can be of any assistance to me in this regard, it would be deeply appreciated.[68]

Like Arthur Reynolds in Washington, D.C., Collins offered to work for free. Nevertheless, the letters yielded no positive responses.[69]

Collins found that most employers would deny any racism on their own part, instead blaming their clients' racist attitudes for their unwillingness to hire him. This attitude was not uncommon. For example, William Levitt, the powerful developer who "invented" the American suburb after World War II, refused to sell to African Americans. He argued that while, as a Jew, he was not prejudiced, allowing African Americans to buy houses in his developments would drive down the selling prices of his homes.[70]

This apparent submission to clients' demands was supported by accounting's main professional organization. The American Institute of Accountants recommended that CPAs consider clients' expectations when hiring new employees. In 1951, the *Journal of Accountancy* published an article about successfully selecting employees through studying their personality traits. While the article did not mention race, it provided the following rationale for choosing employees from a narrow segment of the population:

> Recruiters' first concern is with the applicant's appearance and manner. This is quite understandable because of the nature of their assignments. Almost from the outset they must work in the . . . offices of the firm's clients. . . . The client has little or no direct contact with any of the [low-level employees]. They are *seen*, but not *known*. . . . The client's only basis for forming an impression of the junior is his appearance and manner as judged from casual observation and superficial contacts. No matter how competent and intelligent the man may be, if his appearance is unusual . . . he is very likely to forfeit the client's acceptance. . . . The astute accounting firm seeks juniors whose superficial characteristics will insure their acceptance by their clients.[71]

Those to whom Collins applied for positions apparently felt that their clients would not accept his "superficial characteristics."

When the letters disclosing his race continued to yield no positive responses, Collins adopted two more tactics. First he wrote to the California State Board of Accountancy asking for advice, stating flatly and truthfully, "Due to my race, I have experienced difficulty getting a job with a CPA firm." The board responded with what seems to be a form letter detailing the requirements for becoming a CPA. Several months later, however, the secretary of the Board of Accountancy, Leslie McReynolds, arranged a meeting between Collins and one of his board members. Collins was told that the board could not waive the experience requirement, and he was encouraged to apply to Jewish firms in East Los Angeles.[72]

Unable to find employment with the Jewish firms the state board had recommended, Collins tried a second approach. His clever plan was based on the excuse that most firms provided, that their clients would object to having an African American accountant visit their offices. In late 1957, Collins wrote to the largest black businesses in Los Angeles, including several banks, and asked them who their auditor was. The letter noted, "Since the standard excuse of the firms I have contacted seems to be that their clients object to having Negroes work on their records, I feel that such excuse cannot be used if some of their clients are Negro businesses."[73]

It turned out that all the businesses to which he wrote had the same white auditor, Leo Rosen. When Collins approached him about a job, Rosen displayed no interest in hiring him. Instead, Rosen recommended that Collins work for Safety Savings and Loan, one of the black-owned businesses that had directed Collins to the CPA.[74] Rosen told the savings and loan that Collins was wasted at the post office. Collins believes that Rosen, while unwilling to provide the experience he needed, was eager to have someone of Collins's talent and training as an accountant at the savings and loan to simplify his own job of auditing the organization.

Safety Savings and Loan took Rosen's advice and offered Collins a position. But something surprising happened the very weekend before Collins was supposed to start his new job. In addition to all the applications he sent out, Collins had registered with the placement office at the California CPA Society, and a Mr. Harry Hankin had seen Collins's record and called to request an immediate interview. Hankin and his wife, who was not a CPA but who also worked with the firm, had an office in Beverly Hills. Mrs. Hankin recognized how exceptional Collins was. He recalls her saying, "You've got two bachelor's degrees; you passed the CPA exam; I don't care what color you are. You're going to come work with us on Monday." The secretary of the California State Board of Accountancy had been correct about one thing: when Collins finally found a job working for a CPA, it was with a Jewish-owned firm.

Collins was paid $75 every two weeks by the firm, which he considered "gravy" since he was getting the experience he had craved and he had been willing to work without remuneration. To his knowledge, there was only one client, the Southwest Los Angeles Realty Board, where the Hankins avoided sending him because Mrs. Hankin knew the board did not admit black members. After working for the Hankin firm for two years and thereby completing the requirements for his CPA license, Collins quit to open his own firm, despite the fact that he had a good experience with the Hankins and they wanted him to stay. He was excited about the wide-open field available to an African American CPA in Los Angeles.

Now that he had earned his certification, William Collins sought to educate local black businesses about the value of a CPA.[75] Forty years after opening his own practice, Collins jokes that when he first introduced himself to African American businesspeople as a CPA, they asked if it stood for "Cleaning, Pressing, and Alterations." However, he had no trouble developing a client base and after less than a year he finally was able to quit the post office job he had kept for so long. His CPA firm, with a clientele of black professionals and small businesses, was still thriving at the end of the century.[76]

A RARE ACHIEVEMENT

In becoming CPAs, Richard Austin, Bernadine Gines, Frederick Ford, Benjamin King, Arthur Reynolds, Carroll Lee, Jerome Broadus, Talmadge Tillman, and William Collins all beat the odds and joined a very select group. By 1960 there were 90,000 CPAs in the United States. Yet when Theodora Rutherford, the woman who had to wait thirty-seven years after finishing her master's degree at Columbia to become a CPA, was licensed in 1960, she was only the fifty-eighth African American CPA.[77]

The success of these elite few was noted by the African American press, including emerging national publications published by Charles Beckett's client John Johnson of Chicago. The status of all CPAs had been raised during World War II when the Selective Service System included CPAs as an occupation critical to the war effort, and in the 1940s it became the fastest-growing profession in the United States.[78] Now out of its infancy, the profession of accounting grew in prestige in the African American community, as did the attention given its practitioners.

Chauncey Christian, the third black CPA in the country, who was now working for famous black entertainers in New York, was pictured in the magazine *Our World*. The 1952 *Negro Year Book* featured a section on "Certified Public Accountants," highlighting the work of Mary Washington, Jesse Blayton, Wilmer Lucas, and Richard Austin, and listing twenty-two other African American CPAs. In 1953 *Jet* announced that Elvera Taylor of Chicago had become a member of the American Institute of Accountants, and in 1955 *Jet* noted the thirteenth anniversary of Theodore Jones, also of Chicago, becoming the first black member of the American Institute of Accountants. Another Chicago CPA in the news was Arthur Wilson, who was named to a commission by President Eisenhower in 1957. Despite the fact that William Collins had so much trouble getting a job with a CPA firm, his achievement was appreciated by the African American media. The *Los Angeles Sentinel* announced his passing the CPA exam with the caption "Successful" under his picture.[79]

The mainstream press occasionally noted the milestones that African American CPAs achieved. The *New York Times* joined numerous African American newspapers by featuring a photo of Wilbur Parker when he became the first African American CPA in New Jersey in 1954.[80]

In ensuing decades, becoming a CPA remained an impressive accomplishment, but the barriers faced by those who became CPAs in the 1940s and 1950s were about to weaken. As the incipient civil rights movement spread beyond integration of education to voting and employment rights, the 1960s promised the century's most dramatic change in opportunities for African Americans who wanted to become CPAs.

5

The 1960s: Decade of Change

Robert E. Hill loved books. As a young stay-at-home father in Kansas City in the 1950s, Hill would peruse the shelves at bookstores and read books on a wide variety of subjects. One day he picked up an accounting textbook, and it so engrossed him that he actually worked through the end-of-chapter assignments. Soon thereafter he moved to Los Angeles and, with his newfound interest, enrolled as an accounting major first at Los Angeles City College and then at the University of California–Los Angeles.

Having little familiarity with the field, Hill had not been thinking about becoming a CPA. But as he neared graduation, he learned that all his classmates were applying for positions with the Big Eight public accounting firms. Now the dominant force in the profession, these enormous national firms resulted from rapid growth and multiple mergers in the accounting industry in the late 1940s and 1950s.[1] Hill decided to pursue the same goal. He knew that there were no African American professionals at the firms, and he admits to having been naïve about opportunities. The year 1961 was one of dramatic change, and Hill thought both that it was *time* for the firms to end discrimination and that *he* was a good candidate to break the barrier.

The accounting recruiters got a summary of UCLA students' credentials, and all the major firms requested an interview with this top student. As Hill recounts, "Naturally, everybody wanted to see me. At least they *said* they did. Until they *saw* me." He could see the change in the recruiters' faces as he walked into the interview, and most interviewed him perfunctorily. Two acknowledged that they were surprised to see an African American, and one recruiter bluntly stated that his firm was not ready for integration. The recruiter from Big Eight firm Arthur Young expressed concern and interest. Hill recalls this recruiter's saying that although his firm had not *yet* hired an

African American, he believed that it was time that they did so. He promised to discuss the matter with his superiors.

Hill watched as his classmates—those with both higher and lower grades—counted their job offers and discussed which firm to choose. Hill received nothing but rejection letters from the accounting firms. He was offered a position as an auditor for the California State Tax Board, and Hill resigned himself to the fact that he would have to take the common route of well-educated African Americans in the 1950s and early 1960s and enter government service, forgoing, at least temporarily, his goal of becoming a CPA.[2]

Hill told one of his UCLA professors, Harold Simons, about his experience in looking for a position.[3] When he learned of the response Hill had received from the CPA firms, Simons became visibly angry. Hill recalls him saying, "If this is the way they're going to treat somebody like you, I may have to seriously consider whether I want to continue in this profession."

Hill is not sure if Simons's anger precipitated the ensuing turn in events, but soon thereafter Arthur Young—which, despite the optimistic interview, had sent him a rejection letter—invited him to its office for an interview and subsequently offered him a job. He later discovered that Arthur Young partners had canvassed some of their clients to see how they would feel about having a black auditor. The partners concluded that Lockheed and the Los Angeles Dodgers were the perfect clients for Hill. Lockheed was a major government contractor and therefore subject to federal fair employment requirements, and the Dodgers had several African American players by 1961. The jobs had the additional benefit of being unusually time-consuming—between the two they could keep Hill busy all year, and there would be no need to send him to other clients' offices. Thus, Robert Hill became the first African American in the Los Angeles offices of the Big Eight.[4]

RECOGNITION OF DISCRIMINATION BY THE CPA PROFESSION

Hill's breakthrough into the major public accounting firms signaled the dramatic changes that were to come in the decade. The civil rights movement was nearing its peak, and the accompanying proliferation in social programs greatly expanded the client base of African American CPAs. The civil rights movement also led to a change in public attitudes toward employment discrimination, and by the end of the decade, the accounting profession had endorsed active recruitment of African American professionals.

The first signs that relentless discrimination by the profession was becoming untenable came early in the decade. After complete inattention to the issue on the part of the accounting press, a white accounting professor at Stanislaus State College in California, Kenneth Young, wrote an article on integration for a small-circulation accounting trade journal in 1962.[5] The article underscores how difficult it was for African Americans to become CPAs. Young lamented the fact that his "Negro" and "Oriental" students were granted interviews but never job offers by the accounting firms. Young reported that he, "on numerous occasions," had asked recruiters why they would not offer jobs to the non-Caucasian students, and the recruiters invariably responded that their clients would not accept a nonwhite auditor. Young questioned the recruiters further, finding that none of them had ever queried their clients about the matter. When pushed, sometimes they added that they did not want to disrupt harmonious staff relations.

Young found these responses unconvincing. He taught a diverse group of students who seemed to get along well, and he found it hard to believe that the same students, upon entering professional accounting practice, would suddenly become intolerant of working with people of different races.

Young noted that his best nonwhite graduates, if they were lucky, landed jobs in the federal government and that other minority students often settled for jobs such as mail carriers and bus drivers. He expressed uncertainty over what career advice to give his students because he was hesitant to encourage talented students to pursue a field in which there were no job prospects. He pointed to the shortage of accountants in the early 1960s and the public accounting profession's initiative encouraging young people to choose accounting as a career, concluding that if hiring practices were not changed, "the sales appeal directed to young high school and college students, in which the opportunities and the rewards of a career in public accounting are enumerated, should be clearly and distinctly labeled, 'for Caucasians only.' "[6]

Other publications also began to note the exclusion of African Americans from the accounting profession and the inconsistency between this exclusion and social trends toward diversity. In 1962, Lincoln Harrison, dean of the School of Business at Southern University in Louisiana, published an article on African American CPAs in the *Journal of Negro Education*. Harrison estimated that there were fewer than 75 African American CPAs in the entire country. His respondents reported incomes above the African American average, but their CPA practices were rarely sufficient to provide full-time work. Many of these exceptionally well-educated men and women, over 80 percent of whom held graduate degrees, found their main financial support in government employment or teaching. Their CPA practices were typically confined to small black-owned businesses, which meant they performed mostly tax work and bookkeeping rather than the more lucrative and prestigious jobs of auditing publicly traded companies.

Despite the fact that his survey found little change from the conditions found in I. M. Martin's 1933 survey of "colored accountants," Harrison expressed hope that change was imminent. "As for future prospects, the majority of the Negro CPA's surveyed seem to think that there are rapidly expanding opportunities for qualified accountants, due in part to the increased development of business enterprises owned and operated by Negroes and greater integration of Negroes into the general economic and business life of the nation."[7]

THE CIVIL RIGHTS MOVEMENT

The articles by Young and Harrison were both written during a period of unprecedented public attention to the issue of segregation. The nation was riveted by a rapid series of history-making events. There were important civil rights milestones in the 1950s, particularly the 1954 Supreme Court decision ending legal segregation in the nation's public schools and the 1956 Montgomery bus boycott led by the young Reverend Dr. Martin Luther King Jr. In the early 1960s, the pace of resistance increased. In 1960, students from North Carolina A&T University began a lunch counter sit-in movement that rapidly spread across the South. In 1961, national attention was drawn to the brutal reaction to the Freedom Rides, in which mixed-race groups challenged segregation on interstate buses. In 1962, most Americans were appalled by attacks against James Meredith as he became the first black student at the University of Mississippi. The March on Washington, in which King made his "I Have a Dream" speech, was a major news event in late summer 1963. In 1964, the bodies of three young civil rights workers in Mississippi, James Chaney, Andrew Goodman, and Michael Schwerner, were found after a six-week search that had received national attention. In 1965, the violent response to a voting rights march in Selma, Alabama, horrified the nation.[8]

Widespread television ownership and the advent of live news coverage made these events more immediate, graphic, and dramatic than earlier civil rights struggles had been. People across the country saw well-dressed, polite, nonviolent African American students attacked simply for requesting their basic rights. Southern leaders tried to blunt these effects by pressuring local network affiliates to block coverage. Nevertheless, national awareness was at its peak. President Lyndon B. Johnson had an unprecedented level of contact with the nation's civil rights leaders, who discussed possible strategies to address the overwhelming public response to what was being shown on television.[9]

Television's impact extended beyond coverage of civil rights demonstrations to include changing images of African Americans on syndicated television programs. Programming in the 1950s rarely included African American characters, and when it did they generally played stereotypical, subservient roles.[10] In 1957, the short-lived *Nat King Cole Show*, the first program to feature an African American star, was canceled because fear of a southern boycott meant it could not find a national sponsor.[11] Only a few years later, one of the most popular shows on television, *The Dick Van Dyke Show*, broke a taboo by including a professional African American couple in one episode. Though some of those involved with producing the show were nervous about the audience's reaction, the positive response they received is credited with opening the way in 1965 for Bill Cosby to star as a brilliant Rhodes Scholar in *I Spy*.[12]

The rising awareness of African Americans' rights led to increased donations to civil rights organizations, which benefited African American CPAs. The fastest-growing civil rights organization in the early 1960s was the Southern Christian Leadership Conference (SCLC), led by Martin Luther King Jr. One of its fundraising flyers, entitled "Some Important Fiscal Facts about SCLC," was clearly designed to enhance donors' confidence in the organization's financial responsibility. The third bullet point reads, "Our books are audited by Jesse B. Blayton, C.P.A."[13]

Jesse Blayton, a leading member of the African American business community in Atlanta, was a professor at Atlanta University and a member of Martin Luther King Sr.'s Ebenezer Baptist Church. When the State of Alabama accused Martin Luther King Jr. of understating his 1956 and 1958 income, Blayton was hired to help King's lawyers address the charges.

In a transparent effort to harass the leader of the Montgomery bus boycott, the state accused King of having understated his income by tens of thousands of dollars. It was the first time in Alabama history that anyone had been charged with *felony* tax evasion. By prosecuting King on tax charges, the state may have been attempting to take advantage of the denial of financial expertise to African Americans. If so, they had not counted on Jesse Blayton.

Blayton and his assistant, Willie Boyd Saddler, examined King's records and found that Alabama was counting every deposit into King's account as income, despite the fact that many of these deposits were either gifts or the return of money previously withdrawn. Apparently King routinely withdrew money to cover expenses for his speaking engagement trips. Upon arrival at his destination, however, local civil rights leaders almost invariably hosted him. When he returned to Montgomery, he would redeposit the money he had withdrawn before his departure. Alabama claimed, erroneously, that these deposits were income.

It took Blayton and Saddler weeks to trace King's withdrawals and deposits, but they were ultimately able to disprove the charges.[14] After conducting the investigation, Blayton wrote King's attorney, "The accompanying proposed amended [Alabama state income tax] return will stand the rigors of even the Alabama court."[15] Blayton was correct. King was acquitted after Blayton himself served as the final witness for the defense. King's supporters were surprised by the verdict; they had doubted that he would receive justice from the all-white jury. Later, King joked that perhaps the jurors' antipathy toward the tax authorities outweighed their prejudice against African Americans.[16]

Despite Blayton's key role in helping to solve a problem that had caused King considerable anguish, the experience was not wholly positive for the leaders of the SCLC. Blayton's bill for his services totaled almost $5,000—nearly as much as King's annual minister's salary. Blayton's invoices billed his accounting clerk's time at $1 per hour, his senior accountant's time at $5 per hour, and his own time—"One C.P.A."—at $20 an hour. The average charge for partners' time in Big Eight firms was $35 an hour at the time, and Blayton had been a CPA for thirty years. Nevertheless, the attorneys King had engaged to lead his case found the size of Blayton's bill inappropriately large. They believed he should have reduced his charges because of the political nature of the lawsuit and because of his membership in Ebenezer Baptist.[17]

Despite the discomfort over the bill, Blayton's firm continued its involvement with King and the SCLC. During the peak of the civil rights movement, his employee Willie Boyd Saddler worked for Blayton in the mornings and for the SCLC in the afternoons. She organized groups to count the donations that poured in, especially after Chaney, Goodman, and Schwerner were murdered in Mississippi and after the violent reaction to the Selma voting rights demonstrations. Saddler describes it not as a black or white reaction but as "an American thing." People were so moved by what they saw on television that she had to supervise several volunteers to keep track of the money. Donations came from everywhere, from corporations that sent thousands of dollars and from a semiliterate person whose name was illegible but whose fifty-cent donation—glued to the note—Saddler will never forget. At times there was so much cash that it had to be bagged and retrieved by Brink's trucks each night for safekeeping until it could all be counted and deposited.[18]

Other major civil rights organizations also experienced increases in their fundraising abilities. In 1965, the National Urban League determined that employing a CPA would enhance its fundraising ability, so it hired Audley Coulthurst, a CPA who was working for Lucas & Tucker in New York. Coulthurst reports, "I worked for the Urban League [because] I liked what they were doing. I figured that the students were sitting in at the lunch counters, getting their heads whipped and getting dogs sicced on them . . . but the skills I had as a CPA [meant that] I could contribute to the movement by working for the league, and helping the league raise the funds that would [support] these activities."[19]

LBJ'S WAR ON POVERTY

African American CPAs' work was also changed in the 1960s by new federal government programs resulting from the civil rights movement. Earlier African American accountants had often found that the only available professional positions were with the government. Likewise, in the 1960s their first major auditing opportunities were for government programs. In an effort to address the inequities that were garnering national attention, President Johnson launched the War on Poverty and Great Society programs, which added to the coffers of many community organizations and social programs.[20] These all had a direct effect on African American CPAs' opportunities to make a living.

As a facet of the Great Society program and partly in response to the 1965 Watts riots, which claimed thirty-four lives, President Johnson founded the Department of Housing and Urban Development (HUD) in 1965.[21] HUD sponsored a program in which participants who built low-income housing received special tax credits. Those who wanted to participate in this program required a CPA's certification verifying that the costs involved in building the housing were appropriate. The problem was that no one—including HUD—knew how to complete these certifications. A classmate of Jerome Broadus, one of the "D.C. Four" who had helped each other earn their CPAs in the late 1950s and early 1960s, asked Broadus to help him qualify for the HUD program. Broadus and his CPA firm partner, Carroll Lee, analyzed the requirements and provided the certification for Broadus's friend. Word quickly spread that Broadus and Lee were experts. Soon they were providing certification for other organizations that sponsored low-income housing, including the African Methodist Episcopal Church and the Black Contractor's Association. The two men retained their government jobs, but their "part-time" CPA practice often consumed eighty hours a week.[22]

This increased workload enabled the two men to move into a larger office in 1969. The expansion of the African American professional class had become newsworthy in the late 1960s, and a *Washington Post* reporter published a short notice about the new office. A white CPA saw the notice and brought charges against Lee & Broadus, claiming that the firm was breaking an ethics rule prohibiting CPAs from advertising. The District of Columbia Society of CPAs apparently did not cherish the notion of getting publicity for harassing a neophyte African American firm. The panel it chose to review the complaint included one of the few other African American CPAs in the city at the time, William "Pete" Porter, who had earned his CPA in 1961. The panel found that Lee & Broadus had not violated any of the society's ethics regulations.

While these ethics charges caused Lee & Broadus anxiety and inconvenience, the *Washington Post* article did bring business to the firm. Through it, the Tuskegee Alumni Housing Foundation learned that African American CPAs had opened an office in Washington, and the foundation turned to Lee & Broadus for cost certifications. The men traveled to several states while working for the Tuskegee Foundation. After working for the government all week, on Friday evenings Broadus and Lee would board a flight to Ohio or Florida or wherever they were needed. They would then work on their HUD cost certifications all weekend before returning to their federal jobs Monday morning. In the early 1970s, Carroll Lee was profiled by a local paper and by his alma mater's newspaper because of the busy life he led.[23]

A North Carolina CPA also experienced a change in his employment opportunities due to Johnson administration policies. In 1962, Nathan T. Garrett returned to his home state after meeting his experience requirement by working for Richard Austin in Detroit. His first year in North Carolina he earned only a thousand dollars working for cab companies and grocery stores, and he paid his secretary twice that much. In 1967, Garrett's long-standing involvement in charitable work expanded when he founded and became executive director of the Foundation for Community Development. Garrett helped develop a network of community organizations around North Carolina that could benefit from the newly available federal money. Garrett returned to full-time CPA practice in 1972, providing audits to community-based organizations.[24]

THE CIVIL RIGHTS ACT OF 1964

This change in fortunes of extant African American CPAs was accompanied by a brightening of opportunities for prospective African American CPAs. Robert Hill's entry into the Big Eight in 1961 foreshadowed changes to come. By the end of the decade, all the major firms had begun to hire African Americans.

Several factors led to this dramatic change. From the perspective of African Americans seeking to join the accounting profession, the landmark event of the civil rights movement was passage of the Civil Rights Act of 1964, whose Title VII outlawed discrimination on the basis of race. Several previous attempts to pass meaningful civil rights legislation had been either watered down or squashed, but President Lyndon B. Johnson, the consummate politician, shepherded this legislation through Congress in the wake of the Kennedy assassination, depicting it as a tribute to the slain leader.[25] The public's attitude toward integration is indicated by the 1965 Gallup poll, in which 52 percent of respondents identified civil rights as the most important problem facing the country.[26]

The Civil Rights Act of 1964 did not merely outlaw discrimination; it also created the Equal Employment Opportunity Commission (EEOC), which was charged with enforcing the new legislation. Johnson's nomination of Franklin D. Roosevelt Jr. as director of this new agency only enhanced the awe, and perhaps fear, that the EEOC inspired, as did the fact that the EEOC required that employers submit records on the racial composition of their workforce.[27]

The new legislation and the formation of the EEOC led to a surge of attention to the issue of employment discrimination in white-collar professions in the mainstream business press. Both the *Wall Street Journal* and the *Harvard Business Review* published several articles in the 1960s concerning corporations' need to integrate, not only at the lower levels but also in white-collar jobs, and the entry of African Americans into hitherto segregated fields such as journalism, banking, and executive ranks.[28]

THE AICPA TAKES A STAND AGAINST DISCRIMINATION

The American Institute of Certified Public Accountants (AICPA), the field's leading professional organization, felt the effects of this heightened attention. In 1965, Hugh K. McKee of Alaska, an AICPA council member, proposed that the AICPA adopt the following resolution: "Whereas, we recognize that most CPA firms have long since ceased unwarranted discriminatory practices, it still seems desirable that this Council go on record on that subject. It is Therefore Resolved that it is the consensus of this Council that there should be no discrimination because of race, creed, color, sex, or national origin in the employment practices of individuals or firms engaged in the practice of accounting."[29]

McKee, who was white, supported his proposed resolution with a speech that addressed the objections he expected to encounter. This landmark speech was the first time the AICPA had been addressed on the issue of African Americans in the profession.

> I fully realize that this resolution may produce some controversy. . . .
>
> Before I go into the reasons why I believe this resolution should be adopted, I intend to speak on the reasons which may be advanced against it.
>
> First, it may be said that this resolution is premature. Anyone who follows the day-to-day history of this country could not possibly fail to note that the winds of change are blowing. We should not wait for the ugly charge of unwarranted discrimination to be brought against us by outsiders before we declare our own conscience.
>
> Secondly, it may be said that there is no evidence of such practice by public accounting firms. I can only say that I believe there is such [evidence].[30] We are dealing with something which is difficult to prove or disprove. Let me use a quotation: "To him who believes, no explanation is necessary; and to him who does not believe, no explanation is possible."
>
> Thirdly, it may be argued that this resolution could be destructive of the Institute. I have heard that argument before about other resolutions. If this voluntary union is so weak that it cannot stand a statement of conscience, then it has no right or reason to exist.
>
> Fourthly, it may be argued that this resolution is productive of no useful purpose. And my answer is twofold: one, it will aid in the recruitment

of qualified youngsters of high school age who will admire our stand; and
two, it will aid the public image of the profession in the minds of the adult
world in which we live.

Fifth, it may be said that more time is needed for consideration of this
resolution and that it should be buried in some committee, possibly to be
resurrected at some more propitious time. And I say that either you truly
believe in the equality of opportunity, or you do not. And you cannot substitute the judgment of a committee for your own personal conscience.

And sixth, it may be said that this is just one more example of someone
talking about something he knows nothing about. Before anyone brings
that up, let me say this much about myself: I was born, reared and educated in the State of Mississippi; I am a graduate of Ole Miss. I am proud
of this. I worked in the State of Mississippi, in the States of Alabama,
Georgia and Illinois before I went to Alaska. And let me say further that in
my opinion, based on my own personal experience, discrimination is not
limited to any one region or area of this country.

Now, let me turn to the merits of the resolution.

I believe that it is a clear and concise statement of conscience. It is a
statement of an ideal. You will note that it carries no punitive clause, because I believe that the force of moral persuasion is far stronger than that
of any written rule. Once adopted, this resolution will stand as an objective to be attained, as a goal to be reached, as an expression of hope, and as
a declaration of faith. If this resolution serves to bring one more qualified
recruit into the field of public accounting, or if it causes one member of
this Institute to examine his own personal practices, then I believe that
this resolution is worth passing.

In closing, let me remind the members of this Council of the implication of any action of tabling, postponed consideration, or referring this
resolution to a committee. Any such proposal can have as its purpose only
the defeat of the resolution. . . . I [implore][31] you to consider your own
conscience and vote accordingly.

Mr. President, I move the adoption of the resolution.[32]

The AICPA council president asked for a second to McKee's motion but
received none. Another member, a Mr. Wallace,[33] said, "Mr. President, I
think this is a matter of the individual firms in this area, and accordingly,
I move that the motion be tabled." Wallace's motion was seconded and put to

a vote. The motion was tabled and the issue was not readdressed for the next four years.

The assassination of Reverend Martin Luther King Jr. in April 1968 and the ensuing social disturbances led many institutions to reexamine their policies with regard to equal opportunity. The AICPA was no exception. At that year's October council meeting, President Ralph Kent declared that discrimination was inimical to the profession's values. In December, the AICPA launched the Committee on Recruitment from Minority Groups, chaired by Edwin R. Lang, a white recruiting partner for Haskins & Sells.[34] Five of the eleven members of the committee were African American, including Lincoln Harrison of Louisiana, Robert Hill of California, and Bert N. Mitchell of New York.

The new committee developed a resolution that Chairman Lang proposed to the AICPA council at its May 1969 meeting. Lang stressed the importance of the AICPA's taking a stand against discrimination. In his presentation, he cited economic and educational disadvantages, the fact that many "ethnic minority young people" had no family members who were in business and were suspicious of whether they would be welcome in the accounting field, and the importance of voluntary compliance with the Civil Rights Act of 1964 rather than waiting for federal enforcement. In an interesting twist that underscores the power of government regulation, he reported that at least one client had asked what Lang's firm was doing to recruit African Americans.[35] This ran counter to the argument most African Americans had encountered only a few years earlier when they interviewed with public accounting firms: the firm members claimed they themselves were not prejudiced, but their clients were.

In contrast to four years earlier, in 1969 the AICPA council extensively debated the issue. The transcript of this debate provides a rare glimpse into the AICPA leadership's perspective on the issue. The annual council meeting, held in Colorado Springs, drew approximately 200 members from across the country, including representatives from each state as well as key committee members.[36]

Harry Ward of Texas, who identified himself as a member of the "minority group . . . quiet Anglo Saxon protestants," proposed that the resolution be tabled, saying:

> I think we have to be realistic about these things. Item 3 says that we are going to hire these colored people if they are adequately educated. I can't conscientiously say that I am going to hire somebody who is smart but

whose morals I question or who's been running up and down the college with a gun on his shoulder. . . .

I have another reservation. . . . [The resolution says] that this committee [will] stay in existence until these things are achieved. Well, now, that means this Council is creating a committee in perpetuity. These things are never going to be achieved.[37]

Ward's motion to table the resolution was seconded but failed to pass, as did a motion by Frank Rey of Texas to vote by secret ballot.

Richard Rea of Ohio, a Cornell alumnus, referred to the recent occupation of his alma mater by black student activists and said,

It seems the whole thing started when they lowered their admission standards because their collective guilt complex led them to believe they didn't have enough Negro students.

I think this area of standards is very important, and I think we are going to have to be very careful about how we word it, and perhaps it might be well to admit those who can meet the educational requirements or the standards of the profession. . . .

We've got to get something in there and not lead these people to believe that just because they are black and have got a degree they can get a job, or we may wind up like Cornell with a bunch of people walking in with guns and telling you what they are going to do.[38]

Glenn Welsch of the University of Texas suggested an amendment adding "of high potential" to the description of whom the profession was trying to recruit.[39] Stanley Tunick of New York agreed, though he was willing to accept the term "adequate potential" rather than "high potential." He voiced the same concerns others had expressed.

The people in some parts of the country have problems different from those in others. In the East unfortunately many of the black students have even demanded guaranteed graduation, and this from some of the important colleges in the East. What they are doing is demanding that, and perhaps I sound like a reactionary, and I think I am a very liberal minded person, but they are demanding and asking for guaranteed graduation which means no examinations, no flunks, that the standards of the student body other than the blacks will have to be reduced to the level of these other people, and this I think spells the end of colleges as we have known them for years.[40]

Arthur Dixon of New York objected to the amendment that would add "high potential," arguing that "we must all admit that we are hiring [white] accounting graduates who do not have high potential."

The council meeting apparently included no African Americans because Harold Berlfein of California asked Lang whether the proposed resolution had been shown to members of the black community. When he was told that the African Americans who had seen it had thought it was "outstanding," Berlfein argued that the resolution should be approved without amendment. He argued, "I think that the most important thing is our relationship with the black community. . . . None of these amendments have any meaning if they change in any way the sense of a resolution that had that kind of acceptance in the black community because our problems have been that we have been writing resolutions, but we haven't been listening. . . . If . . . the black community . . . has accepted [the resolution], I think we should approve it."[41]

Robert Trueblood of Illinois agreed, referring back to the proposal that had been submitted in 1965:

> It was four years ago this month at a meeting of this Council in this same hotel when a similar motion was proposed and tabled. I think probably that parliamentary action was appropriate. The motion had not been presubmitted. There has been no institutional work put into the motion, but here we are, a number of years later, and we have an increasingly acute problem, a problem of equal opportunity, of course, but we have now had dedicated work done by a group of people for whom I have very much respect.
>
> They have submitted a proposal on the floor. It is not the same proposal I would have written. It is not the same proposal perhaps any one of you would have written, but I think it would be completely inappropriate to attempt to redraft a proposal on the floor of Council. I wonder if it's not also a little bit inappropriate for each of us to try to superimpose our judgments on those who have studied the problem deeply.[42]

Sidney Davidson of Illinois disagreed, arguing for inclusion of the phrase "of high potential":

> I am sure Ed Lang has talked to members of the black community about this resolution, but it's frequently difficult to determine who speaks for the black community, and I have had some experience in talking with black college students, and I think the one thing that disturbs them more

than anything else is the tendency toward a patronizing attitude, and I think it is especially important that we speak with a voice that will be appealing to them. . . .

The students to whom we are appealing don't want to enter the accounting profession merely because they are black. They want to enter this profession because they can make a positive contribution to it, and to give the inference that merely because they are disadvantaged gives them a right to enter is going to do more harm than good in my opinion.

We must emphasize the fact that what we want are Negroes who do have the intellectual capacity to hold up their heads in the accounting profession.[43]

Committee on Recruitment from Minority Groups chairman Edwin Lang addressed the issue of amending the proposed resolution:

None of these suggestions gives me problems at all personally. In fact, I think they are good suggestions except this matter of high potential.

You can't define high potential. We are not recruiting all "A" students from any segment of our society. . . .

I agree with [Sidney Davidson of Illinois] that the black student and the faculties that are teaching these black students don't want to be babied along—they really don't. They want an equal opportunity. After that, they will carry the ball, and if you have to release us because we don't perform, you go ahead and release us, as long as we have the first initial opportunity.[44]

The council voted 95 to 89 to amend the resolution by adding "high potential."[45] James Money of Alabama then made by far the strongest speech against adopting the resolution, stating:

I believe that Mr. Lang did make an excellent presentation. Sometimes when we people from the Deep South make a discussion, we explain what we are not. An illustration of that is that I am not a George Wallace Democrat. I have been an independent and have voted Republican for the last four times, so that's one thing I am not. . . .

For years we have been trying to get . . . better students. . . .

If this main motion is passed with the high potential in there, then most of the objection to it on my part will be resolved. I realize that we will not get any unanimous opinion and perhaps there might be more opinion against me than with me on this, but there is certainly some substantial authoritative support for the fact that the black race is actually mentally inferior.

I have material before me at this point here [indicating that blacks are inferior]. . . .

I believe we will weaken the profession by making an effort to recruit these people whom I believe, and I can read it to you . . . who I believe are not at the level of attainment which we would want.

If you say that it is not inheritance, that it is environment, it is still environment and the attainment level is not there. I believe that we are going in two directions, trying to reach a black group, and also trying to reach the group of high attainers which we have tried to reach in the last ten years.[46]

The other council members did not engage in a discussion of these ideas. Immediately after Money stopped talking, William Westphal of North Carolina called for suppression of debate and moved to vote. The following resolution passed by voice vote:

Whereas, the Council of the American Institute of Certified Public Accountants recognizes that only relatively few individuals from disadvantaged groups have entered the accounting profession, that an inadequate number of students of high potential from disadvantaged groups are now being educated for accountancy, and that both of these situations represent a challenge to our profession—

BE IT NOW RESOLVED, that the Council of the American Institute of Certified Public Accountants urges:

1. that a special campaign be undertaken to encourage young men and women of high potential from disadvantaged groups to attend college and major in accounting;

2. that special efforts be made to provide educational opportunities for young men and women from disadvantaged groups so that they may enter the accounting profession without educational disadvantage;

3. that such men and women be hired by individuals and firms in order to integrate the accounting profession in fact as well as in idea.

FURTHER RESOLVED, that the Institute's committee for recruitment from disadvantaged groups continue to advance these objectives until they are achieved.

FURTHER RESOLVED, that copies of this resolution be sent to presidents, deans, and chairmen of business and/or accounting departments throughout the academic community, and that individual and firm prac-titioners be advised in an appropriate manner.[47]

MEDIA COVERAGE OF THE CHANGE

The historic changes of the 1960s were also reflected in the accounting profes-sion's publications. The most important article of the period appeared in October 1969 when the *Journal of Accountancy* published Bert Mitchell's study entitled "The Black Minority in the CPA Profession."[48] With a grant from the Ford Foundation, Mitchell surveyed accounting professionals and found that the underrepresentation of African Americans among CPAs was much worse than in other professions, including law and medicine. He revealed that out of 100,000 CPAs in the United States, fewer than 150 were African American. In response to Mitchell's survey, the major accounting firms maintained that the barrier to employing African Americans was not their *own* bias, but bias on the part of their *clients*. The *Journal of Accountancy*'s editors' introduction to the article also elided CPAs' responsibility. While, for the first time, they acknowledged that the profession had discriminated against African Ameri-cans, the editors stated that this discrimination was a matter of "oversight and indifference" rather than "deliberate hostility."[49]

Mitchell had firsthand knowledge of the barriers African Americans faced. When he graduated at the top of his accounting class at the City University of New York in 1963, his qualifications were unrivaled. He was an outstanding student who had supported himself throughout college by working for small Jewish-owned CPA firms. When he graduated he wanted to work for one of the major firms, preferably one of the Big Eight. He walked from the southern tip of Manhattan all the way to midtown, stopping at every major CPA firm to apply for a position. In two weeks of walking, twenty-five firms had refused to hire him, usually attributing their decision to their clients' attitudes. Finally, at 53rd Street and Fifth Avenue, having worked his way up five miles, he became the first African American employee at J. K. Lasser and Company. Lasser was a national firm, but not one of the Big Eight.[50]

Mitchell's study of African American CPAs led the way for many other articles on the topic in the late 1960s and early 1970s. They appeared not only in accounting journals but also in Big Eight firms' internal newsletters.[51] The articles revealed the sudden change in the profession's willingness to hire African Americans as well as its interest in self-protection. Several of these

Bert Mitchell. Photo courtesy of Bert Mitchell.

articles were written by AICPA Minority Recruitment Committee Chair Edwin Lang, who emphasized the barriers to attracting African Americans to the CPA profession, including the absence of role models, lack of familiarity with the profession, shortage of business education at predominantly black colleges, and disaffection from business-oriented professions because of a history of employment discrimination. The article also emphasized that it would be preferable for the profession to initiate its own efforts to end discrimination rather than facing inevitable direct government pressure to do so.[52] All of Lang's articles downplayed any possible past misconduct on the part of the profession.

Lang acknowledged some difficulties in communicating with faculty at black colleges, many of whom did not trust a profession that had excluded them when they completed their own degrees. Nevertheless, he lay blame for the underrepresentation of African Americans on wider social conditions over which CPAs had little influence. Even less convincingly, he frequently implied that the shortage was due to lack of interest: "Since the number of ethnic minority youngsters aspiring to become CPAs has been infinitesimal, there has been little demand for adequate educational preparation in the predominantly black colleges."[53] Another of Lang's explanations also directly conflicts with the experiences of pioneering African American CPAs. "[Certified public accountancy] is actually the most segregated of all the professions in [the] U.S. today, not because ethnic minority people are barred from employment in public accounting *directly* because of race, but because they are barred *indirectly.* . . . They are barred because they lack the adequate education that the whole social history of their race has kept them from getting. The ethnic minority individuals who have been properly educated for accountancy have been exceptions—rare exceptions."[54]

Lang did not note that even those "rare exceptions" who were "properly educated for accounting" had been barred from employment in virtually all CPA firms. This is despite the fact that the AICPA committee Lang led included five such African American CPAs. One of them, Lincoln Harrison, earned a Ph.D. in accounting from Ohio State University, yet he had never been able to attain a position with a CPA firm. In addition, he was denied membership in the Louisiana State Society of CPAs until 1970.[55] Another member was Bert Mitchell, who in 1963 had found it impossible to find employment in the Big Eight.[56] Lang, who had been national personnel partner of Haskins & Sells, one of the Big Eight, also did not note that his own firm refused to hire African Americans a very short time before he accepted the post of chair of the AICPA committee charged with increasing diversity.

THE BIG EIGHT

This change in focus at the AICPA and in the accounting journals was paralleled by changes in employment opportunities at the major firms. For the first half of the 1960s, it was still virtually impossible for an African American to find employment with a major firm. In 1966 and 1967, a few firms hired African Americans, but those that did hired only a handful nationwide.[57]

In the late 1960s, the New York State Human Rights Division launched investigations into professional employment of African Americans, including an investigation of the Big Eight. The Human Rights Division found that in 1968, there were only eighteen African American professional employees in the Big Eight in New York City, a mere half of 1 percent of the nearly 4,000 professional employees in these firms at the time.[58]

The negative publicity accompanying the minuscule numbers reported by the Bert Mitchell study and the New York State Human Rights Division did lead to dramatic changes. An AICPA survey—part of its new minority recruitment effort—revealed that 60 of the nation's largest firms employed 197 African American accountants in 1969 and 700 in 1970.[59] When the firms decided to hire African Americans, they suddenly seemed to be able to find candidates.

These increases resulted from a variety of efforts. The AICPA's Committee on Recruitment from Minority Groups included an internship program for African American accounting students between their junior and senior years in college. Some African American faculty were given the opportunity to work in Big Eight firms or major corporations during the summers, and the firms suddenly began recruiting at schools they had never visited before, the African American colleges in the South.

Not all these changes went smoothly. While Big Eight recruiters visited these colleges, they were often unwilling to employ African Americans in their southern offices, and they asked the students to move to northern cities such as Chicago and New York. The African American colleges had not yet had a chance to improve their accounting programs in response to the new demand for their students. The work of an entry-level auditor was not difficult—it mainly involved matching reported revenues and expenses with corresponding bank deposits and invoices. But lack of confidence in their preparation discouraged many of the new African American employees. A recent graduate of New York University, for example, might not be embarrassed to turn to his superiors, who had gone to comparable schools, with a seemingly simple question. But graduates of southern black colleges lacked this comforting network. This communication barrier, combined with the culture shock of moving north and frequent discomfort on the part of their new colleagues and supervisors, resulted in disappointment, discouragement, and enormous attrition rates.[60]

The firms' alleged fear that large numbers of clients would not tolerate African American auditors did not materialize. Nevertheless, several African Americans who worked with the Big Eight in the late 1960s or early 1970s noted that clients were accommodated when they asked that African Americans not be sent to their offices. One African American CPA did not learn until he left the Big Eight firm for which he had worked that one of his earliest clients had requested that he not return to the audit the following year.[61] One white staff member of a Big Eight firm noted the difference in treatment while monitoring the area designated for staff who had not been assigned to visit clients. He found that it was not uncommon for half of the people in the area to be African American, even though African Americans constituted less than 2 percent of the total employees in his firm.[62] Back in Detroit in the 1940s, Richard Austin had been fortunate to find work with a white CPA, but he had not been allowed to visit client offices. In the late 1960s, these attitudes still affected the work opportunities of African American employees of major firms.

A 1971 survey of African American professionals in Big Eight firms revealed an overall favorable impression among the 168 respondents, the vast majority of whom had been hired after 1968.[63] Nevertheless, many of those surveyed felt that they were not given career-developing assignments. Often they noted that while their firm's leadership expressed commitment to ending discrimination, their immediate supervisors, usually people with only three or four years of experience, were not responsive or supportive of them. Noting that efforts to transform the profession had just begun, the study's author concluded that the door to African American entry was ajar, but not fully open.

THE NATIONAL ASSOCIATION OF BLACK ACCOUNTANTS

The change in the composition of the firms and the challenges faced by newly hired African American employees led several of the pioneering African American employees in the Big Eight firms to form a support network to help deal with the transitions that were occurring. In 1969, the National Association of Black Accountants (NABA) was founded in New York by nine African American men: Earl Biggett, Donald Bristow, Kenneth Drummond, Bertram Gibson, Richard McNamee, George Wallace, Ronald Benjamin, Frank Ross, and Michael Winston, the latter three of whom were CPAs. The group's members provided networking and support for each other as well as professional advice for African American–owned businesses.[64]

The founders of NABA carefully chose the name of the group. The word "national" was commonly used in African American professional organiza-

Six of the nine NABA founders with NABA's president at the annual convention in 2000.
Standing, left to right: Frank Ross, Bert Gibson, Earl Biggett, and Michael Winston.
Seated, left to right: Donald Bristow, NABA president Daniel Moore, and Ronald Benjamin.
Photo courtesy of Frank Ross.

tions: the National Medical Association and the National Bar Association
were African American professional organizations. However, NABA's founders could not choose the name "National Accounting Association" because that name was used by an organization of accountants who worked in
industry.[65]

Introducing the word "black" into the organization's title caused some
controversy. The nonviolent civil rights movement that had earlier provoked
widespread sympathy had waned by the end of the 1960s and was replaced by
other methods of confrontation. "Black power" became the phrase of choice
for many young civil rights activists and many whites associated this term
with the violence that had followed the King assassination and with the Black
Panther organization, which was widely perceived as militant. Black power
was associated with increasing student activism, including anti–Vietnam
War protests and demands for African American studies programs, and was

viewed with suspicion by many whites in business, as is reflected in numerous *Wall Street Journal* articles of the era.[66]

NABA's founders considered it important to designate explicitly theirs as a black organization, so they committed to the name. Some African Americans in major accounting firms did not join NABA for fear that their new white colleagues would regard it as too militant. Others wondered why the men were "segregating themselves" and recommended that they work through existing organizations such as the AICPA Committee on Recruitment from Minority Groups and similar state committees.[67]

Despite these concerns, NABA was successful from its very inception. One of its earliest activities was to sponsor a meeting to which partners from all the Big Eight firms were invited. This meeting assuaged some fears about the possible militancy of the organization. Many of NABA's founding members were highly regarded by the firms that employed them, which also contributed to NABA's credibility. NABA quickly became a prominent national organization: four years after its founding, it had 1,100 members.[68]

GUN-TOTING CPA

Home to headquarters for NABA, the AICPA, and most of the Big Eight firms, New York was the center of change in the profession in the 1960s. But on the opposite coast, in Los Angeles, the changes of the 1960s also had dramatic impact on the accounting career of Korean War veteran Henry T. Wilfong Jr.

Wilfong was in the top 20 percent of his class at UCLA in 1958, just three years before Robert Hill graduated from the same university and became the first African American in the Los Angeles Big Eight. As with Hill, all the Big Eight firms interviewed Wilfong, and all denied him a job. After this disappointment, Wilfong decided to accept a job with the State of California. Then a Jewish partner at Haskins & Sells, a Big Eight firm, told him that it was time that the firm end its ban on hiring blacks and offered Wilfong a job. Wilfong was elated: unlike the position with the state, this job would count toward the requirements for becoming a CPA. Within a week, however, the national office of Haskins & Sells forced its Los Angeles office to rescind the offer. Wilfong recalls that the recruiter called to tell him that the New York office had decided that Haskins & Sells did not want to be the first Big Eight firm to hire a black professional.[69] Wilfong accepted the government job and used his GI Bill to get an M.B.A.

His experience trying to get a job with a CPA firm surprised Wilfong. Born in Arkansas and having lived most of his life in Los Angeles, he was aware of racism. But he had come to believe, through his military experience in the Korean War as well as his successful participation in athletics, that he would succeed based on his merits. He reports becoming "radicalized" by the CPA firm's rejection. Because of it, he refused to join the AICPA for more than a decade. He did join other organizations, however, including the Congress on Racial Equality (CORE), the National Association for the Advancement of Colored People (NAACP) and the Student Nonviolent Coordinating Committee (SNCC).

In 1963, Wilfong was finally hired by a white-owned CPA firm. During his employment there, his peers in the civil rights movement led a demonstration against one of Wilfong's employer's largest clients. When Wilfong informed his employer that he would be joining the picket, his supervisor reminded Wilfong of how difficult it had been to convince the firm to hire an African American. Wilfong participated in the demonstration, saying that he would have quit if the firm had pressured him not to join the civil rights activists.

After working for the white-owned firm long enough to meet his experience requirement, Wilfong opened his own small firm. One of his early clients was a construction firm owned by a white family for whom Wilfong's mother had done domestic work. Other clients initially included small African American–owned businesses, but his client profile soon changed dramatically. In the aftermath of the Watts riots in 1965, funding for community programs increased and Wilfong's work rapidly expanded. He became the auditor of major Los Angeles War on Poverty programs such as the Compton Willowbrook Enterprise Community Action Agency.

As a result of his connections in the civil rights movement as well as the proliferation of the War on Poverty and Great Society programs, Wilfong's firm became the auditor for the twenty-five largest community action agencies in California, Nevada, and Arizona. Wilfong's daily preparations for going to work were unusual for a CPA. He reports:

> For much of my professional life when I got up and dressed in the morning, I had a three-five-seven Magnum hanging under my arm and a twenty-five automatic with hollow-point shells in my boot. I'm a CPA going to work. . . . Because where we went and the activities we were involved in, you better have one in case something happened. . . . In the sixties, now, remember the Black Panthers. Much of the groups that I audited

and dealt with were heavy with nationalists and other kinds of groups. You didn't go out on Central Avenue in Watts in most instances unless you were packing.[70]

In the early 1970s, one of Wilfong's employees discovered that some money had been embezzled from an agency in a tough neighborhood in San Francisco. Five of his auditors were run off the job at gunpoint. Wilfong showed up in San Francisco wearing, as usual, a big Black Panther–style leather coat and accompanied by some of his Black Panther friends from Oakland. One of the agency leaders tried to intimidate Wilfong by opening his coat to reveal his .38 special. In response, Wilfong let his suit jacket open a little to reveal his .357 Magnum.

Wilfong reports that he had no further problem with the organization. He says that "audit is much more than having a calculator" and that his experience in the Korean War helped him prepare for some aspects of his job.[71]

This gun-toting CPA made a seemingly unlikely connection in the late 1960s, a close alliance with the Nixon administration. To many, Nixon's election in 1968 signaled an end to the social progress of the 1960s. Johnson's War on Poverty and Great Society programs had already been weakened as the Vietnam War strained federal budgets, and Nixon was not regarded as a promoter of racial justice.

But given the times and the very recent assassination of Dr. Martin Luther King Jr., it was impossible for any credible presidential candidate to ignore integration issues. Nixon consciously appropriated the term "black power" and asserted that it was consistent with his promotion of "black capitalism." When addressing civil rights issues, Nixon focused on economic equality rather than social equality. He spoke of creating "100 Black Millionaires" and in 1969 created the Office of Minority Business Enterprise (OMBE) under Commerce Secretary Maurice Stans, a CPA and former president of the AICPA. While many questioned Nixon's and Stans's sincerity and effectiveness, the program had a direct impact on the small group of African American CPAs.[72]

Henry Wilfong was active in the Republican party. His connections with other African American Republicans and his credibility as a CPA led to an introduction to John Jenkins, a black official in the OMBE. Wilfong and Jenkins discussed the need for African Americans to manage their own money. Wilfong argued that minority-owned firms, not the Big Eight, should audit the new minority business enterprises supported by the Nixon administration. Wilfong was particularly insistent because the Big Eight had refused to

Henry Wilfong with Richard M. Nixon. Photo courtesy of Henry Wilfong.

hire African Americans, including Wilfong himself, just a few years earlier. The OMBE gave Wilfong a $12,000 grant to pursue his plan for establishing the National Association of Minority CPA Firms (NAMCPAF).[73]

While Wilfong was working with the OMBE on increasing African American self-determination, the AICPA had also won a grant from the organization. Secretary of Commerce Maurice Stans provided an OMBE grant to encourage CPAs to provide free professional services to minority-owned businesses. Both the AICPA and the OMBE touted their collaboration and publicized the thousands of hours members donated to minority-owned businesses.[74]

But Wilfong was not pleased with this joint venture. At a time when African American CPAs finally had an opportunity to expand their clientele, he believed that the OMBE was undermining their efforts by funding the AICPA's plans to offer accounting services for free. African American businesses, he reasoned, should learn that hiring a CPA was just like any other cost of doing business, and he wanted the newly expanded African American business class to hire members of the NAMCPAF, not get free support from the AICPA.[75]

NEW COMPETITION FOR BLACK CLIENTS

There were other unanticipated effects of increasing integration. While the AICPA was impinging on traditional African American CPA territory, white CPA firms were also exhibiting a new interest in African American clients. As community organizations and small African American–owned businesses grew, major white accounting firms began courting their business. In North Carolina, some of the community organizations Nathan Garrett had helped develop felt pressure to move to larger, white-owned CPA firms for their audits. As these organizations expanded and sought loans from major banks, the banks often demanded that the organizations use recognized CPA firms, which inevitably meant white CPA firms.[76]

The change was not limited to community organizations. Enhanced attention to African American issues meant that readership of *Ebony*, *Jet*, and other major black publications mushroomed. John Johnson, the Chicago publisher of these periodicals, was one of those who felt the pressure to change from his African American CPA, Charles Beckett, to a major auditor. He refused.[77]

A similar shift occurred at African American colleges. Increased educational and professional opportunities led to an expansion of funding for these schools. Small African American colleges had been Jesse Blayton's largest clients before integration, but as the colleges got bigger, they added more white members to their boards. The new board members often insisted on hiring Big Eight accounting firms to conduct their audits, and Blayton lost several clients.[78]

Despite these setbacks, overall the decade of the 1960s had been one of dramatically increasing opportunity and unprecedented optimism for African American CPAs. The two new national organizations, NABA and the NAMCPAF, led African American–owned CPA firms across the country to network, and several of them decided that it was time for a national African American–owned CPA firm. Bert Mitchell, managing partner of the oldest African American–owned firm in the country, Lucas & Tucker in New York, led the effort.

Mitchell proposed a merger between several of the African American–

owned firms and formed an alliance with small firms across the country including Lee & Broadus in Washington, D.C. The merger served to raise the profile of African American CPA firms, thereby mitigating some of the client loss to larger white-owned firms. It also helped the CPAs take advantage of burgeoning business, including increased opportunities with community organizations, growing African American–owned businesses, and government agencies. Lucas & Tucker's own gross revenues had skyrocketed to $688,000 in 1969 when it accepted $451,000 in work from the City of New York.[79] The group of firms was optimistic about future growth: it had landed a contract with the city of Newark, New Jersey, to install accounting systems for new federal programs. Other clients of the merged firm included the National Urban League and the Freedom National Bank of New York.

As these newly networked CPA firms looked to the future, they anticipated continued expansion of opportunities. The 1960s had been a turbulent decade for African American CPAs in practice, and African American accounting educators also felt the impact. The new willingness of major firms to hire African American graduates led to a complete transformation of business schools at black colleges.

6

Accounting Programs at Black Colleges

Prior to the civil rights movement, the handful of African Americans who earned their Ph.D.'s in accounting were obligated to go north to gain their education and then return to the South in order to teach in the only institutions that would hire them, the African American colleges. While most African American CPAs in the early decades of the twentieth century left the southern United States to work in cities such as Chicago, New York, and Detroit, accounting educators did not have this option. Only African American colleges would hire African American faculty, and virtually all of these colleges were in the South. Therefore, most African Americans who earned Ph.D.'s in accounting prior to 1970 lived in the South and faced Jim Crow barriers that northern black CPAs did not.

The civil rights movement transformed African American education in accounting. In the late 1960s and early 1970s, accounting students in African American colleges had opportunities that had been denied to their professors. The sudden willingness of accounting firms and businesses to hire African American graduates required black colleges to alter their curricula radically in order to prepare their students for these jobs. The new opportunities led to new challenges for African American accounting educators.

AFRICAN AMERICAN COLLEGE PROFESSORS

Many great American universities got their start from federal land grants under the Morrill Act. In the midst of the Civil War, Abraham Lincoln signed the act, ceding federal land to the states in order to facilitate the expansion of American higher education. In 1890, a second Morrill Act was passed providing substantial increases in both federal land and financial support.

The new legislation required that grant recipients either admit African American students or use part of the funds to establish separate colleges for African Americans. The universities resulting from the southern states' refusal to integrate are currently known as "historically black colleges and universities" or HBCUs.[1]

Before the civil rights movement, the vast majority of African American college students attended either the HBCUs or private African American colleges. As late as 1954, when the Supreme Court decided *Brown v. Board of Education*, less than 1 percent of college freshmen in majority-white colleges were African American. Most majority-white universities refused to enroll more than a token few African Americans, and virtually none would hire African American faculty members.

Allison Davis broke through this barrier in 1941 by becoming the first African American full-fledged faculty member at a majority-white institution. Davis was well qualified for the position, holding two master's degrees from Harvard, one in English and the other in anthropology, as well as a Ph.D. from the University of Chicago. When he broke new ground by being appointed to the University of Chicago faculty, there were 330 other African American Ph.D.'s in the United States, all of whom were restricted to HBCUs or nonteaching positions.[2]

Some progress did occur during World War II. Nevertheless, a study of 500 majority-white universities in 1946 found only 78 African Americans in teaching positions, two-thirds of whom had part-time or temporary status. One of these teachers was Adelaide Cromwell Hill, the daughter of the first African American CPA, who taught sociology at her alma mater, Smith College.[3] By 1960, nearly twenty years after Davis's breakthrough, the number of African American faculty members in majority-white institutions remained minuscule at fewer than 200.[4]

The vast majority of African American faculty in all fields taught at the HBCUs. In business fields, many HBCU faculty members had been not only excluded from teaching at majority-white institutions but also prevented from practicing their professions. They turned to teaching due to lack of other opportunities. A 1994 survey of the earliest African Americans to earn master's degrees in business administration (M.B.A.'s) at leading universities reveals how few were able to find opportunities in business and how many became teachers in HBCUs. H. Naylor Fitzhugh earned his M.B.A. at Harvard in 1933 and spent the next thirty years teaching business at Howard University. Only in 1965 was he able to move to a corporation. Luzine Bikham, who earned a University of Michigan M.B.A. in 1947, told his colleagues at Texas Southern University, "I won't be here long. I'm going into the business world." Bikham remained on the faculty for forty-two years. George Owens used the GI Bill to earn his M.B.A. at Columbia University in 1950, but after finding it impossible to obtain a position with an accounting firm in New York, he taught at HBCUs. He considered education "a slight detour and fully expected that [he]'d go back [to business]." But forty years later he was still working for an HBCU.[5]

LINCOLN HARRISON: "IMBUED WITH THE SPIRIT OF THE PROFESSION"

Like the early M.B.A.'s, early African American CPAs often taught in HBCUs. One of these was Lincoln Harrison. While a student at Southern University in Baton Rouge, Louisiana, in the 1930s, Harrison, along with most of his classmates, majored in education. He decided not to pursue a career in teaching after seeing press accounts of African American millionaires in the black newspapers of the time. Instead, he wanted to become a "big-time businessman."[6]

Only one school in the South offered graduate education in business to African Americans, Atlanta University.[7] Harrison headed to Atlanta, where Jesse Blayton taught his accounting courses. The fact that Blayton was the richest African American Harrison had ever met magnified the attraction of business and convinced Harrison to become a CPA.[8] However, the business opportunities he was looking for did not materialize. Following the well-worn path of other well-educated African Americans, Harrison became a teacher at his undergraduate institution, Southern University.

Still determined to become a CPA, Harrison faced several obstacles. He needed more accounting courses because Atlanta University lacked the resources to offer the entire accounting curriculum requisite to prepare for the CPA examination. Louisiana State University, just a few miles from Harrison's home, provided the necessary courses but barred him from attending. Segregation also impacted his ability to take the CPA examination: in Louisiana, the examination was given at the Roosevelt Hotel in New Orleans, where African Americans were not permitted.[9]

Undeterred, Harrison learned that the University of Illinois offered the required courses *and* gave the CPA examination on campus. In 1945, he took a one-year leave of absence from Southern University and moved 700 miles to take the courses that were not available to him in the South. At the University of Illinois, he met Professor A. C. Littleton, one of the leading accounting theorists of the era.[10] Littleton encouraged Harrison in his pursuit but warned him that his educational background was weak and that it would require a couple of years of study to prepare for the rigorous examination.

Harrison lived in the Kappa Alpha Psi fraternity house, where he met future Chicago CPAs Isaac Little and Frederick Ford. These new friends teased him for not participating in social activities, but Harrison remained focused on his goal. In order to reduce his spring course load, Harrison spent Christmas break on campus teaching himself cost accounting from the textbook. Before the year was out, he took the examination, passed it, and had his results transferred to Louisiana. He became Louisiana's first African American CPA in July 1946.[11]

Asked if he considered staying in Chicago, with its unparalleled opportunities for African American CPAs, Harrison replied, "No, I was eager to return to Southern [University] and brag about being a CPA. I was young in those days."

Harrison returned to Baton Rouge, but soon he was recruited to teach at one of the few black colleges located outside of the South, Central State in Ohio. There he learned of the new Ph.D. program in accounting at Ohio State University.[12] Ever ambitious, he pursued the degree. His friends and colleagues were incredulous that this already exceptionally educated man—a CPA with master's degrees from both Atlanta University and the University of Illinois—would feel the need to pursue more education.

The four or five other students in Harrison's doctoral program were hired as teaching assistants; he was not. The other students were on a first-name basis with the faculty; he was not. The other students had offices; he did not. Nevertheless, accustomed to hard work and isolation, Harrison simply turned his attention to his coursework, his teaching responsibilities at Central State, and his dissertation. He used the theories of A. C. Littleton, who had encouraged him at Illinois, to write a dissertation on accounting textbooks' failure to incorporate modern accounting theory.

In 1948, Harrison learned that the American Accounting Association, the professional association for accounting faculty, was holding a conference in Memphis. He knew in advance that he would not be allowed to stay in the Hotel Peabody, where the conference was held, so he arranged to stay with family friends. "Imbued with the spirit of the profession," he was excited

about attending the two-day meeting. In the aftermath of the war, the conference featured presentations such as "National Accounting Systems and
Their Role in the European Recovery Program" and "Interpretation of Income in a Period of Inflated Prices," delivered by professors from major
universities and other leading accounting professionals.[13] But Harrison never
made it to those sessions.

When he arrived at the Hotel Peabody lobby for the meeting he encountered another African American who taught at a small college in Arkansas.
The two talked and then entered the first session together. There they were
met by a white hotel attendant, who set a smoking stand and two chairs about
ten feet behind the rest of the group. Indicating that Harrison and his new
acquaintance should sit there, the attendant said something to the effect that
he would not stay somewhere he was not wanted. Harrison left the meeting
after the first session.[14]

Back in Ohio, Harrison earned his Ph.D. in 1953. For a few years he worked
for North Carolina College for Negroes. In 1958, he returned to Louisiana to
teach at Southern University. Like African Americans with Ph.D.'s in other
fields, Harrison knew that he was a rare commodity and could maximize his
salary by encouraging colleges to compete to employ him and by moving
from school to school.[15]

With over 4,000 students, Southern University was now the largest HBCU
in the country.[16] Despite the size of the school, the business faculty was so
small that Harrison, as a CPA with a Ph.D., was by far the best-qualified
faculty member and thus was required to teach a wide variety of business
courses. A student of his later reported that Harrison taught fully half of her
business courses.[17]

As a CPA in Louisiana, Harrison returned the application he was sent invit-
ing him to join the Louisiana Society of CPAs. Harrison's education at Southern University and Atlanta University clearly indicated that he was African
American, and his membership was denied. Years later, in 1970, he was talking
to a white CPA who casually asked, "Why don't you come out and join the
society?" Harrison told him that his membership had been rejected. The
white CPA expressed consternation as well as certainty that Harrison would
now be welcomed. He applied again that year and was accepted. At his first
meeting, one of the members took him aside and recommended that his wife
not try to join the women's auxiliary because they often met at segregated
restaurants.[18]

When asked if the treatment at the Peabody Hotel in 1948 and the exclusion from the Louisiana CPA Society until 1970 made him angry, Harrison had two responses. The incident at the Peabody Hotel in Memphis had been quite upsetting because he had been excited about joining the *American* Accounting Association and had made quite an effort to attend the meeting of this national organization.[19] The Louisiana Society of CPAs was a different matter. Accustomed to the Jim Crow South, he did not expect to be admitted, and only applied because of his mother's encouragement. At the time he was not angry, though it made him angry to think about it decades later. In the intervening time, he reported, he "felt much better" about the profession as he became involved on committees of both the American Accounting Association and the AICPA.[20]

MILTON WILSON: THE STATE OF TEXAS FIGHTS INTEGRATION

A contemporary of Harrison's also headed north for his graduate education and then south to teach at an HBCU. Milton Wilson was a graduate of West Virginia State, where one of his professors inspired him to become a CPA. Wilson learned that the State of Indiana accepted graduate education in lieu of an experience requirement, so he moved to Bloomington and earned a master's degree in commercial science at Indiana University in 1945.

Wilson was able to take advantage of opportunities for professional African Americans that opened up during World War II, and he moved to Washington, D.C., as a cost accountant for the federal Office of Emergency Management. Wilson's supervisor soon made it clear that, as an African American, Wilson did not have the same opportunities for promotion as his white colleagues. Unwilling to accept this constraint, he began to teach, first at Hampton Institute in Virginia and then at Dillard University in New Orleans. Equipped with a master's degree from Indiana University, Wilson was inordinately qualified for teaching. Still, when he asked the vice president for academic affairs at Dillard for a raise, he was told that he was already the highest-paid member of his department and that if he wanted more money he was going to have to earn his doctorate.

Meanwhile, a landmark desegregation case was taking shape in Texas. The NAACP, having been successful in Missouri and Maryland, attacked the segregated graduate schools in Texas. When Heman P. Sweatt applied for admission to the University of Texas Law School in Austin, his application was denied solely because of the color of his skin.[21]

While pressing for Sweatt's admittance to the University of Texas at Austin, the NAACP also demanded that Texas comply with the "separate but equal" doctrine and provide graduate and professional education for African Americans, as there was no law school in the state that would admit African Americans. The state quickly established the Texas State University for Negroes in Houston. In an attempt to avoid future lawsuits demanding entry into other graduate or professional schools, the legislation specified that the new school would offer *any* requested courses not otherwise available to black Texans.[22]

In 1950 the U.S. Supreme Court decided in Heman Sweatt's favor, and he enrolled in the University of Texas at Austin's law school. But the state, hoping to avert an influx of African Americans demanding to attend the state's flagship institution, persisted in developing the Texas State University for Negroes. The name was changed to Texas Southern University (TSU) in 1951, in order to avoid the implication that the state was operating segregated institutions.[23]

In the small world of well-educated African American HBCU faculty, Milton Wilson had known the new president of TSU when they worked together at Hampton Institute. The president first asked Wilson to prepare the university's financial statements, which he did part-time while retaining his job at Dillard. He was then asked to join the faculty of TSU. But Wilson, mindful of the salary implications, stated that he was determined to earn his doctorate. The TSU president helped Wilson obtain a scholarship to earn the degree at Indiana University in 1951.

Upon completion, Wilson immediately became dean of the new School of Business at TSU. When Texas granted reciprocity to Wilson, he also became the first African American CPA in the state. As a new state resident, Wilson attempted to join the Texas State Society of CPAs. To apply for society membership, he needed the endorsement of two members. One of his employees, a Jewish accounting professor, signed his application and found a colleague to provide the other signature. But the state society denied his membership, arguing that it was a social organization with the right to choose its members. Wilson recalls that the society feared that he would attend their dances and jokes that he would have been an ideal member of the organization, since dancing was the least of his interests. He was not admitted to the society until 1969, when a white partner in a Big Eight firm became outraged to hear that Wilson had been excluded and sponsored his membership.[24]

LARZETTE HALE: THE FIRST AFRICAN AMERICAN
FEMALE PH.D. IN ACCOUNTING

Like Lincoln Harrison and Milton Wilson, the first female African American Ph.D. in accounting faced Jim Crow restrictions on her professional development. Larzette G. Hale became interested in accounting in the 1930s as a bookkeeper's assistant at the Oklahoma orphanage in which she spent her teenage years. She then attended Langston University, the only HBCU in the state, and pursued a business major, where she took typing and shorthand as well as accounting.

Hale had a history of endearing herself to the adults in her life. While she was at Langston, her former supervisor from the orphanage took her shopping each year to ensure that Hale had new clothes and linens. Her college accounting teacher took her under her wing and regularly invited Hale to her home. Reporting the story fifty years later in a hotel room after a banquet in her honor, she laughed as she said, "We would go to her home and work accounting problems all weekend. And just have fun! And now that sounds so stupid, but I was in awe of having the teacher ask me out. I couldn't believe it, and I just had so much fun."

Not allowed to attend her state's two major institutions, the University of Oklahoma and Oklahoma State University, in 1942 Hale headed for the University of Wisconsin, where her new husband had relatives. The State of Oklahoma paid her tuition. The virtually all-white environment of Madison, Wisconsin, was an enormous change for Hale, but her academic excellence smoothed the way. She took intermediate accounting from Fayette Elwell, the dean of the business school, and she reports that he was "so surprised and so happy" when she earned an "A" in the class. Once again she had found a mentor. Elwell provided both financial support in the form of scholarships and moral support by making the rest of the faculty aware of his interest in her success.

Hale studied with a Jewish girl who also felt isolated—Hale reports that the male students "couldn't be bothered with women." The engineering students with whom she took a statistics course provided her greatest challenge. They did not address her directly, but she frequently overheard their disparaging and racist comments. She felt vindicated when she received her high grade.

Hale survived and excelled because, as she reports, "One of the things that people learned in my day was how to be alone. Blacks had to realize that they were not going to be accepted widely and you had to have a good opinion of yourself. And if you had a family support group, that helped. . . . I was very fortunate to marry somebody who wanted both of us to succeed."[25]

After earning her master's, she and her husband returned to the South to teach in HBCUs. After a few years they moved to Atlanta, where she became a professor of accounting at Clark College, part of the Atlanta University complex.

Atlanta was home to the "Dean of Negro Accountants," Jesse Blayton. When Hale arrived at Clark College, "The first thing J. B. [Blayton] said was 'You will have to get your CPA.'" In addition to teaching, she worked on Blayton's staff and enthusiastically studied for the CPA examination with a group of other aspirants Blayton had organized. Unlike Lincoln Harrison, who was not allowed to take the examination in Louisiana, Hale took the CPA exam in a government building in downtown Atlanta. She was required to sit in the back of the room and was not allowed to use the lunchroom with the other examinees. Once again, she overcame these barriers through unassailable success: she became a CPA in 1951.

Hale joined the AICPA, but did not bother to apply to the Georgia Society. She joined the American Women's Society of CPAs (AWSCPA), but was not allowed to join its Georgia chapter. When the national AWSCPA held a meeting at a segregated hotel in Atlanta in the 1950s, a Jewish woman in the Atlanta chapter obtained special permission for Hale to attend the event.[26]

Hale's mentor from the University of Wisconsin had kept in contact over the years. Each winter, Dean Fayette Elwell stopped in Atlanta on his way to vacation in Florida. On one visit he suggested that she return to Wisconsin to get her doctorate before he retired. She did, and in 1955 she became the first graduate of the University of Wisconsin Ph.D. program in accounting as well as the first African American female Ph.D. in accounting in the United States.[27]

Lincoln Harrison, Milton Wilson, and Larzette Hale all became faculty members prior to the major changes the civil rights movement effected on higher education in the United States. They were lone pioneers; by the mid-1960s, only seven African Americans had earned doctorate degrees in accounting.[28] The group remained minuscule for decades, but after the civil rights movement its members faced a dramatically different environment.

THE CIVIL RIGHTS MOVEMENT AND THE HBCUS

The HBCUs were an integral part of the civil rights movement. They were often the center of organized opposition to segregation including the lunch-counter sit-ins and the Freedom Rides. This leadership often came at tremendous personal cost. In 1968, students from South Carolina State College demonstrated to integrate a bowling alley in downtown Orangeburg. State troopers killed three of the students. In 1970, members of the Mississippi Highway Patrol fired into a dormitory at Jackson State University, killing two. In 1972, two more students were killed in a confrontation between the police and demonstrators at Southern University in Louisiana.[29]

The era was also one of academic transformation at these institutions, which continued to educate the majority of African American college students. In drawing attention to the disparities between whites and African Americans, the civil rights movement focused unprecedented attention on the HBCUs. Expanding opportunities and new federal funding resulted in a dramatic increase in the number of African Americans attending college.[30] It also led to a widening of occupational options for African Americans and thus to a demand for greater educational choices and faculty expertise.

The HBCUs benefited financially from several accomplishments of the Lyndon Johnson presidency. Most dramatically, federal aid to the colleges, including direct aid, student loans, and work-study opportunities, mushroomed. Largely driven by the Higher Education Act of 1965, federal funds for HBCUs rose from $18 million in the 1962–63 school year to $123 million in the 1968–69 school year. Federal funding to all colleges and universities tripled during the period, but the HBCU share of funding rose disproportionately, increasing from 1.3 percent to 3.1 percent of the total.[31]

As noted earlier, the Civil Rights Act of 1964 contributed to the end of the complete exclusion of African Americans in several occupations. The same act forbade discrimination in college admissions by any institution receiving federal funds, which included most universities. Despite intense resistance, this led to the end of the complete exclusion of African Americans that had persisted at many southern universities.[32]

Increased federal funding and pressure to desegregate had a ripple effect. Several southern states increased budgets for the HBCUs: the per-student budget at Alabama State doubled between 1962 and 1964. At the time, an African American educator in Alabama explained the increase in funding to a *Wall Street Journal* reporter as follows: "They've finally realized they can't keep Negroes out of state-supported schools, so now they're trying to keep them happy in Negro schools."[33]

The new social and political climate also enhanced other funding sources.

The Ford, Carnegie, and Rockefeller Foundations dramatically increased scholarship support for African American students. Donations to civil rights organizations grew during this period, including those to the United Negro College Fund, which funneled the money to the HBCUs.[34]

African American accounting faculty benefited from the increased financial support. The members of the AICPA's new committee on minority recruitment toured several HBCUs in 1969 to assess the schools' greatest needs. It then raised $350,000 from AICPA members to improve libraries, provide internships for faculty, and hire CPAs to teach part-time at the colleges.[35] As director of development and chair of the business administration department at Langston University during this period, Larzette Hale was able to raise funds to increase salaries, improve the library, and grant leaves of absence for faculty to study for doctorates. She also earned a grant to start an Upward Bound program at Langston. This federal program paid for students to spend part of the summer on campus to enhance their skills and their likelihood of success.[36]

JOBS FOR HBCU ACCOUNTING GRADUATES

One reason for the increase in funding for the HBCUs is that companies had discovered that these schools were the most effective place to begin recruitment of African American students. Prior to the late 1960s, students at HBCUs considered business—and accounting in particular—as among the least hospitable professions for African Americans. Perceptions changed gradually, as the number of companies recruiting at the HBCUs for white-collar jobs rose dramatically in the late 1960s. Engineering, the sciences, and accounting positions in corporations became available to African Americans for the first time.[37] The *Wall Street Journal* published several front-page articles touting this rush into HBCU placement offices and quoted several claims that African American applicants were getting more and better job offers than their white classmates.[38]

Accounting professors at the HBCUs recall the increase in recruiters, but they were not as optimistic about the change as the *Wall Street Journal* articles might suggest. Of the 241 students who graduated from HBCUs as accounting majors in 1968, only sixteen were hired by CPA firms, most in large northern cities.[39] Students at Virginia Union in Richmond could land positions in

Professor Ruth Harris, right, with graduates Louise White and Willie Williams at
Virginia Union University, June 1966. Photo courtesy of Ruth Harris.

Boston, New York, or Chicago, but not in Richmond itself. Recruiters from
the Big Eight firms came from the national headquarters, not the local offices.
When Virginia Union accounting professor Ruth Coles Harris asked the firms
about local jobs, the firm's recruiters told her that their Richmond offices were
too small and were not hiring. But faculty at Virginia Commonwealth, a local
majority-white school, told her that their students were obtaining jobs in the
Big Eight in Richmond. Harris reports, "There was even one instance where I
received a call from a local office of one of the 'Big Eight,' asking me whether
we had a degree program in accounting, how many students were enrolled in
it, etc. I invited him to come to the campus to visit and offered to send him a
catalog and some literature. He turned down all that I had offered and had the
nerve to tell me that he was calling because the national office had instructed
him to do so."[40]

It was not until the 1980s that Professor Harris's students were hired for
positions in the Richmond offices of the major accounting firms.[41]

NEW PRESSURES FOR HBCUS

Despite the financial aid increases and the newfound interest in their gradu-ates, the HBCUs remained underfunded and had difficulty competing for students and faculty. A study of HBCUs in 1971 showed that, notwithstanding the progress made in the 1960s, these schools had fewer faculty members with doctorates, smaller libraries, smaller endowments, and poorer facilities than their white counterparts.[42]

Competition for students came from new sources. White colleges in the South began—after vicious resistance—admitting African American students, though typically in small numbers. Northern white schools began recruiting African American students rather than merely accepting a token few. Harvard University, the University of Chicago, Northwestern University, and other major business schools instituted scholarship programs for African American M.B.A. students in the last half of the 1960s. In 1970, there were enough African American students in M.B.A. programs to start a new professional group, the Black M.B.A. Association.[43]

This new competition for students put pressure on the HBCUs that had not been felt previously. Spelman College in Atlanta had long attracted the daughters of prominent African American families, but now many of these young women were going north. The future of integration was hotly debated, and many wondered whether the HBCUs would survive.[44]

New competition not only affected the HBCUs' ability to attract students, but it also reduced their ability to retain faculty. Suddenly the white colleges became willing to hire African American faculty, who were typically lured by higher salaries, lower teaching loads, and facilities that supported research.[45]

Efforts were made to stop this "brain drain." The Ford Foundation and the Urban League arranged professional internships at major corporations for HBCU faculty where they learned current business practices they could share with their students. Under a similar AICPA program, Lincoln Harrison, dean of the business school at Southern University, spent the summer of 1969 working with Price Waterhouse, a Big Eight firm.[46]

The Higher Education Act of 1965 was designed to improve faculty quali-fications by sponsoring cooperative programs in which HBCU faculty ex-changed places with faculty at majority-white colleges or spent time in corpo-rations.[47] But these faculty exchange programs had substantial drawbacks. They came at a time when white schools had finally become willing to hire

African American faculty and turned to the HBCUs to find candidates. The president of Morehouse College in Atlanta was wary of faculty exchange programs; he called them "neatly disguised recruiting programs." The *Wall Street Journal* reported that "federal pressure to integrate faculties" meant a loss of faculty at HBCUs: Southern University, for example, lost six professors in 1967.[48]

These new conditions represented a radical change. The first five African Americans to earn Ph.D.'s in accounting had had no chance at full-time positions in majority-white institutions. The first African American Ph.D., William L. Campfield, earned his Ph.D. at the University of Illinois in 1951 and soon became the fourth most prolific publisher in the most prestigious journal among accounting academics, the *Accounting Review*. He was a CPA in both North Carolina and California. Yet he was not employed by one of the leading institutions of his time. Instead, he spent one year as a lecturer, not a professor, at the University of San Francisco (USF), a Catholic school. While USF was the first majority-white institution to hire an African American Ph.D. in accounting, Campfield's credentials outshone those of the other business administration faculty, not one of whom—including the dean—had a Ph.D.[49]

After his year at USF, Campfield returned to his accounting position in the federal government and punctuated his work there with visiting positions at various colleges.[50] His former students—both black and white—remember him as an encouraging and exceptionally demanding professor.[51]

In 1957, Milton Wilson, who like Campfield had earned his Ph.D. in 1951, took a one-year leave from TSU to teach at the Harvard Business School.[52] In 1970, he was offered a full-professor position at his alma mater, Indiana University, but he chose instead to become dean of Howard University's School of Business. Although he was interested in the Indiana job, Wilson and his wife agreed that his mother, who had been a teacher, would have preferred that he continue his efforts to improve educational opportunities for African American students.[53]

The first African American in a full-time, permanent position in an accounting department at a majority-white institution was Joseph J. Cramer Jr. Cramer had been Milton Wilson's student at TSU, and Wilson had recommended him to his own alma mater, Indiana University, where Cramer earned his doctorate in 1963. Upon completion, Cramer accepted a position at Pennsylvania State University, where he was ultimately promoted to professor.[54]

In 1972, Larzette Hale also became one of the few African American accounting faculty members at majority-white schools: she moved from Langston University in Oklahoma to Utah State. Despite the lack of diversity in Utah, Hale found it a much more hospitable environment than she had experienced in the South. She was welcomed in the Utah Association of CPAs and quickly assumed leadership positions, including becoming a member of the board of directors.[55]

TRANSFORMING THE BUSINESS SCHOOL CURRICULUM

These changes among students and faculty, combined with the sudden appearance of industry recruiters on campus, meant that the courses offered by the HBCUs had to be transformed to meet the needs of their new constituents. No longer viewed as solely teacher-training institutions for the segregated school systems of the South, the HBCUs prepared students for wider roles, including business and accounting. Prior to the civil rights movement, most business programs at HBCUs prepared students to be high school business teachers or secretaries. Typing, shorthand, and bookkeeping constituted a substantial proportion of the curriculum.[56]

As opportunities began to unfold, there was a dramatic increase in business majors at the HBCUs. In 1963, only seven HBCUs offered accounting as a major; by 1968 that number had risen to twenty-four. Between 1967 and 1968, HBCU graduates with accounting majors jumped 50 percent, to 241. In 1971, the AICPA reported that the number of African American accounting majors had continued to rise. At Southern University, for example, where Lincoln Harrison was dean of the business school, there were nine accounting majors in 1964 and eighty-three in 1971. A 1972 survey of college freshmen revealed that African American students were slightly more likely than whites to want to major in business, even though white students were three to four times more likely to have a father who was a businessman.[57]

The HBCUs were ill-prepared for this transition. Because of exclusion in the profession, there were few CPAs on HBCU faculties. A 1968 study identified twenty-seven CPAs of all races, part-time and full-time, on the faculties of the twenty-four HBCUs that offered an accounting major. Ten of these schools did not have a single CPA on their faculties.[58] There were also few African Americans with Ph.D.'s, seven in 1965 and only eleven by 1973.[59] These pioneers bore substantial responsibility for the requisite transformation in the curriculum.

As dean of the TSU School of Business, Milton Wilson oversaw rapid expansion and led the school to become the first HBCU to be accredited by the American Assembly of Collegiate Schools of Business (AACSB).[60] Pressure to obtain accreditation increased at HBCUs during this period of trying to meet the standards of major white institutions.

Various independent organizations offer accreditation to colleges and universities by evaluating an institution's conformity with educational standards. Such accreditation provides legitimacy and improves a school's ability to attract students, foundation support, and recruiters for its graduates. The AACSB is the premier accreditation agency for schools of business. It became dominant after World War II, when certain GI Bill funding was available only to accredited schools. The AACSB defined standards for faculty credentials, courses offered, course loads for faculty, and institutional support such as libraries and, later, computer facilities.[61]

The AACSB requirement that a substantial proportion of the faculty have terminal degrees in their fields was one of the most difficult standards for HBCUs to meet. Because most accreditation requirements for accounting faculty were designed to prepare students for work as CPAs, either a Ph.D. or a combination CPA and M.B.A. met the standard. Heavy teaching loads encompassing a wide variety of courses, another common feature of HBCUs, were not allowed in AACSB-accredited schools. The leading colleges offered twelve to twenty different accounting courses, eight to ten of which were required.[62] With their limited resources, HBCUs found meeting these standards a severe challenge.

In 1947, shortly before Wilson's arrival at TSU, the department of business administration had only three faculty members, all at the lowest level, instructor. In the 1960s, Wilson won a $600,000 grant from the Ford Foundation to help improve the School of Business. By 1967, when the school earned AACSB accreditation, TSU's School of Business still had three instructors, but it also had two full professors, five associate professors, and four assistant professors. Consistent with its growth in faculty, the university also offered a much wider selection of courses.[63]

Wilson's unprecedented success in accrediting TSU led to several job offers, including the position as dean of Howard University's new School of Business. Howard University was considered by many to be the premier institution for African American college students. Yet in the 1950s it did not have a business school. Wilson helped Howard's new business school take its place among the other outstanding departments at the university, raising money from corporations, the Big Eight accounting firms, foundations, and federal programs. He led the school to AACSB accreditation in 1980, becoming the only dean to have accomplished this at two African American colleges. He also oversaw fundraising and the opening of a $13 million facility for the School of Business and Public Administration in 1984.[64]

QUIESTER CRAIG: "I WAS NAIVE, ENERGETIC, AND PROUD"

When Quiester Craig became the first dean of the new School of Business at North Carolina Agricultural & Technical State University (A&T) in 1972, he was hired to imitate Wilson's accomplishments and earn the school AACSB accreditation. Only the tenth African American to earn a doctorate in accounting when he completed his degree at the University of Missouri in 1971, his background was similar to those of his predecessors from earlier decades. Like so many others, Quiester Craig's first encounter with an African American CPA came when, as an undergraduate at Morehouse College, he met Jesse Blayton. He attended graduate school at Atlanta University in the mid-1950s, the only southern school at that time providing graduate business education for African Americans. Part of his expenses were paid by the state of Alabama—Craig called these out-of-state scholarships "pacifying money."

Craig did not want to enter teaching, but finding no opportunities in business, he found himself teaching at various HBCUs, ultimately landing at Lincoln University in Missouri. Soon he was teaching all the accounting courses that Lincoln University offered, including financial accounting, cost accounting, advanced accounting, and taxes. "I can't tell you the difficulty of trying to prepare for this, even though I had taken these courses. I worked every problem in every chapter and I put an 'X' in the middle of the chapter to mark where I was going that day, and that's as far as I went. I would not permit a student to take me past that point because I wasn't ready. . . . Ultimately I taught eight different accounting courses . . . four different accounting classes every semester. . . . I was young; I was naive, energetic, and proud and . . . it never occurred to me that *nobody* taught four different accounting classes each semester."[65]

Apparently he was not busy enough because he decided to pursue a Ph.D. at nearby University of Missouri and get "all his union cards." It was there that he met other college accounting instructors and learned that "*no one* else was doing this." By 1971 Craig had both a Ph.D. and a CPA. He moved to Greensboro, North Carolina, to become dean of the new School of Business at North Carolina A&T, the largest black college in North Carolina and the birthplace of the lunch counter sit-in movement.[66]

Craig was hired expressly to lead the school to AACSB accreditation and the program quality it necessitated. He did not know exactly what this entailed until after he had confidently accepted the challenge. He had noted that nursing, engineering, and other programs at A&T were accredited, and he did not see why he could not accomplish the same thing for the business school.[67] It was only after accepting the job that Craig learned that only two out of fifty-five colleges in the state of North Carolina had AACSB accreditation and that the only HBCU in the nation with such accreditation was Milton Wilson's Texas Southern University.

The university had expanded during the 1960s, but it was still far behind where it needed to be to meet AACSB standards.[68] When Craig arrived, he had twenty-three faculty members, none of whom had Ph.D.'s in accounting and none of whom were CPAs. Much of the curriculum was designed to produce teachers and secretaries, with coursework focusing on typing, shorthand, and similar skills.[69]

Accreditation by the AACSB meant that the curriculum had to be completely revamped to offer more advanced accounting courses and courses in other business fields such as finance, marketing, information systems, quantitative management, and management strategy. Many members of the business faculty did not welcome changing the curriculum because it meant that their courses, which had constituted the core of the curriculum, would now be marginalized or even eliminated. Craig lost an initial effort to vote the typing course out of the accounting curriculum. He called the chancellor to tell him that the business education faculty, due to its size, was never going to let him institute the necessary reforms. Craig recalls the Chancellor's response: "I hired *you* to solve this problem. I was told *you* could figure out these things."

Craig did not object to typing courses, but he knew that he would never be able to compete with schools that offered strategy, quantitative methods, and finance if students were required to take a year or two of typing. Some faculty firmly believed—based on their experience in the very recent past—that there was no point in developing courses in subjects in which the students would find no job opportunities, and they knew that the students could get jobs as teachers or clerical professionals.

Craig lobbied the other faculty, educating them on the AACSB requirements and on the fact that these changes would benefit the entire school. The next vote was taken at a meeting where faculty raises constituted a major part of the discussion. He also gained authority to transfer the business education faculty into the School of Education. Fortunately, he never had to carry through with this transfer. Typing ceased to be a required course.

The business education major shrank as professors retired and were replaced by faculty in other fields such as marketing, accounting, and finance, and as students saw that accounting majors had become more marketable. Craig's efforts to improve the school included raising donations from several foundations, corporations, and public accounting firms to build library facilities and for faculty development. Some of the grant money was used to send faculty to doctoral programs. Many faculty members benefited from the new AICPA fellowship program for African Americans pursuing doctorates in accounting. Craig also encouraged—some might say pressured—his faculty to earn their CPAs in order to become better role models for their students.[70]

In 1971, North Carolina A&T had formed the first student chapter of the National Association of Black Accountants. In 1979, the A&T business school became the third HBCU in the country to gain AACSB accreditation at the undergraduate level, and in 1986, it became the first to earn separate AACSB accreditation for its accounting program. By 1998, over 300 North Carolina A&T graduates had earned their CPAs, constituting more than 5 percent of all African American CPAs in the nation.[71]

The changes accompanying the civil rights movement transformed the accounting programs at the nation's black colleges. The period had been one of challenge for Lincoln Harrison, Milton Wilson, Larzette Hale, Quiester Craig, and other accounting educators, but it had also been a time of great promise. Seeing their students experience opportunities they had only dreamed about, these educators hoped for continued strides toward educational and employment equality in the CPA profession.

7

The Momentum Is Lost

The beginning of the 1970s was a time of high expectations for African Americans in the public accounting profession. The American Institute of Certified Public Accountants (AICPA) had called for efforts to integrate, the major firms had ended their decades of absolute exclusion, the National Association of Black Accountants (NABA) was growing rapidly, accounting departments in historically black colleges were expanding, and African American–owned CPA firms found their clientele burgeoning under the newly created antipoverty programs.

This period of excitement was short-lived, however. Near the end of the decade, the U.S. Supreme Court made its first decision weakening affirmative action, signaling an end to the period of escalating efforts to include African Americans in all aspects of American life. A shift away from public concern with integration laid the groundwork for the 1980 election of Ronald Reagan, whose administration reversed many of the programs developed in the 1960s and 1970s. The effect on CPA firms was immediate: after only a decade of growth in African American employment in white-owned firms, the 1980s was a period of decline. Reagan's cutbacks in social programs reduced or eliminated War on Poverty programs, which had been the major clientele of many African American–owned CPA firms.

Changes in the public accounting profession in the 1970s and 1980s reflected the changes taking place in the larger business world. In the early 1970s, the *Wall Street Journal* regularly heralded African American "firsts," such as the addition of African Americans to the boards of directors at several major corporations, the admittance of African Americans to various stock exchanges, and unprecedented promotions to executive positions.[1] One of these landmark events was the establishment of a new journal for African Americans in business, *Black Enterprise*. Launched in 1970, the magazine's early columnists included two African American CPAs, Bert Mitchell and NABA founder Frank Ross, who provided financial advice to *Black Enterprise* readers.[2]

The optimistic atmosphere of the 1970s was bolstered by progress in the profession. In 1968, only 30 percent of African American CPAs worked in public accounting—most had no choice but to work for the government or as teachers. By 1971, 60 percent of African American CPAs worked for public accounting firms. The AICPA reported continuous increases in the number of African Americans working for the major accounting firms. Surveyed firms reported 197 black employees in 1969, 478 in 1971, and 1,005 in 1973.[3] NABA membership skyrocketed. After starting with nine members in 1969, it grew to 1,100 members in 1973 and 2,000 members by 1975. In a sign of the changing times, a 1973 *Black Enterprise* article noted that the accounting profession offered excellent opportunities to African Americans, and Bert Mitchell's 1975 follow-up study of progress by African Americans in the profession since 1968 found that the number of CPAs had tripled to 450 and that 89 percent were glad they had chosen the field.[4]

By 1976, members of the profession had donated more than $1.25 million to the AICPA's scholarship fund for minority students. The AICPA's Committee on Minority Recruitment secured a grant from the U.S. Department of Health, Education and Welfare to fund fellowships to enable teachers in historically black colleges and universities (HBCUs) to earn Ph.D.'s. The grant provided financial support for the doctoral student and funds for the HBCU to hire temporary replacements. The National Urban League sponsored a Black Executive Exchange Program (BEEP), which brought African American professionals to HBCU campuses to provide role models as well as updates on professional opportunities. In addition, the AICPA invited HBCU faculty to annual seminars at which current developments in the profession were discussed.[5]

Many of the same people who, only a few years earlier, had struggled to find employment suddenly saw opportunities open. In 1963, Bert Mitchell had been unable to obtain employment with any of the Big Eight firms. In 1972, he became the first African American on the governing council of the AICPA, and in 1974, he became the first African American to serve on the New York State Board for Public Accountancy.[6] In 1950s Los Angeles, top students Talmadge Tillman and William Collins had faced tremendous barriers to becoming CPAs. In 1969, organizers for the Western Regional Meeting of the American Accounting Association, the national organization for accounting professors, asked Tillman and Collins to lead a panel discussion on opportunities for African Americans in the profession. Other African American CPA pioneers, previously all but invisible, found their contributions honored by the newly established NABA.[7]

"FROM BEGINNER TO PARTNER"

The *Journal of Accountancy*, which had been silent on the subject of African Americans in the profession between 1933 and the late 1960s, now reported regularly on the AICPA's efforts to diversify the profession as well as on the successes of African American CPAs.[8] One of the landmark achievements described in the *Journal of Accountancy* was the 1974 promotion to partnership of William Goodall, who worked for the majority-white firm Lester Witte & Company, headquartered in Chicago. The article, entitled "Black CPA Advances from Beginner to Partner," profiled one of the first African American CPAs to have worked his way up through a majority-white firm to achieve partnership.[9]

Arthur Witte, the senior partner in the firm and son of its founder, had attended the 1968 AICPA meeting where the major topic of discussion was the need to integrate. Witte reports, "It was striking. Remarkable. There was a sea of faces out there—2,500 faces, and none of them black."[10] Witte returned to his office in Chicago determined to address this problem, and soon thereafter he hired William Goodall.

Goodall exemplified the economic mobility made possible by the integration of the profession. The son of a coal miner, Goodall took a full college course load while working full-time as a motorman for the Chicago Transit Authority. He was twenty-eight years old when he graduated from Roosevelt University and joined Lester Witte & Company. He told the *Journal of Accountancy* that his race did not impede his success: "These people were not interested in where I came from or my color. You sit down and start making an intelligent analysis of the problem and you are talking about money in a client's pocket."[11]

In the article, Arthur Witte attributed Goodall's rise from staff in 1968 to partner in 1974 to Goodall's talent in understanding and improving clients' accounting systems. Witte believed that because his firm was small—roughly twenty professionals in the Chicago headquarters—he was able to defuse any negative interactions by making all his employees aware of his commitment to making integration work. Witte also told the *Journal of Accountancy* that when he first hired Goodall, he informed each client that a black man was going to represent his firm, and he reported meeting no resistance whatsoever.[12]

On reflecting on this experience twenty-five years later, Goodall agrees that his problems with clients were minor. Occasionally a client would make it clear—subtly—that Goodall was not wanted. The adjustment was more difficult when it came to his fellow staff members and supervisors.

Goodall recalls having fifteen job offers when he graduated from college in 1968. He was well aware that the AICPA had recently introduced a push for integration, and he knew that an African American accounting graduate was a rare and newly valued commodity. Price Waterhouse, a Big Eight firm, offered him $15,000—double what he was making as a driver for the Chicago Transit Authority. Goodall believes that if he had been twenty-two instead of twenty-eight, he might have accepted that offer. He knew that Price Waterhouse was a premier firm in which he would get excellent training. He liked the people he met when he visited the Price Waterhouse office. However, he did not meet any African American professionals, and he lacked confidence that the firm would be a comfortable place to work.

Lester Witte & Company offered Goodall $8,500—only $1,000 more than he was making as a motorman. But the recruiter for Witte, Todd Lundy, and Arthur Witte himself made a tremendous impression on Goodall. Before he joined the firm he spent five hours one Saturday talking to the two men, asking them tough questions about how they would handle employing an African American. He left with a strong sense that these men would back him up if he encountered unfair treatment.

Goodall worked hard to prove himself at the firm. When several weaknesses were brought to his attention in his first six-month review, including his speed on the calculator and his knowledge of accounting regulations, he strove to improve. In fact, Lundy told Goodall at a friendly lunch that he was not required to *memorize* the citations for all the accounting pronouncements. But Goodall believed that he had to overprepare in order to survive.

After a year, Lundy conducted Goodall's second six-month review. Goodall soon realized that several of the comments reported to him were verbatim repetitions of what he had heard during his first review. One manager who had submitted a negative review of Goodall's work had not even supervised him during the period the review covered. When he pointed this out to Lundy, Lundy insisted that the two of them meet with the senior partner, Witte. When Witte and Lundy ascertained that the manager had indeed fabricated a review of Goodall's work, they were furious. From then on, Witte insisted that Goodall only work on Witte's own clients—clients he and his father had known for decades. Under this plan, anyone who wanted to critique Goodall's work had to justify his critique to the senior partner in the firm. As Witte had told the *Journal of Accountancy* in 1974, he sent a strong message that he was committed to integrating the firm.

This change, plus the mentoring that accompanied working only on Witte's clients, made an enormous difference for Goodall. Soon he was not only supervising audits himself but also providing growth-promoting advice to clients. As the clients' revenues grew, the fees they paid to Lester Witte also grew. Instead of the usual twelve years it took to become a partner, Goodall became a partner in six. Arthur Witte's confidence in him had made all the difference, and Goodall never regretted the choice he had made. "Not for one day" did he wish he had taken the higher-paying position at Price Waterhouse.[13]

AFRICAN AMERICANS IN THE "BIG EIGHT"

Unlike William Goodall, many African Americans did enter Big Eight public accounting firms in the late 1960s and early 1970s. Prior to mergers in the 1980s and 1990s, the Big Eight consisted of Arthur Andersen; Arthur Young; Coopers & Lybrand; Ernst & Ernst; Haskins & Sells; Peat, Marwick and Mitchell; Price Waterhouse; and Touche, Ross. These eight firms employed thousands of professional accountants, had offices in all major cities, and audited over 95 percent of the 500 largest companies in the United States.[14]

While the Big Eight offered tax and management consulting services, new staff members were almost invariably assigned to the audit function because it was only through audit experience that an accountant could meet the experience requirement to become a CPA. Auditing exposes new staff members to a variety of clients and issues, and it is typically considered the best training for new professionals. These auditors spend very little time in their employer's office—auditing requires spending time at the clients' offices. As part of the audit, staff accountants work in clients' file rooms to verify that invoices match payments, visit warehouses to ensure that inventory records are correct, and spend time with cashiers to check that cash on hand matches cash receipts and payments reported. This constant contact with clients is one difference between working for a large law firm and working for a large accounting firm. Auditors are invariably visible to their clients. In contrast, lawyers can remain in their firms' offices researching and writing. A mid-1960s study revealed that there were only three African Americans in the largest law firms in New York, and that two of the three *never* met with clients.[15]

The hierarchical structure of the Big Eight contributed to many of the problems with integrating the firms. While some partners recognized the importance of complying with government mandates to integrate, lower-echelon supervisors, called seniors, frequently did not consider this a priority. Most African American members of the firms, as new employees, had little contact with partners. A 1971 NABA survey of 168 African American professionals in the Big Eight reflected several problems with lower-level staff. Seniors chose the members of their audit teams, and they were often hesitant to include African Americans. When they were assigned to teams, African Americans frequently reported being assigned to less desirable audits such as government or not-for-profit work rather than the high-profile, lucrative Fortune 500 audits that would provide more visibility within the firms. While 60 percent of the new hires rated their salary advancements as "good," "excellent," or "outstanding," 61 percent rated social relationships between black and white staff as "poor" or "fair" and 66 percent rated firm's efforts to motivate black staff as "poor" or "fair." African American women were less content with their jobs than were African American men: one-third of the men rated their overall work experience with the Big Eight as "fair" or "poor," whereas three-quarters of the women chose these ratings.[16]

The early 1970s were undoubtedly the period during which most attention was given to recruiting African Americans into the major firms. Years later, white recruiters for the Big Eight firms recalled the early and mid-1970s as a time when they would "hire *anybody*" who was African American and had the requisite credentials.[17] In 1984, an African American partner at a major firm concurred. Referring to the early 1970s, he said, "If you could walk and chew gum at the same time, and were black, you were hired."[18]

While the big firms hired African Americans in unprecedented numbers, African American CPAs who graduated in the 1970s report that many barriers to hiring remained. The social and sartorial norms of the firms could stand in the way: for example, sporting a fashionably large Afro might count against a candidate.[19] Women were often unwelcome, and African American students from the South frequently found that the Big Eight were only interested in employing them in northern offices. When she graduated from South Carolina State in 1973, Gwendolyn McFadden was told by the recruiter for one Big

Eight firm that his office was not ready for "someone like you"—she was not sure if it was because she was African American, a woman, or both. The only Big Eight recruiter to offer her a job would not employ her in her native South Carolina; he offered her a job in Milwaukee. To her, that seemed like moving to the moon.[20]

Although the Big Eight had reversed their decades of complete exclusion, smaller white-owned firms were widely regarded as being less willing to hire African Americans.[21] A 1975 study examined Florida CPA firms' experiences with women and African Americans. Of the forty-eight nonnational firms that participated in the study, only one employed an African American.[22] In contrast, fifteen of twenty-six national firms employed African Americans in their local Florida offices.[23] The researchers concluded that the Big Eight firms were more visible and thus under more pressure to integrate.

The study confirmed that race affected job assignment and hiring. Two-thirds of the national firms that employed African American staff acknowledged that possible client disapproval played a role when assigning work to African American staff. Half of the firms reported having experienced negative client reaction to their assignment of an African American professional.[24] All respondents were asked, "Would you hire a black if the individual was qualified, was interviewed, desired to come to work with your firm and a position was available?" Every national firm replied "Yes." Of the forty-eight nonnational firms, thirteen—more than one-quarter—said "No." The main reasons given for this lack of willingness to hire African Americans were anticipated client resistance, doubts about qualifications of black candidates, and anticipated office staff resistance.[25]

BLACK IS BEAUTIFUL

The number of African Americans working in the major CPA firms had increased dramatically, but African Americans who worked for these firms typically did not follow the same career paths as their white counterparts. White staff members of CPA firms often joined the firms directly after college, met the experience requirement and passed the CPA examination, then left public accounting to pursue opportunities in corporations eager to hire Big Eight–trained CPAs.[26] Becoming a partner in a Big Eight firm could be very lucrative, but many were unwilling to defer the financial rewards that came with partnership because corporate salaries for CPAs were generally higher than the prepartnership salaries in CPA firms.

While many African Americans did leave for corporate positions, they also frequently left the major CPA firms to open their own firms.[27] In a 1975 survey, Bert Mitchell found that half of the African American CPAs in public practice worked in African American–owned CPA firms. While these professionals were likely to have met their experience requirement in the national, majority-white firms, most of the African American partners in CPA firms in the United States were partners in African American–owned firms.[28]

Mitchell himself had left the white firm for which he worked, J. K. Lasser, and after becoming disenchanted with his position as managing partner of the venerable black firm Lucas & Tucker, he started his own firm. Mitchell reports that he largely enjoyed working for J. K. Lasser, even though many clients assumed that his white subordinates were in charge of the audit teams he led. He left Lasser because he wanted to work within and for the African American community; it "was the tenor of the times." Black entrepreneurship, economic self-determination, and "black is beautiful" were the popular phrases of the early 1970s, and Mitchell wanted to contribute to creating a new African American destiny.[29]

Antipoverty programs and government audits expanded opportunities for African American–owned CPA firms, as most economic power in the African American community was concentrated in noncorporate organizations. African American leaders had more economic clout in HBCUs, civil rights organizations, and antipoverty programs than in commercial enterprises.[30]

A 1971 *Journal of Accountancy* article addressed the crucial role played by African American CPA firms in Great Society programs. It emphasized the fact that directors of the programs had social activist, rather than financial, backgrounds and stressed the importance of African American CPAs in helping these organizations meet their goals. The article included interviews with African American CPAs who had many such clients, one of whom was the ubiquitous Bert Mitchell, who said, "What happens is that you are asking people to manage money who, because of racial discrimination forced on them for ages, have had no exposure to financial controls. . . . Any social program should have two objectives. The primary objective [is addressing a social issue] and the other objective should be the training of financial personnel to help achieve the primary objective."[31]

In 1973, Mitchell and his partner Robert Titus began their firm with one major not-for-profit and five small African American–owned businesses as clients. Their not-for-profit clientele expanded rapidly, ultimately including the Dance Theatre of Harlem, the National Urban League, and the NAACP. Government contracts were a major source of growth for the new small African American–owned firms. Following the New York City fiscal crisis in 1975, the city began to require independent audits. Mitchell-Titus participated in the city's first audit, which was led by Big-Eight firm Peat, Marwick and Mitchell. Starting in the 1970s, federal, state, and local set-aside programs encouraged or required government contractors to work in joint ventures with minority-owned firms. For the first time, the Big Eight *needed* minority CPAs in order to qualify for some important clients. Because of Mitchell's prominence, reputation, experience, and expertise, his firm was in a perfect position to maximize these opportunities, landing contracts, among others, with the U.S. Departments of Commerce and Energy. Mitchell-Titus grew rapidly, and by 1981 the firm had seventy-five employees.[32] At the turn of the century, it was the largest African American CPA firm in the country.

Changes in New York were paralleled by changes in Chicago, where Mary Washington's firm, now Washington, Pittman, and McKeever (WPM), was also expanding. Chicago's late-1960s riots had led to the establishment of Chicago United, an organization that encouraged major corporations to utilize the products and services of African American–owned business. As a leader in the African American business community, WPM partner Hiram Pittman attended the first meeting of Chicago United. Through these new contacts, the clientele of WPM began to transform. In its first major venture beyond African American–owned businesses, WPM audited Commonwealth Edison's employee benefits plan. This audit led to work for several other major corporations, including the Amoco Foundation and Quaker Oats.[33]

The transformation also included joint-venture work with Big Eight firms. In the early 1970s, WPM audited Cook County Hospital as part of a team led by Ernst & Ernst. The firm was a boon to WPM's development because it was willing to share work in both the public sector and the more lucrative private sector. In addition, Ernst & Ernst invited WPM employees to participate in its staff training programs.

Like other African American–owned CPA firms, WPM benefited from the election of an African American mayor. The Voting Rights Act of 1965 and the changing demographics of many northern cities had resulted in unprecedented elections of African American officials. When Harold Washington was

The founders of Banks, Finley, Thomas and White, early 1970s. *From left to right*: George Thomas, James White, Frank Banks, and Mack Finley. Photo courtesy of Frank Banks.

elected Chicago's first black mayor in 1983, he signed an executive order mandating that 25 percent of city contracts be spent with minority-owned companies. WPM benefited directly from this change. Along with Big Eight firms, WPM worked on audits of the City of Chicago, the Chicago Public Library, and the Chicago Housing Authority.[34]

Although most were located in major northern cities like New York and Chicago, African American–owned CPA firms were also formed in the South. One of the largest African American firms of the 1970s, Banks, Finley, Thomas and White, was based in Birmingham, Alabama. Frank J. Banks graduated from Xavier University in New Orleans in 1964 and worked as an accountant for social agencies until the end of the 1960s, when opportunities opened in the Big Eight. He then worked for Ernst & Ernst for two years before joining a black-owned CPA firm in Memphis. In 1973, he and his partners, Mack Finley, George Thomas, and James C. White, formed a firm with offices in four southern cities: Memphis, Birmingham, Atlanta, and Jackson. Within a year after establishing their firm, they won a Department of Labor contract to conduct 124 audits in eight states, and soon they had federal contracts for various social programs. They developed financial procedures for Great Society creations such as Head Start programs and the Comprehensive Employment Training Act.

Like other African American–owned CPA firms in the post–Voting Rights Act era, Banks's business was tied to African American politicians. Soon, in addition to the federal work, he was managing the campaign finances of African American office seekers across the South. Although the firm was forced to utilize northern banks because of lack of cooperation from white southern bankers, Banks believed that the newly developing black professional community in the South offered networking opportunities unavailable in the established black business communities of major northern cities.[35]

Other young southerners also saw their opportunities transformed. When Michael Bruno graduated from Southern University's New Orleans campus in 1971, Ernst & Ernst hired him to work for its Jackson, Mississippi, office. His new colleagues informed him that one of the primary reasons that Ernst & Ernst hired an African American in its Mississippi office was because the firm had many federal contracts in that state.[36] He became the first African American employed by the Big Eight in the entire state of Mississippi, and he spent most of his three years with the firm auditing federal contracts.

Although Bruno worked in Mississippi, he intended to return to New Orleans and therefore became certified in Louisiana. Had he pursued the Mississippi CPA, he might have been surprised when he received his certificate. Until the mid-1980s, the Mississippi certificate featured two illustrations. On the top right-hand corner was a drawing of a ship navigating the river for which the state is famous. The top left-hand corner was occupied by a drawing of several African Americans picking cotton. The latter illustration was removed only after Marvel A. Turner Sr., the first African American to serve on the Mississippi State Board of Accountancy, joined the board in 1984.[37]

Bruno felt poorly prepared for his new position. His professors had inspired him to excel, and he believed that his accounting background was strong. Nevertheless, he was unfamiliar with the business world. For his first six months in Jackson he worked until 5:30 or 6:00 each evening, went home for dinner, and then returned to the office, working until midnight or later, trying to get up to speed by reading business periodicals and federal

Certified Public Accountant certificate, State of Mississippi, 1980. The illustration in the upper left-hand corner depicts African Americans picking cotton. Courtesy of Marvel Turner.

regulations pertaining to the job assignment. Before he accepted the position, he expected that socializing with his new colleagues would not be an option, and that expectation was realized. His colleagues were cordial, but Bruno felt isolated. He and his family were very proud, however, that he was able to buy his own home within six months of his employment with the firm.

Without realizing that he was part of a trend among African American CPAs in the 1970s, once he had gained a wealth of experience in auditing federal programs, Bruno left Ernst & Ernst to join a black-owned CPA firm in Memphis, Tennessee, that specialized in auditing social programs and African American colleges in Mississippi and Alabama.

In 1977, Bruno returned to New Orleans to join an African American firm owned by one of his former professors, Reynard J. Rochon. Rochon contacted Bruno because he needed additional employees to help with auditing federal funds awarded to the city for employment programs. In 1978, New Orleans elected its first African American mayor, Ernest "Dutch" Morial, who immediately appointed Rochon chief administrative officer for the City of New Orleans.[38] Rochon considered selling his business to one of the Big Eight, but the firm was unwilling to hire his employees other than Bruno. So Bruno himself bought the firm from Rochon, taking a loan for four times the value of his home. Over the years his firm took part in joint ventures with the Big Eight on many government audits. The firm, Bruno & Tervalon, has become one of the largest CPA firms in the New Orleans metropolitan area.[39]

THE METCALF REPORT

In 1976, the CPA profession came under intense and unprecedented scrutiny from the federal government.[40] Several corporate failures of the era were blamed on faulty accounting practices, and many of the failed corporations had been audited by Big Eight accounting firms. Legislators believed that the public was losing faith in accounting regulations, and the accounting firms had to struggle to maintain their independence from federal oversight. The result was an investigation of the Big Eight by the Senate Committee on Government Operations, led by Democratic senator Lee Metcalf of Montana. Although the main focus of the investigation was on auditing procedures and concerns about CPA firms' objectivity, the Senate subcommittee also asked each of the Big Eight to report the number of female and black partners it employed. Their responses provide rare insight into the Big Eight perspective on the issue of African Americans in the profession.

Despite the pressure they were under, some firms balked at the request, maintaining that this data was irrelevant to the issue under scrutiny. Nevertheless, only Touche, Ross refused to cooperate with this aspect of the investigation. Five of the Big Eight noted that they had no African American partners, though Arthur Andersen expressed its intention to promote two African American partners later in the year. Two firms, Ernst & Ernst as well as Coopers & Lybrand, reported that they each employed one African American partner. Several firms noted that they had instituted strong affirmative action programs and that they anticipated an expansion in African American partners once the group they had hired beginning in the late 1960s had the opportunity to spend the requisite ten to fifteen years with the firms to become partners. Ernst & Ernst's response is typical: "You will recognize that, in past years, the accounting profession was not one which was sought out by women or minorities, and that it is therefore taking time to develop and train personnel in these groups who are qualified for partnership in our firm."[41] While several of the firms pointed to the recent entry of African

Americans in the profession, none acknowledged any responsibility for the prior exclusion.

In 1978, the Minority Recruitment and Equal Opportunity Committee of the AICPA sponsored a career development seminar to assess the experiences of African Americans in major CPA firms. Fourteen of the country's largest firms sent forty-nine African American professionals to Chicago to the seminar. The discussions identified many of the same barriers revealed by NABA's 1971 study.[42] African American CPAs reported feeling underutilized, being excluded from crucial informal communications networks in the firms, and having only circumscribed contact with clients.

In the report developed by Senator Metcalf's Committee (*Metcalf Report*), one Big Eight firm attributed its shortage of African American partners to the attraction of higher salaries African Americans could earn in corporations compared to public accounting. The 1978 career development seminar found that many African Americans did seek higher salaries outside of public accounting but that the main reason for departure was perceived lack of opportunity. They worried that becoming partner would be impossible because attracting clients was a major criterion for partnership and they lacked the lucrative social and business contacts of some of their white peers. Compounding the problem, many of the social organizations in which business contacts were made did not admit black members. Participants in the seminar also reported that corporations were more aggressive and sincere in their recruitment efforts.[43]

The *Metcalf Report* identified only two African American partners in 1976, one at Ernst & Ernst, and one at Coopers & Lybrand. Ernst & Ernst had become the first Big Eight firm with an African American partner in 1971, when it acquired the CPA firm of Elmer Whiting of Cleveland.

FIRST BLACK "BIG EIGHT" PARTNER

Whiting's accounting career paralleled those of the other African American CPAs of his era. He graduated from Howard University in the 1940s, and upon returning to his hometown of Cleveland, found it impossible to meet the experience requirement. He sought out the help of white leaders in the profession, and they allowed him to count his own bookkeeping work as meeting the requirement. He passed the examination on his first attempt and became the first African American CPA in Ohio in 1950.

Whiting's CPA firm provided the experience requirement to the next five African American CPAs in the state, including his brother Thomas. Whiting reports that, unlike white CPAs in Ohio, "I didn't have to recruit; I had a parade of kids coming in here looking for a job. Hell, there was nobody else to go to."[44]

Whiting's practice consisted mainly of tax and bookkeeping work for small black businesses and African American professionals. But Whiting also had a couple of white clients. One had looked in the phone book for the closest CPA and found Whiting. Concluding from his address that Whiting was probably African American, he hired the CPA after some of his African American employees assured him that Whiting had an excellent reputation. Another white business owner whose wife had hired Whiting later confessed that he had "raised hell" when he found out that Whiting was African American. The client's attitude changed when Whiting resolved a major problem the man was having with the Internal Revenue Service.

Like many other black CPAs, Whiting benefited from his association with an African American mayor. Whiting was a lawyer as well as a CPA. He had attended law school at Cleveland State University with Carl Stokes, who became the first African American mayor of a major U.S. city in 1967. Whiting maintained Stokes's campaign finance records, and after the election, he was appointed to a city finance committee. On this committee Whiting met several white CPAs who worked for Big Eight accounting firms, one of whom asked his advice about recruiting African Americans. Whiting offered suggestions, but he was struck by the fact that this was the same firm that had refused to hire African Americans only a few years earlier.

Whiting's firm conducted several joint-venture audits with Big Eight firms because, under Mayor Stokes, the city had introduced minority participation goals. Whiting's staff returned from a joint-venture audit of Cleveland's utility department and reported, "[The Big Eight employees] don't do anything differently than we do." Whiting replied, "I'm happy you're telling me that we're keeping up with high professional standards."

Through his friends who were CPAs in other cities, Whiting had heard that Ernst & Ernst was exploring the possibility of buying an African American CPA firm. He also heard that Ernst & Ernst had offended the partners in one firm by suggesting that they join as managers instead of full partners. Like them, Whiting—who had twenty years of experience as head of his own CPA firm—would not tolerate this arrangement. So when Ernst & Ernst suggested a merger, with Whiting entering the firm as a manager, he quickly defused this suggestion. Ernst & Ernst remained interested and offered to make Whiting a partner. Another barrier arose, however, when the Big Eight firm, eager to hire Whiting's five male employees, was reluctant to hire his two female accountants. Whiting insisted that *all* of his employees be welcome. The firms merged in 1971, and Whiting became the first African American partner in the Big Eight.[45]

"REVERSE DISCRIMINATION"

The numbers of African Americans in the Big Eight continued to grow in the 1970s. But before long the momentum changed. In the 1978 case *Bakke v. Regents of the University of California*, the U.S. Supreme Court decided that certain aspects of affirmative action could be construed as discrimination against white males. A new term, "reverse discrimination," entered the lexicon. After decades of complete exclusion and a mere ten years from the time that major accounting firms began employing African American CPAs, the pendulum reversed direction.

Many commentators worried publicly that the *Bakke* decision would halt the limited progress that had been made toward integration.[46] An article in *Black Enterprise* expressed concern about the "New Racism." Attributing the reversals in part to "national fatigue with civil rights and black nationalism," *Black Enterprise* editors also noted that growing opportunities for middle-class African Americans contributed to "the breakdown of a unified black political movement in this country." The late 1970s mood was pessimistic; the article cites several prominent examples of articles and books on "reverse discrimination."[47]

The complex response to the changes in the profession and the attitudes prevailing at the turn of the decade can be observed in a 1981 book, *The Big Eight*, which introduced the mammoth CPA firms to a wider audience. A small section describes the composition of the firms, and the description underscores the changes that occurred as well as the resentment they could engender:

> There is no such thing as a "typical" Big Eight partner. The group is a mixed bag of personality types, religions, ages, skills, educational backgrounds and regional identities. The impact of affirmative action has seen to that, putting an end to the genteel WASP club that once was the Big Eight.

"They really were the good old days back when I was an active partner," says a retired Big Eight auditor who still dresses in white shirt and tie every day to go shopping or putter around the house. "It was a gentleman's business, that's what I liked about it. Now it's like the UN there. I wouldn't be with the firm today, not under these conditions. You don't have anything in common with your partners.

"I drop in to see the fellas every once in a while—a few of my contemporaries are still around—and it's a shock every time that I do. I just can't get used to it. I mean, in my day lunchtime was a relaxed affair. A good meal and good conversations with men of your own ilk. Now if you want to tell a joke, you have to look around the table first. One of your partners may be Negro, Spanish, a Jew, or a woman. You know how sensitive they are."

Still the majority of Big Eight partners are white Anglo-Saxon Protestants, mostly from the Midwest. Although affirmative action has brought some mix to the ranks, it is still worlds away from the U.N.[48]

REAGAN ERA

While progress was slowed by the *Bakke* decision in the late 1970s, President Jimmy Carter's Department of Justice continued to push for integration, and Carter appointed African Americans to an unprecedented number of prominent federal posts. The most dramatic reversals were ushered in with President Ronald Reagan's election in 1980.

While Reagan's Departments of Justice and Labor continued to pursue some of the equal employment lawsuits that had been filed in the 1970s, the lawsuits they initiated were more likely to involve white employees who believed that affirmative action programs had denied them opportunities. Civil rights and integration were yesterday's objectives; Reagan spoke of a "level playing field" and a "color-blind society," sending the message that the efforts made in the late 1960s and 1970s were no longer necessary or desirable.

The effects of Reagan's policies were widespread. In contrast to the reports on progress that had appeared in the 1970s, in the 1980s articles on African American opportunity emphasized decline. As federal financial aid shrank, there were across-the-board declines in the number of African American students in college and graduate school, including business schools. Many African Americans who had been hired as equal employment opportunity

African American Professionals in Majority-Owned CPA Firms, 1977–1989

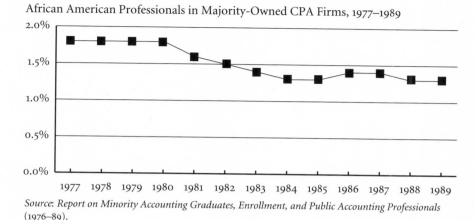

Source: Report on Minority Accounting Graduates, Enrollment, and Public Accounting Professionals (1976–89).

officers in the 1970s saw their jobs eliminated during the "downsizing" of the 1980s.[49]

Reagan's influence permeated the Supreme Court, to which he appointed four justices. As the 1980s wore on, these justices began reversing some of the progressive legislation of the 1960s and 1970s. In 1989 the Court dealt a fatal blow to many African American CPA firms by denying state and local governments the right to give minority-owned businesses a specific share of public-works contracts. This dramatically reduced the interest of major public accounting firms in embarking upon joint ventures with African American–owned firms.[50]

Other Reagan initiatives compounded the problems for African Americans in the profession. Throughout his presidency, Reagan continually attacked the Small Business Administration (SBA). Although he was never able to achieve his goal of eliminating the SBA, he significantly reduced its influence.[51] Many African American businesses that had started in the 1970s—including both CPA firms and clients of African American CPA firms—would not have been able to survive without the loans and favorable consideration in federal contracts that the SBA provided. The administration also sharply cut federal social programs, eliminating many of the clients African American CPA firms had developed in the 1960s and 1970s.[52]

In 1981, the Reagan administration ceased funding the National Association of Minority CPA Firms (NAMCPAF), which had been founded in 1971 under President Nixon's Commerce Department.[53] NAMCPAF had provided a vital service in connecting small African American CPA firms with oppor-

Minority Representation in Major Public Accounting Firms, 1977–1989

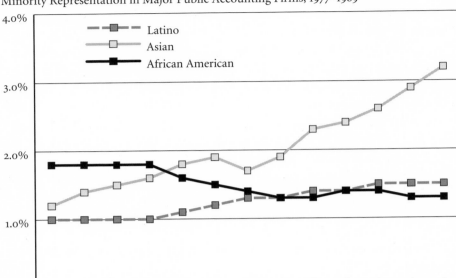

Source: *Report on Minority Accounting Graduates, Enrollment, and Public Accounting Professionals* (1976–89).

tunities for federal contracts. The end of NAMCPAF, the deterioration of the SBA, cutbacks in federal social programs, and the elimination of incentives for the Big Eight to engage in joint ventures on audits of local governments all resulted in a decline in both the number and size of African American–owned CPA firms.[54]

In 1980, the year Reagan was elected, there were only 1,000 African American CPAs—less than one-half of 1 percent—and fewer than 20 out of 7,000 partners in the Big Eight firms—less than one-third of 1 percent—were African American.[55] The profession had barely begun to diversify when the damage done by the Reagan administration took effect.

The 1980s witnessed decline in the representation of African Americans among professionals employed by large public accounting firms. Every measure of African American progress in public accounting firms declined in the 1980s: percentage of African Americans hired, percentage of African Americans remaining with the firms, percentage of African Americans promoted, and percentage of HBCU graduates hired.[56]

While the percentage of African Americans was declining, the percentages of white women, Latinos, and Asian Americans in the firms were growing. Many observers believed that the increases in these groups lessened pressure to increase African American recruitment. As more "minorities" entered the field, many firms publicly discussed only their total "minority" statistics; this obscured the decline in African American staff. Studies repeatedly indicated that while women, Asian Americans, Latinos, and African Americans were all underrepresented compared with their respective representation in the population of the United States, African Americans were most underrepresented in both hiring and retention. The number of total professional employees in the AICPA's annual survey doubled between 1976 and 1989. During this period, the number of Latino professionals in major CPA firms tripled and the number of Asian Americans and women increased by a factor of six. The number of African Americans rose by only 43 percent.[57]

Turnover was more extreme among African Americans. During the period for which the AICPA kept records, for every one hundred African Americans the large white-owned firms hired, eighty-eight left. Corresponding numbers for Latinos, women, and Asian Americans are seventy-two, sixty-three, and sixty, respectively.[58]

Interviews in 1989 with African American partners at six of the largest firms in New York revealed a consensus that the progress of the 1970s came to an end in the 1980s. As one put it, "Once the Reagan administration started, all pressure was off. . . . No clients care about whether we hire blacks." Another said, "Most of my . . . partners . . . are nonminorities. They have no particular interest in minority recruitment, I assure you." This diminished interest was reflected in the accounting media—the flurry of articles on African American successes in the profession and affirmative action efforts by both the AICPA and the firms that had characterized the 1970s slowed markedly in the 1980s.[59]

AFRICAN AMERICAN SELF-HELP

The one group whose attention did *not* wane was African American CPAs themselves. The 1980s was a discouraging decade for those whose hopes had been ignited by the recently expanded opportunities of the 1970s. While the AICPA continued to provide annual scholarships, the push to integrate weakened. Many African Americans were disappointed when, in 1984, the AICPA

A NABA presentation circa 1975 at California State University at Long Beach, where Talmadge Tillman was on the faculty. *From left to right*: Brainard Simpson, Melba Williams Simpson, Talmadge Tillman, Andrew Smith, and Fred Moultrie. Photo courtesy of Talmadge Tillman.

identified the fourteen major issues facing the profession, and none concerned the need to increase minority participation in the profession.[60] Leadership in the area would have to come from elsewhere.

It came from the National Association of Black Accountants. NABA's rapid expansion led to the establishment of many programs consistent with its motto, "Lifting as we climb." Local NABA chapters held annual scholarship banquets, formed student chapters, and held awards dinners honoring outstanding African American accountants, including many of the earliest African American CPAs.[61]

In the mid-1970s, NABA discovered that the major public accounting firms were reducing their recruiting efforts at the HBCUs. In order to ensure that students' opportunities did not decline, NABA developed regional student conferences that served as recruiting fairs and provided professional development sessions. By the end of the decade, 1,200 students and all the Big Eight firms—as well as dozens of corporate recruiters—were attending the four regional conferences. NABA also reached out to high school students by providing career awareness programs at campuses across the country.[62]

NABA's annual convention, begun in 1972, offers technical sessions, networking opportunities, and professional development. In 1989, over 1,000 NABA members attended the event. NABA also provided matching services for job seekers and potential employers, and $100,000 in scholarships annually. At the end of the decade, it had nearly 3,000 members, 42 professional chapters, and 80 student chapters.[63]

During the 1980s, many African American CPAs rose to prominence. Bert Mitchell became the chairman of the New York State Board of Accountancy in 1983 and the president of the New York State Society of CPAs in 1987. Thomas McRae became the first African American vice president of the AICPA. In Los Angeles, African American CPA Fred Moultrie made news for his work for celebrities such as Michael Jackson and Prince.[64]

Despite these unprecedented achievements, African American representation in the profession was declining. By the end of the decade, during which mergers had reduced the Big Eight to the "Big Six," these firms had 9,000 partners, fewer than 50 of whom were African American. African Americans constituted nearly 13 percent of the population, but less than 1 percent of CPAs. A comparative study of African Americans in the professions concluded that only airline pilots had a lower representation.[65]

8

Entering a New Century

In the absence of outside pressure, the CPA profession has demonstrated little interest in increasing opportunities for African Americans.[1] Prior to the Civil Rights Act of 1964, African Americans were virtually excluded from the profession: white CPA firms openly refused to hire African Americans, and those few who became CPAs did so through extraordinary perseverance and with the support of a small network of African American CPAs. In the late 1960s, when the civil rights movement had resulted in social, political, and legal changes, the CPA profession finally acknowledged that it needed to make some efforts to compensate for its past discriminatory behavior. These efforts were short-lived, however. Throughout the 1980s, when most pressure to integrate had evaporated, the profession's gains in recruitment and retention of African Americans deteriorated.

Though the social and political climate regarding African American employment changed radically between 1968 and 1981, a complete reversion to the pre–civil rights era was impossible. Many of the changes that had been made, such as improvements in the accounting programs at historically black colleges and the relative increase in the number of African American CPAs, were institutionalized and irreversible. In addition, now that white society at large—and the CPA profession in particular—had acknowledged that the outright discrimination of the past was unacceptable, complete exclusion could no longer be tolerated.

For the most part, African American participation in the CPA profession in the 1990s remained at the level of the late 1980s. After several years of decline in African American representation, the American Institute of Certified Public Accountants (AICPA) suspended its annual report on minority participation in the profession, which it had produced from 1976 to 1989. Four reports were compiled in the 1990s, and they revealed stagnant numbers: in white-owned CPA firms African Americans constituted approximately 1 percent of the professional staff, four in every one thousand CPAs, and less than one in one thousand partners.[2] In 1990, the only major profession with a lower representation of African Americans had been airline pilots. By the turn of the century, after several major airlines stepped up minority recruitment to settle federal lawsuits, CPAs had fallen to the lowest level of African American representation in the professional workforce.[3]

Historically, CPA firms attributed the lack of opportunity for African American CPAs to the unwillingness of their *clients* to tolerate a black auditor reviewing their books. In the landmark 1968 survey of African Americans in the profession, three-quarters of the respondents felt that race discrimination by clients was a major barrier to their advancement, and three-quarters believed that race discrimination by firm members was also a major barrier. In 1990, a study led by the same author found that while a *third* of his black respondents perceived client bias as a major reason for limited professional growth,[4] *half* attributed lack of opportunity to bias on the part of their CPA-firm employers.[5] Apparently the negative reaction of clients, while still a problem, was diminishing faster than bias within the firms themselves.

Late in the century, there remained regional differences in opportunities for African American CPAs. No state CPA societies excluded African Americans from membership, as had been the case in Texas, Louisiana, and other southern states through the 1960s. Prospective CPAs no longer had to move north for educational and employment opportunities or take the CPA examination in the back of the testing facility. But some locales have proved more hospitable to African American CPAs than others, and they parallel the states where the trailblazers got their starts. Maryland, Georgia, California, and Washington, D.C., are among the places that have the highest numbers of African American CPAs, black-owned CPA firms, and African American professionals working in large white-owned CPA firms.[6]

THE 150-HOUR REQUIREMENT

State boards of accountancy set their own standards for CPAs within their jurisdictions. Though its suggestions are not binding, national leadership comes from the AICPA, and in 1987, its membership voted overwhelmingly to recommend that the states adopt a 150-hour educational requirement. By this time, most states required the equivalent of an undergraduate degree in accounting in order to take the CPA examination. The change would require examinees to have earned 150 credit hours, or the equivalent of a master's degree. Because approximately 20 percent of applicants were passing the CPA examination on their first attempt, the AICPA believed that the adoption of stiffer educational requirements would attract a higher caliber of student and raise the status of the profession.[7]

As various states considered whether to adopt this recommendation, professional accounting publications ran numerous articles debating the issue. One major focus of the debate was whether the new requirement would have a negative impact on diversity in the profession. In contrast to previous policy debates, African Americans were influential in this discussion.

Accepting the 150-hour requirement as a fait accompli, perhaps prematurely, the National Association of Black Accountants (NABA) issued position papers urging state organizations to provide funding to mitigate the negative impact on economically disadvantaged African Americans as well as on historically black colleges and universities (HBCUs). The HBCUs themselves protested that the new rule would result in another obstacle for their typically economically disadvantaged students. The HBCUs had developed full undergraduate curricula in accounting relatively recently; the development of graduate programs would be prohibitively expensive for most.

The issue gained some national prominence when Jesse Jackson was enlisted in the cause. He wrote a letter to the AICPA stating that the proposed change would "greatly impede . . . African American[s' ability] to successfully pursue careers in the field of accounting." Other African American leaders were also influential: as the Massachusetts legislature considered the new requirement, its black caucus was instrumental in postponing the adoption of the legislation in that state, saying, "This legislation will . . . discourage public accountancy as a career path for African American and other minority students." The issue of the disproportionate impact on African Americans was also successfully used in stalling adoption of the legislation in California and New York. The AICPA expected all states to have adopted the 150-hour requirement by the turn of the millennium, but only 41 states and jurisdictions had done so.[8]

In the midst of the commotion, the AICPA's *Journal of Accountancy*, the most widely read accounting journal, published an article arguing that the impact on African Americans would not be substantial. It noted that black CPAs were already much more likely to have master's degrees than were their white counterparts. Similarly, it pointed out that because African Americans were more prevalent among doctors and attorneys than among CPAs, the stiffer educational requirement might *increase* the number of African Americans interested in entering the profession.[9]

On the surface, this argument is somewhat persuasive. As was true in early decades, in the 1990s, on average, African American CPAs were better educated than their white peers.[10] This is not necessarily a good argument supporting the adoption of tougher educational requirements; it may just be another indication that African Americans need to work harder to achieve the same goals as whites.

The most provocative argument in the *Journal of Accountancy* article, however, was that educational requirements were of little import when it came to African American participation in the profession. "Minority access is limited *with* or *without* [the 150-hour requirement]. African American participation has remained relatively constant [since the changes in the 1970s]. . . . Although a great deal of energy and money have been devoted to scholarships, with the exception of a small number of firms the profession has not attempted to recruit and retain those in whom they have invested. Minority access has been, and continues to be, limited."[11]

The author responded to calls that the profession provide scholarships to compensate for the 150-hour requirement by saying that, given the lack of hiring and retention, this might be a "nonproductive investment."[12]

The 150-hour requirement debate, coupled with the realization that the representation of African Americans was declining, did draw some attention back to the topic after the 1980s hiatus. It was far from the pressing issue it had been in the late 1960s. But many of those who had earlier believed that a laissez-faire approach was sufficient could not deny the fact that, in the absence of proactive efforts to increase African American participation in the profession, the representation of African Americans in the firms was minuscule and declining. In 1969, when attention was first brought to the issue of African American CPAs, the editorial board of the *Journal of Accountancy* admitted to the drastic shortage but attributed it to "oversight and indifference" rather than to any negative action by the profession's members. In the 1990s, the profession recognized that its record on African American hiring and retention was unimpressive. The *CPA Journal* entitled a 1994 article, "The Profession Continues to Lag in Minority Hiring." Also in 1994, a member of the AICPA's Women and Family Issues Executive Committee testified before the U.S. Department of Labor that "minority leadership representation in the profession remains woefully inadequate." Around the same time, a KPMG spokeswoman referred to "an alarming scarcity of African Americans in the profession."[13]

While not denying that a representation of African Americans below 1 percent at the professional level and below 0.1 percent at the partner level is "woefully inadequate," the profession at large does not consider this paucity a central issue. Many of those involved in efforts to diversify the profession were disappointed when the AICPA engaged in a long strategic-planning process in 1992 and came up with seven "critical thrusts," none of which concerned minority recruitment.[14]

When, in 1969, the AICPA began its initiatives to promote African American participation in the profession, one of the harshest opponents, Harry Ward of Texas, predicted, "These things are never going to be achieved."[15]

Given a decade of stagnation in representation of African Americans in CPA firms—stagnation that followed a decade of decline—Ward's prediction may have been right.

"DIVERSITY IS GOOD FOR BUSINESS"

Despite the stagnant statistics, there were some signs of progress in the 1990s. But the initiatives led by white members of the profession were couched in a different term than the "equal opportunity" to which the firms purportedly aspired in the 1960s. In the 1990s, the slogan "diversity is good for business" emphasized the fact that CPA firms could increase profitability by hiring a diverse workforce, especially because business ownership was becoming increasingly diverse.[16] All of the Big Five firms—KPMG, Arthur Andersen, PricewaterhouseCoopers, Ernst & Young, and Deloitte & Touche—devote portions of their Web pages to the importance of diversity, especially in meeting the needs of a diverse clientele.[17] As Jon C. Madonna, the chairman of KPMG, put it, "Providing opportunities for African Americans is the right thing to do; however, there is also a very clear additional business imperative. Over the last several decades industry has made measurable progress to integrate blacks. A client service team which lacks diversity is simply out of step with the makeup of many client workforces. Clients are demanding integration."[18]

In light of the stories of pioneering African American CPAs, the fact that the chairman of a Big Five firm would explain his firms' initiatives regarding enhancing African American participation in the profession by pointing out that *clients* demand integration is ironic, to say the least. The very profession that earlier blamed clients for their own lack of willingness to hire African Americans again ducked leadership and emphasized, instead, their responsiveness to client demands.

"Diversity is good for business" also often obscured the unique issues African Americans faced, as firms gained cover by using a broad definition of diversity. None of the Big Five Web sites include the proportion of African Americans at various levels in the firms, though some provide information on women or for minorities as a whole. When Deloitte & Touche was charged with race discrimination in a 1995 suit, the firm responded that it had an excellent diversity record, pointing to its award for innovative "family-friendly" work policies designed to make the firm more attractive to women. In a statement it released after being threatened with a class-action race discrimination suit, Deloitte & Touche said, "There is no pattern of discrimination at Deloitte & Touche. D&T has a strong record on equal employment opportunity. Its initiatives regarding diversity and the advancement of women have received recognition from several outside organizations as being among the best in American business."[19]

The 1990s included some new initiatives designed at least in part to enhance African American participation in the profession. Several of the Big Five, including Deloitte & Touche, appointed national directors of diversity in the mid-1990s.[20] In 1993, Ernst & Young was chosen as one of the best companies for minorities.[21] The AICPA continued granting scholarships and developing support programs for students. In 1999, the AICPA started an advertising campaign in *Vibe* magazine and *New Accountant* saying "Be a star in business. . . . Be a CPA" with photos of famous athletes, including Barry Sanders and Lisa Leslie, with their African American CPAs.[22]

THE PHD PROJECT

The 1990s' most serious attack on the shortage of African American CPAs came not from the AICPA nor from incremental changes at individual firms, but from an innovative new program that took a long-term, more comprehensive approach. In 1994, the KPMG Foundation launched the PhD Project, a multimillion dollar effort to increase the number of African American Ph.D.'s in accounting. The program was later expanded to include Latinos and Native Americans and to involve other business fields outside of accounting.

Building on research indicating that African American role models in front of the classroom were one of the major determinants of African American students' choice of major, the PhD Project sought to redress the paucity of African American accounting faculty.[23]

Under the leadership of its foundation president, Bernard J. Milano, KPMG founded the PhD Project in 1994. Citigroup Foundation, the Graduate Management Admission Council, the AICPA, and other organizations are major partners in the $10 million project, but the KPMG Foundation supplies almost half of the funding. In 1994, when the initiative began, there were forty-two African American doctoral students in accounting; in 2001, there were fifty-nine. In 1999, eleven African Americans, all of whom had received support from KPMG, earned doctorates in accounting; for the previous sixteen years the average number of recipients was four.[24] This increase is all the more impressive because it occurred in a period during which the total number of doctoral students in accounting declined.[25]

The PhD Project takes a multipronged, long-term approach to addressing the shortage of African Americans, Latinos, and Native Americans among CPAs. By expanding the number of African American faculty in accounting, it is providing more role models in a field that sorely needs them. The PhD Project seeks to "diversify the front of the classroom" and thereby increase the number of African Americans majoring in accounting, just as Professor Jesse Blayton inspired CPAs of the 1940s, 1950s, and 1960s to pursue their dreams.

In the early 1990s, in over 600 four-year accounting programs in the country, there were only 75 African American professors with Ph.D.'s in accounting, half of whom were clustered at a few HBCUs. It is therefore not surprising that 40 percent of the African American doctoral students in accounting had never met an African American with a Ph.D. in accounting.[26] The PhD Project's annual meetings for all African American doctoral students in accounting provide the opportunity for the students to share ideas and strategies as well as to meet African American faculty from other institutions. At the first meeting, pioneering African American accounting professors and CPAs Milton Wilson and Larzette Hale spoke about their experiences earning doctorates in the 1950s.

In addition to the PhD Project, the KPMG Foundation sponsors efforts for HBCUs to earn American Assembly of Collegiate Schools of Business (AACSB) accreditation. As noted, AACSB accreditation adds legitimacy to business schools and improves their ability to attract students and employers

The first meeting of the African American Accounting Doctoral Student Association, Montvale, New Jersey, August 1994. Larzette Hale and Milton Wilson are seated in the middle of the front row. Courtesy of KPMG Foundation.

for their graduates. When the KPMG program started in 1994, five HBCUs had AACSB accreditation; since then, six more schools that KPMG funded have received accreditation, and twelve more are being supported toward the goal of earning accreditation.[27] Because of its support for the PhD Project and HBCUs, *Black Issues in Higher Education* ranked the KPMG Foundation among the top fifteen U.S. foundations supporting African American education.[28]

EXTERNAL PRESSURE

Externally, there are three potential fronts upon which the profession could be influenced to increase its representation of African Americans: government intervention, client pressure, and pressure from job applicants.

Government intervention has taken several forms. The federal government (and some states) influenced change in the profession from its beginnings. The federal government, particularly after World War II, was more willing to hire African Americans as accountants than was any other sector of the economy. Many of the earliest African American CPAs held government accounting jobs while maintaining their CPA practices. These professional positions, particularly in the 1950s in the District of Columbia, provided African American accountants an opportunity to meet and strategize together on how, against daunting odds, to earn a CPA.

The federal government made an even bigger difference in the 1960s with the passage of equal employment legislation that ended the legitimacy of relentless discrimination within the professions. It was in the immediate aftermath of this legislation that the largest gains were made in African American employment in the firms.

After decades of de jure discrimination, the equal opportunity legislation of the 1960s was not sufficient, especially once it was weakened beginning with the 1978 *Bakke* decision, which placed limits on affirmative action. Federal intervention is all the more appropriate in the CPA profession because, since the 1930s, the federal government has granted CPAs monopoly power over the right to audit publicly traded companies. The Securities and Exchange Commission, overseen by Congress, continues to grant CPAs that right. Just as Congress applied some pressure on the firms during the Metcalf Hearings of the late 1970s, it remains within its purview to do so again today. However, with the current climate of resentment toward affirmative action, it is unlikely that new and substantive federal legislation will result in the kind of renewed pressure needed to reignite major change.[29]

In every decade in this study, CPA firms have attributed their motivations and decisions to meeting the needs and demands of their clients. Historically, that meant *refusing* to hire African Americans. Today, many firms say their clients are insisting that they hire a more diverse staff in order to meet clients' needs. This underscores two points: corporate America has done a better job of diversifying than has the CPA profession, and CPA firms are still reacting rather than leading when it comes to African American recruitment. While the motivation may not be ideal, this reaction can have very positive effects. When KPMG representatives discuss the PhD Project, the justification for their impressive program typically starts with the importance of diversity to KPMG clients.

But while "diversity is good for business" has led to some important changes in firms' activities, the diffuse term "diversity" also provides cover for the firms' poor records regarding African Americans. In the past twenty years, the proportions of white women, Asian Americans, and, to a lesser degree,

Latinos, have grown, while the proportion of African Americans declined and then stagnated. The firms often point to their success in "diversity" while obscuring the persistent dearth of African Americans in the firms.

The diversity issue also applies in considering why the public accounting firms do not feel pressure from educational institutions to diversify. As the percentage of accounting graduates has hovered around 50 percent female for the past decade, the firms have responded to the need to modify work loads and create "family-friendly" environments as a tool to recruit and retain female employees. Several firms have adopted flexible work arrangements and the AICPA's Women and Family Issues Executive Committee is a higher-ranking committee than the significantly older Minority Initiatives Committee.

In the legal profession, there are many law firms and relatively few top schools from which to recruit. The students in these desirable schools put pressure on the firms to report their success in hiring and promoting African Americans and other groups. Each year the information on associates and partners is printed in a recruiting guide, and the few firms that refuse to provide numbers risk alienating those they would like to employ. In accounting, the employment situation is reversed. The Big Five firms have over 150,000 professional employees in the United States alone, and they recruit from hundreds of schools. The schools are competing to get the highest percentage of their students placed with the Big Five, rather than the other way around. It is impossible to get firm-specific data on employment level by race from the Big Five firms, and there is no meaningful pressure for them to provide this information.

In the next century, it is unlikely that government, client, or prospective employee pressure will make a substantial difference in African American participation in the profession. Studies indicate that the majority of white members of CPA firms have little interest in recruiting a diverse professional staff, but those few whites who take an interest in the issue can make an enormous difference in the experiences of African American CPAs.[30] In the 1930s through the 1950s, a few Jewish CPAs in New York, Detroit, and Los Angeles made it possible for Wilmer Lucas, Richard Austin, and William Collins, among others, to meet their experience requirement and join the profession.[31] In the same period, white accounting professors who cared about equality supported, advocated for, and were critical to the success of their black students. In the late 1960s, the all-white AICPA council debated and adopted a resolution to end discrimination in the profession. More recently, the success of the PhD Project is attributed primarily to the leadership of KPMG Foundation president Bernie Milano.

Since whites are the overwhelming majority in the profession, especially in powerful positions, their leadership is critical. But during the 1980s and 1990s, it was leadership by African Americans, through NABA or through those who had achieved leading roles in industry or public accounting, that continued to be the most important contributor to expansion of opportunities.[32] In a NABA publication, Betty Maple, national director of diversity at Deloitte & Touche, underscored the importance of African American CPAs taking on the responsibility for hiring more African Americans. Expressing an opinion shared by many black leaders in the profession, she said, "If [we] do not do it for [ourselves], no one else is going to do it for [us.]"[33]

In a 1999 children's book on occupations, there is a picture of an African American boy wearing a tie and holding a calculator—he wants to be an accountant.[34] The trail to that goal has been blazed by hundreds of African American CPAs. But bumps remain, and the opportunities that readers of the children's book will face when they grow up will depend upon changes instituted now. It has been thirty years since the profession declared its commitment to integration—a decade of progress, a decade of decline, and a decade of stagnation. The past twenty of those thirty years have been squandered. In order to make a difference for the coming generation, we must make the most of the next twenty.

Appendix

The First 100 African American CPAs

1.	John W. Cromwell Jr.	1921	New Hampshire
2.	Arthur J. Wilson	1923	Illinois
3.	Chauncey L. Christian	1926	Kentucky
4.	Jesse B. Blayton Sr.	1928	Georgia
5.	Wilmer F. Lucas	1929	New York
6.	Paul G. Stewart	1937	Illinois
7.	Louis Rawlings	1937	Illinois
8.	Alfred W. Tucker	1938	New York
9.	*Theodore A. Jones*	1940	Illinois
10.	*Charles A. Beckett*	1941	Illinois
11.	*Richard H. Austin*	1941	Michigan
12.	William L. Campfield	1941	North Carolina
13.	Mary T. Washington	1943	Illinois
14.	G. Steven Marchman III	1944	Illinois
15.	*Lincoln J. Harrison*	1946	Louisiana
16.	George L. Unthank	1948	New York
17.	Jesse H. Turner Sr.	1948	Tennessee
18.	Parnell Drayton	1949	New York
19.	*Hiram L. Pittman*	1949	Illinois
20.	Elvera Taylor	1949	Illinois
21.	Milton S. Monjoy	1949	Michigan
22.	Cary B. Lewis Jr.	1950	Kentucky
23.	Walter P. H. Harris	1950	Pennsylvania
24.	George Washington	1950	Michigan
25.	*Elmer J. Whiting Jr.*	1950	Ohio
26.	*Isaac Y. Little*	1950	Illinois
27.	*Milton Wilson*	1951	Indiana
28.	*Larzette G. Hale*	1951	Georgia
29.	*Frederick C. Ford*	1952	Illinois
30.	*Benjamin H. Crockett*	1953	Illinois
31.	*William S. Anderson*	1953	Illinois
32.	Charles T. Cartwright Jr.	1954	Illinois

33.	Hubert W. Mullings	1954	New York
34.	*Bernadine Coles Gines*	1954	New York
35.	Wilbur Parker	1954	New Jersey
36.	Oliver Walcott	1954	New York
37.	*Calvin L. Cooke*	1955	Texas
38.	Evelyn McLendon Beasley	1955	Indiana
39.	Bruce L. Murray	1955	New York
40.	Andrew M. Bradley	1955	Pennsylvania
41.	Mizura C. Allen	1955	Oklahoma
42.	*Ernest H. Davenport*	1956	Michigan
43.	Lewis W. Vaughn Jr.	1956	Pennsylvania
44.	George D. Faulkner	1957	New York
45.	Thomas J. Whiting	1957	Ohio
46.	Curtis C. Duke	1957	Virginia
47.	Melvin J. Bergeron	1957	Louisiana
48.	*Benjamin L. King Sr.*	1957	Maryland
49.	Cecil Bogan	1957	Illinois
50.	*Arthur M. Reynolds Sr.*	1958	Maryland
51.	Emanuel Whiting	1958	Pennsylvania
52.	Clarence R. Newby	1958	California
53.	Arthur Macklin	1958	Illinois
54.	Donald Eugene Farrar	1959	Connecticut
55.	Joseph Watson	1959	New Jersey
56.	*William D. Collins*	1959	California
57.	Julius M. Cayson Jr.	1959	New York
58.	*Theodora F. Rutherford*	1960	West Virginia
59.	Emsar Bradford	1960	Maryland
60.	Broadus Sawyer	1960	Maryland
61.	*Lester H. McKeever Jr.*	1960	Illinois
62.	William P. Reiland	1960	Illinois
63.	Joseph J. Cramer Jr.	1961	Texas
64.	Donald C. Haley	1961	Ohio
65.	Sanford M. Perkins	1961	Virginia
66.	James W. Price	1961	California
67.	*Carroll D. Lee*	1961	Maryland
68.	William Porter	1961	District of Columbia
69.	Edward V. Hipps Jr.	1961	Illinois
70.	Thomas W. McCrae	1961	California
71.	Herman Johnson	1962	New York
72.	Otha L. Brandon	1962	Tennessee
73.	Emerson E. Blue	1962	Illinois

74. *Edmond N. Fambro*	1962	Illinois
75. Gregory H. Moses Jr.	1962	New York
76. *David A. Kelly*	1962	Illinois
77. Ted A. St. Leger Jr.	1962	Illinois
78. Calvin P. McCord	1962	California
79. William L. Jones	1962	California
80. *Jerome R. Broadus*	1963	Maryland
81. Bert W. Smith Jr.	1963	District of Columbia
82. Joyce Turney	1963	Ohio
83. *Ruth Coles Harris*	1963	Virginia
84. James Tatum Jr.	1963	New York
85. William Hughes	1963	Illinois
86. *Edward A. Williams*	1963	Illinois
87. *Robert E. Hill*	1963	California
88. Wayman F. Smith Jr.	1964	Missouri
89. Robert W. Coles Jr.	1964	Ohio
90. Donald T. Morgan	1964	California
91. *Henry T. Wilfong Jr.*	1964	California
92. *Johnnie L. Clark*	1964	Georgia
93. Charles Seymour	1964	New Jersey
94. *Nathan T. Garrett*	1964	North Carolina
95. Delmar Barnes	1964	Ohio
96. *John E. Wilson*	1965	Illinois
97. *Audley E. Coulthurst*	1965	New York
98. Alvin J. Freeman Jr.	1965	Illinois
99. Wilson C. Stockey	1965	Illinois
100. *Bert N. Mitchell*	1965	New York

Note: Names in italics indicate CPAs interviewed for this book.
Source: Adapted from *The History of Black Accountancy: The First 100 Black CPAs* (Washington, D.C.: National Association of Black Accountants, 1990).

Notes

ABBREVIATIONS

AICPA Library	American Institute of Certified Public Accountants Library, Jersey City, N.J.
BE	*Black Enterprise*
Blayton File	Atlanta University, Atlanta, Ga., Clipping File: Jesse B. Blayton
JoA	*Journal of Accountancy*
King Papers	Boston University, Boston, Mass., Martin Luther King Jr. Papers
NABA	National Association of Black Accountants
NYT	*New York Times*
Schomburg Center Clipping File	Schomburg Center for Research in Black Culture, New York Public Library, New York, N.Y.
WSJ	*Wall Street Journal*

CHAPTER ONE

1. Miranti, *Accountancy Comes of Age*; Abbott, *System of Professions*; Krause, *Death of the Guilds*; Larson, *Rise of Professionalism*.
2. In the late 1990s, about 0.1 percent of partners in the major firms were African American; in the 250 largest law firms in the United States, 1.2 percent of partners were African American; *Miles to Go*.
3. Miranti, *Accountancy Comes of Age*.
4. Occasionally the pay was meager or even nonexistent, but it still differed from the British system where the apprentice had to pay for the right to gain experience.
5. Prior to and in the 1960s, these firms were known as the "Big Eight." Mergers in the 1980s and 1990s have left only the "Big Five."

CHAPTER TWO

1. Edwards, *History of Public Accounting*, 344; Christian interview, 31 May 2001. Typically the CPA examination comprises four or five sections, and most states allow examinees to retake only the parts failed on previous attempts, as long as a minimum score was obtained on the earlier attempt. In Christian's case, he took the four-part examination in May 1926, failing only one part. In November, he successfully completed the fourth part.
2. "CPA examination," *JoA* 24, no. 1 (1917): 12; Edwards, *History of Public Accounting*, 131, 184.

3. *History of Black Accountancy*, 8, 18, 22; Previts and Merino, *History of Accounting in America*, 215.

4. Du Bois, *College-Bred Negro*, 42; Du Bois, *Souls of Black Folk*, 132; U.S. Department of Commerce, *Statistical Abstract*, 55.

5. Aptheker, *Documentary History*, 835.

6. Du Bois, *College-Bred Negro*, 73.

7. Anderson, *Education of Blacks*, 190, 194–95.

8. Ibid., 211–21.

9. Johnson, *Negro College Graduate*, 104.

10. Hine, *Black Women in White*; Organ and Kosiba, *Century of Black Surgeons*; Crawford, *Talladega Manual*; "Editorial Comment: Vocational Guidance"; Johnson, *Negro College Graduate*, 136, 206–7; "Business and Industry," *The Messenger* 9 (January 1927): 50.

11. Rutherford interview.

12. Du Bois, *College-Bred Negro*, 38; Horton, "Black Education at Oberlin College."

13. Rutherford interview; Edwards, *History of Public Accounting*, 111. Professor Thornton's exclusion presumably took place in Maryland and Virginia, since the District of Columbia did not begin licensing CPAs until 1923, becoming the last jurisdiction to grant licenses. Maryland began granting licenses in 1900, and Virginia followed in 1910.

14. *Annual Catalogue 1920*, 133.

15. *History of Black Accountancy*, 8–15; Rutherford interview.

16. *Annual Catalogue 1924*, 338.

17. *The Bison.*

18. "Harvard University and Racial Discrimination," *The Messenger* 4 (August 1922): 59; "Fair Harvard," *The Messenger* 4 (November 1922): 518. At about the same time, Harvard chose to limit the number of African Americans enrolling at the school. Despite their outstanding tradition of including African American students, Oberlin also participated in a "gentleman's agreement" to restrict entry.

19. Mabee, *Black Education in New York State*, 285.

20. L. Berger, "Howard Honors Its Own," *Washington Post*, 2 March 1983, B9; "Graduate Study in Accounting," *JoA* 79, no. 4 (1945): 270. *Columbia University One Hundred and Seventieth Annual Commencement Program*, 4 June 1924, Columbia University Library. Rutherford (then Fonteneau) earned a master of science in business with an emphasis in accounting, since Columbia's master's degree programs in accounting were not formalized until 1936 and 1945. She was the only African American in her class of fourteen. Nevertheless the class was diverse; it included students named Mesrob Housep Atikian, Surendra Desai, and Jui Huang Sun.

21. Rutherford interview.

22. Previts and Merino, *History of Accounting in America*, 215; J. E. Masters, "Qualifications and Responsibilities of Public Accountants," *JoA* 22, no. 6 (1916): 440. *Certified Public Accountants Laws*, 13–27, AICPA Library.

23. "Business & Industry," *The Messenger* 9 (September 1927): 290.

24. Rutherford interview.

25. Simmons, *Men of Mark*, 898–907; "Notes," *Journal of Negro History* (1927): 564–66, Schomburg Center Clipping File: John W. Cromwell Sr.; Meier, *Negro Thought in Amer-*

ica, 44, 50, 56; Gatewood, *Aristocrats of Color*, 56–57, 99, 217–19, 253, 309; Logan, *Howard University*, 8.

26. Du Bois, *College-Bred Negro*, 35–38; Greene, *Holders of Doctorates*, 168.

27. Du Bois, *College-Bred Negro*, 38.

28. Gibson, *Dunbar Story*.

29. Poor treatment of aspiring black professionals was not unusual in the nation's capital. The law library at the federal courthouse excluded blacks until forced to open up in 1951 due to a lawsuit. African Americans were not allowed to take bar review courses in Washington until 1957. See Littlejohn and Hobson, "Black Lawyers," 1635.

30. *Certified Public Accountants Laws*, 13–27, AICPA Library; Edwards, *History of Public Accounting*, 336–63.

31. "Annual Report of the Secretary of Finance of the African Methodist Episcopal Church," J. W. Cromwell, CPA, auditor, 3 April 1946; Letter from John Cromwell, controller, to Emmett Scott, secretary/treasurer, Howard University, 17 November 1931 (copies provided by Adelaide M. Cromwell).

32. *History of Black Accountancy*, 8–15.

33. "Editorial: What the Profession Offers," *JoA* 27, no. 6 (1919): 437.

34. "Editorial: Exemption for Accountants," *JoA* 26, no. 3 (1918): 212–15.

35. "Editorial: Accountants' Services in Wartime," *JoA* 23, no. 5 (1917): 364–68; C. C. Waters, "Public Accountants and Industrial Preparedness," *JoA* 23, no. 6 (1917): 445–49; "Distribution of Personnel," *JoA* 26, no. 2 (1918): 109–10.

36. "Editorial: What Is a Certified Public Accountant?" *JoA* 30, no. 1 (1920): 57.

37. "Editorial: Accountants' Services in Wartime," *JoA* 23, no. 5 (1917): 367; Lena E. Mendelsohn, "A Woman's Mind as Applied to Accountancy," *JoA* 27, no. 2 (1919): 107–10; "Editorial," *JoA* 30, no. 2 (1920): 138; "Editorial: What Is Accountancy?" *JoA* 34, no. 3 (1922): 203; "Editorial: Opportunities for the Young Accountant," *JoA* 35, no. 1 (1923): 34.

38. "Editorial: Women in Accountancy," *JoA* 36, no. 6 (1923): 444.

39. *Accountants' Indexes*.

40. Bernard E. Anderson, former faculty member at Wharton, e-mail to author, 28 February 2000.

41. I. Maximilian Martin, "Accounting as a Field for Colored Men," *JoA* 55, no. 2 (1933): 112–16. Martin was an accountant, but not a CPA, in Philadelphia. He later became president of the Berean Savings Association in Philadelphia. "New York and Philadelphia HUD Regions Join in Fair Housing Conference," *PR Newswire*, 7 June 1988; "I. Maximilian Martin, Accountant and Auditor, 6 North 42nd Street, Philadelphia," advertisement in *The Crisis* 45 (July 1938): 241.

42. *History of Black Accountancy*, 8; *Certified Public Accountants Laws*, 13–27, AICPA Library. There is some discrepancy between Martin's study of CPAs and the National Association of Black Accounts (NABA) study. Martin identified two African American CPAs in Georgia, instead of one, and one in West Virginia where NABA found none. The latter jibes with Theodora Rutherford's understanding that there was a CPA on the West Virginia State faculty, but she reports that when she arrived at the school, she learned that the other teacher was not really a CPA. I cannot account for a second CPA

in Georgia, though I have spoken with many CPAs who worked in Georgia as early as the 1940s, none of whom know of any CPAs besides Jesse B. Blayton.

43. Lucas interview; "Black Accounting Firms," *BE*, February 1972, 30–34.

44. The national president of Beta Alpha Psi, Northwestern University Professor Eric Kohler, wrote the following in a memorandum to the Beta Alpha Psi Council: "The Hebrew membership of the Boston Chapter has become well known in the East and in the Middle West, and I have even heard comments from members of our chapter in Evanston to the effect that they understand we have a Jewish branch of the Fraternity and I have been asked whether this Jewish chapter came under the jurisdiction of our Grand Council. The members of the Chapter are Jews to the last man and the only way I see of remedying this situation is to suspend the chapter for a period of two years" (Sheldahl, *Beta Alpha Psi*, 173). Boston University did not regain its chapter membership until 1983, when the school applied to become a chapter without even knowing there had ever been a Beta Alpha Psi chapter at the university. Then president of Beta Alpha Psi David Tinius of Seattle University reinstated the chapter with its original designation as "Eta" chapter; Tinius interview; letter from Terry K. Sheldahl to Professor Philip Meyer at Boston University, 21 June 1983 (copy provided by Kenneth Schwartz). During World War II, a Jewish CPA firm in Cincinnati sponsored and employed a Japanese-American CPA from California so he would not be forced to live in an internment camp; Laurie Mason, "CPAs and the Changing Demographic," *Outlook* 66 (Winter 1999): 38.

45. "Gen. Lucas Dies at 82," *New York Amsterdam News*, 10 May 1980, 4; Mitchell interview; Adelaide M. Cromwell, letter to author, 2 December 1997; Lucas interview; Military Records and "Biographical Outline—Colonel Wilmer Francis Lucas," n.d. (copies provided by Wilmer F. Lucas Jr.).

46. "John W. Cromwell, Noted Historian, Dead in Capital," Schomburg Center Clipping File: John W. Cromwell Sr.

47. On growth and expansion of the profession at this time, see Edwards, *History of Public Accounting*, 136–40.

48. Asa Gordon, *Sketches of Negro Life*, 148; Du Bois, *Negro in Business*, 124, 160; Washington, *Negro in Business*, 50; Walker, *History of Black Business*.

49. Asa Gordon, *Sketches of Negro Life*, 148–51; Albon L. Holsey, "Negro Business: Its Real Test Is Still Ahead," *The Messenger* 9 (November 1927): 321; Thomas Dabney, "Can Negro Business Survive?" *The Messenger* 10 (April 1928): 75–76, 92, 95.

50. Thomas Dabney, "Can Negro Business Survive?" *The Messenger* 10 (April 1928): 75–76, 92, 95; Abraham Harris, *Negro As Capitalist*, 198; Washington, *Negro in Business*, 111–12.

51. "Louisville Business: From Yesterday to Tomorrow," *Louisville Courier-Journal*, 23 February 1997, K3; "Neighborhoods East End," *Louisville Courier-Journal*, 20 February 1991, N1.

52. C. L. Christian vs. Samuel Plato, claim (ca. 1940), n.d. (copy provided by Chauncey L. Christian Jr.). As noted earlier in the chapter, twelve Kentuckians passed the CPA examination in 1926.

53. *History of Black Accountancy*, 20.

54. "Dean of Negro Accountants," *Color*, July 1951, 5.

55. Ibid.; Seder and Burrell, *Getting It Together*, 124–30; "Blacks in the Accounting Indus-

try," *New York Amsterdam News*, 17 February 1973, D6; "Jesse B. Blayton," *Atlanta Daily World*, 20 September 1977, 6; "Blayton, Pioneer Atlanta Businessman, Dies of Heart Attack Leaving Barber Shop," *Jet*, 29 September 1977, 7; Mason, *Going Against the Wind*, 79; Ellen Sweets, "Out of Africa," *Dallas Morning News*, 29 July 1994, G1.

56. "First Black CPA in U.S. Dies [John Cromwell]," *Jet*, 6 January 1972, 17; "Blayton, Pioneer Atlanta Businessman, Dies of Heart Attack Leaving Barber Shop," *Jet*, 29 September 1977, 7.

57. Seder and Burrell, *Getting It Together*, 125.

58. Ingham and Feldman, *African-American Business Leaders*, 533–47.

59. Seder and Burrell, *Getting It Together*, 128–29; Ingham and Feldman, *African-American Business Leaders*, 80–91; Pierce, *Negro Business*, 275; "Negro Banks Fill Real Economic Need, Declares J. B. Blayton," *Atlanta Daily World*, 22 December 1936, no page number, Blayton File; Barlow, *Voice Over*, 133, 247.

60. Robert C. Vowels, "Atlanta Negro Business and the New Black Bourgeoisie," *Atlanta Historical Bulletin* 21, no. 1 (1977): 56; Ingham and Feldman, *African-American Business Leaders*, 80–91.

61. "Get Blayton as Chief Speaker," *Atlanta Daily World*, 15 December 1936, no page number, Blayton File.

62. "Blayton to Speak for 'Guide Right' This Sunday," *Atlanta Daily World* , 24 April 1936, no page number, Blayton File; "Get Blayton as Chief Speaker," *Atlanta Daily World*, 15 December 1936, no page number, Blayton File.

63. Blayton, *Better Records*.

CHAPTER THREE

1. Duncan and Duncan, *Negro Population of Chicago*, 300; Lemann, *Promised Land*; Grossman, *Land of Hope*; Sinclair, *Available Man*, 84–91, 214–17; Sitkoff, *Depression Decade*, 90–91; Drake and Cayton, *Black Metropolis*, xxxv.

2. Drake and Cayton, *Black Metropolis*, 34–50, 258, 516.

3. Ibid., 81, 111, 254, 342–49; Sullivan, *Days of Hope*, 134, 170; Sitkoff, *Depression Decade*, 31, 98; "Black Rulers of White Folk," *The Crisis* 37 (January 1930): 14.

4. Houston, "The Need for Negro Lawyers," 49–52; Drake and Cayton, *Black Metropolis*, 196, 511; "Along the Color Line," *The Crisis* 39 (January 1932): 466; Dulaney, *Black Police in America*, 23.

5. David Moberg, "Scholar's Life Bears Stamp of Greatness," *Chicago Tribune*, 16 February 1994, C1. Two African Americans worked as researchers in white universities, but none as full-fledged members of the faculty.

6. Drake and Cayton, *Black Metropolis*, xxxvii, 61, 79, 80, 104, 112, 162, 216, 219–21, 257–59, 272, 275, 300–301, 513–14; "Mr. James Crow," *The Crisis* 40 (August 1933): 186; Michael Briggs, "A Freedom Ride to Washington," *Chicago Sun-Times*, 29 August 1993, 20; Robert R. Taylor, "Low Cost Housing in America," *The Crisis* 42 (March 1935): 76, 86; "Relief in Chicago," *The Crisis* 48 (January 1941): 50.

7. "A Look at Chicago's Black Business History; Contributions Date Back to the Early Nineteenth Century," *Chicago Sun-Times*, 9 July 1993, 4; "Along the Color Line: Work, Waste, Wealth," *The Crisis* 40 (November 1933): 257; "Along the Color Line: Homes,"

The Crisis 40 (February 1933): 40; Ingham and Feldman, *African-American Business Leaders*, 201.

8. Ingham and Feldman, *African-American Business Leaders*, 75–80. Drake and Cayton, *Black Metropolis*, 64, 82, 403, 466, 721–22; Reed, *Chicago NAACP*, 58–59; John Wilson interview; advertisement for Binga State Bank, *The Crisis* 37 (April 1930): 141; "Plans, Work, Binga's Secret for Success: Colored Banker Tells of Struggles," *Chicago Daily Tribune*, 8 May 1927, 1.

9. W. E. B. Du Bois believed that the collapse of black banks in Chicago during the depression could have been prevented if white banks had been willing to extend credit. W. E. B. Du Bois, "Postscript," *The Crisis* 37 (December 1930): 425; W. E. B. Du Bois, "Postscript," *The Crisis* 39 (July 1932): 234.

10. John Wilson interview.

11. Travis, *Autobiography of Black Politics*, 120.

12. "Branch News," *The Crisis* 43 (June 1936): 184; Drake and Cayton, *Black Metropolis*, 108; "Along the Color Line," *The Crisis* 37 (September 1930): 311; "Along the NAACP Battlefront," *The Crisis* 44 (May 1937): 150–51.

13. Pittman interview, 9 December 1992; John Wilson interview; McKeever interview; "Nation's First Black Woman CPA Honored," *Jet*, 23 February 1978, 19.

14. Ingham and Feldman, *African-American Business Leaders*, 244–49; Pamela Sherrod, "S. B. Fuller: The Dean of Black Entrepreneurs," *Chicago Tribune*, 9 June 1987, 1; "S. B. Fuller: A Man and His Products," *BE*, August 1975, 47–50; Walker, *History of Black Business*, 296–98. In 1947, because his business was thriving and he had excess cash to invest, he purchased a white-owned beauty products company, Boyer International. He rescued Boyer from financial difficulties, but the transaction had to be completed clandestinely because the majority of the company's customers were southern whites. Neither Boyer's owners nor Fuller wanted it to be known that an African American owned the company. His business was successful—in the 1950s and early 1960s it was the largest black-owned company in the country, and Fuller was one of the wealthiest African Americans in the United States. His concern for secrecy proved to be well-founded, however. In the mid-1960s his empire collapsed when southern white citizens councils (formed to oppose the civil rights movement) discovered and publicized his ownership of Boyer International and led boycotts, which, along with a few missteps of his own, destroyed his business and forced him to file for bankruptcy.

15. Pittman interview, 13 August 1996; Francis Ward, "Black CPAs in America," *PUSH Magazine*, Fall 1991, 16–21, 56.

16. John R. Hawkins, "Why the Negro Should Vote for Mr. Hoover," *The Crisis* 39 (October 1932): 313–14; Reverdy C. Ransom, "Why Vote for Roosevelt?" *The Crisis* 39 (November 1932): 343; Lester A. Walton, "Vote for Roosevelt," *The Crisis* 39 (November 1932): 343–44; Roy Garvin, "Alf Landon as I Know Him," *The Crisis* 43 (May 1936): 139, 142; Francis E. Rivers, "The Negro Should Support Landon," *The Crisis* 43 (October 1936): 296–97, 308; Democratic National Committee, "Roosevelt, the Humanitarian," *The Crisis* 43 (October 1936): 298–99; Eugene Lyons, "Roosevelt—and the American Labor Party," *The Crisis* 43 (November 1936): 332, 345; Walter White, "An Estimate of the 1936 Vote," *The Crisis* 43 (February 1936): 46–47; Goodwin, *No Ordinary Time*, 163–65; Sitkoff, *Depression Decade*, 93, 303; Sullivan, *Days of Hope*, 143.

17. Sitkoff, *Depression Decade*, 147–49, 228–31, 242; "Supreme Court Rules Out White Primaries," *The Crisis* 51 (May 1944): 164–65. In 1935, the Court determined that the exclusion of African Americans from juries in Alabama meant it was impossible for the "Scottsboro Boys" to get a fair trial. With the international media focused on this notorious rush to injustice, in which an all-white jury had convicted nine young African American men of rape and sentenced eight of them to death, the Court overturned their convictions; Sullivan, *Days of Hope*, 148.

18. "Along the NAACP Battlefront: First Lady Speaks," *The Crisis* 42 (June 1935): 184; Robert Weaver, "A Wage Differential Based on Race," *The Crisis* 41 (August 1934): 236–38; John P. Davis, "NRA Codifies Wage Slavery," *The Crisis* 41 (October 1934): 298–99, 304; Charles H. Houston and John P. Davis, "TVA: Lily-White Reconstruction," *The Crisis* 41 (October 1934): 290–91, 311; "Editorials: Social Security—for White Folk," *The Crisis* 42 (March 1935): 80; George Edmund Haynes, "Lily-White Social Security," *The Crisis* 42 (March 1935): 85–86; John P. Davis, "A Black Inventory of the New Deal," *The Crisis* 42 (May 1935): 141–42, 154–55; Sitkoff, *Depression Decade*, 65; Chadakoff, *Eleanor Roosevelt's My Day*, 113, 209; Goodwin, *No Ordinary Time*, 161–64; political advertisement, *The Crisis* 47 (November 1940): 367. Franklin Roosevelt was alone in the advertisement taken out in 1936.

19. Drake and Cayton, *Black Metropolis*, 84; W. E. B. Du Bois, "Postscript: Boycott," *The Crisis* 41 (April 1934): 117; Vere Johns, "To Boycott or Not to Boycott? A. We Must Have Jobs," *The Crisis* 41 (September 1934): 258–60, 274.

20. Sitkoff, *Depression Decade*, 38; Drake and Cayton, *Black Metropolis*, 430–33.

21. "State-Wide Battle on Illinois Jim Crow," *The Crisis* 44 (February 1937): 43, 61–62.

22. Gustavus Adolphus Steward, "The Negro Student Prefers Prejudice," *The Crisis* 42 (August 1935): 245–46.

23. "Forrester B. Washington Resigns," *The Crisis* 41 (September 1934): 265; George S. Schuyler, "New Job Frontiers for Negro Youth," *The Crisis* 43 (November 1936): 328–29.

24. A review of the names of the known African American CPAs in the 1920s through the 1940s against AIA membership reveals that Mr. Jones became the first African American member of the institute in 1942. The AICPA (formerly AIA) has no record of the discussion of Jones's admission, and it is unclear whether or not other African American CPAs had applied to join the institute. However, as further evidence that Jones was first, Wilmer Lucas, who had become a New York CPA in 1929, did not join the institute until 1944. In 1955, *Jet* Magazine noted that Theodore Jones had become the "first Negro ever elected to the [American Institute of Accountants]" on 14 October 1942; "People," *Jet*, 20 October 1955, 7.

25. Jones interview.

26. "Editorial: Admission Requirements of the American Institute," *JoA* 34, no. 1 (1922): 39.

27. Edwards, *History of Public Accounting*; Carey, *From Technician to Professional*; Carey, *To Responsibility and Authority*; Allen and McDermott, *Accounting for Success*; Spacek, *Arthur Andersen & Co.*; Miranti, *Accountancy Comes of Age*; Hamilton, *History of the West Virginia Society*; *History of the CPA Profession in Missouri*; Derrick, *South Carolina Society*; *History of Florida Institute*; *History of the Oklahoma Society*; Grant, *New York State*; Alkire, *Accounting Profession in Washington State*. I searched for all society

and large-firm histories, and the only state that directly addressed African American CPAs was Texas, in both Tinsley, *History of the Texas State Board*, 15, and Tinsley, *Texas Society*, 171–72.

28. *Proceedings, Council Meeting, American Institute of Accountants*, 11–12 May 1942, 154–55, AICPA Library.

29. Victor Stempf, "Practical Aspects of Professional Ethics," *JoA* 69, no. 4 (1940): 281. African Americans desiring to become CPAs would certainly notice this invisibility. Though African American college libraries in general had paltry business collections, the *JoA* was one of the ten business periodicals most likely to be found in their libraries. See Pierce, *Negro Business*, 257.

30. *Minutes, fifty-fourth annual meeting, American Institute of Accountants General Sessions*, 15, 18 September 1941, 47–48, AICPA Library.

31. It is likely that these jokes are representative and not anomalous. I encountered them while searching for information on Theodore Jones's admission to the AIA and did not peruse the minutes of all AIA meetings, which presumably contain similar jokes. This attitude, of course, was not unusual among white professionals, and such stories were not uncommon at the time. In 1937, civil rights champion Eleanor Roosevelt told a similar joke in her column, recommending a book called "Chocolate Drops from the South" by E. V. White, which comprised, in Roosevelt's words, "humorous stories about American Negroes" (Chadakoff, *Eleanor Roosevelt's My Day*, 52). Roosevelt did not, however, use the term "nigger."

32. "Along the Color Line," *The Crisis* 37 (March 1930): 97; "Supreme Liberty Life Insurance Company of Chicago," *The Crisis* 48 (April 1941): 111; Ingham and Feldman, *African-American Business Leaders*, 203.

33. "Chicago Branch Wins Four-Year Fight," *The Crisis* 43 (February 1936): 56; Ernest E. Johnson, "Supreme Court 1940," *The Crisis* 48 (July 1941): 220–22; Reed, *Chicago NAACP*, 118, 120; Harold L. Ickes, "The Negro as a Citizen," *The Crisis* 43 (August 1936): 230–31. See also "Editorials: FEPC Is Captured by the South," *The Crisis* 49 (September 1942): 279; "Along the NAACP Battlefront—Ask FEPC Hearing Go Forward," *The Crisis* 36 (February 1943): 56–57; "Editorials: The New FEPC," *The Crisis* 50 (August 1943): 231; "Editorials: Freezing 'Negro' Jobs," *The Crisis* 51 (January 1944): 7; "Editorials: FEPC Again," *The Crisis* 51 (May 1944): 136; "Editorials: Slander in the Senate," *The Crisis* 51 (July 1944): 217; "Editorials: FEPC," *The Crisis* 52 (July 1945): 193; "National Defense Labor Problems, The Weaver Appointment," *The Crisis* 47 (October 1940): 319, 322.

34. Sullivan, *Days of Hope*, 157–58.

35. Allen and McDermott, *Accounting for Success*, 85; Spacek, *Arthur Andersen & Co.*, 161; "Editorial: Manpower," *JoA* 73, no. 4 (1942): 290–91; "Editorial: Accountants in War," *JoA* 73, no. 5 (1942): 385–86; "Women in Accounting," *JoA* 73, no. 4 (1942): 295–96; Florence L. Sivertson, "Letters to the Editor: Women in Accounting," *JoA* 74, no. 1 (1942): 67; John L. Carey, "The Accounting Profession in War," *JoA* 73, no. 5 (1942): 449; S. Paul Garner, "The Scope and Extent of the Defense Training Program in Accounting," *JoA* 73, no. 6 (1942): 541; Robert D. Gracey, "Staff Training," *JoA* 74, no. 4 (1942): 326–31; R. E. Glos, "Postwar Collegiate Accounting Education," *JoA* 77, no. 2 (1944): 122–24; Jennie Palen, "The Position of the Woman Accountant in the Postwar

Era," *JoA* 80, no. 1 (1945): 27–30; Wescott and Seiler, *Women in the Accounting Profession*, 51–54.

36. Spacek, *Arthur Andersen & Co.*, 161.

37. As noted in chapter 2, John Cromwell, the first African American CPA, taught Weaver at Dunbar High School in Washington, D.C.

38. Carl H. Nau, "The Aims of the Institute," *JoA* 31, no. 5 (1921): 326.

39. "Editorial: To Encourage the Young Accountant," *JoA* 36, no. 1 (1923): 29.

40. Kenneth R. Manning, "The Complexion of Science," *Technology Review*, November/December 1991, 64; "Validity, Legality of ABA Accreditation Question," *Weekend Edition*, 18 February 1995, Transcript number: 1111–14, National Public Radio.

41. David Moberg, "Scholar's Life Bears Stamp of Greatness," *Chicago Tribune*, 16 February 1994, C1.

42. Drake and Cayton, *Black Metropolis*, 127, 552, 566.

43. "World's Greatest Weekly and Why," advertisement for the *Chicago Defender*, *The Crisis* 43 (May 1936): 130.

44. Beckett and Chambliss interview.

45. Ibid.

46. Blayton, *Better Records*.

47. Johnson and Bennett, *Succeeding Against the Odds*, 133, 164.

48. Beckett and Chambliss interview.

49. Yenser, *Who's Who in Colored America*, 59.

50. Pierce, *Negro Business*, 266–70, 290.

51. Drake and Cayton, *Black Metropolis*, 293, 508–10, 514–15. See also Delany and Delany with Hearth, *Having Our Say*, 137.

52. Anderson interview; Fambro interview; Crockett interview; *History of Black Accountancy*. Two others became CPAs in Illinois in the same period: Paul Stewart in 1937 and G. Steven Marchman III in 1944. Stewart worked with Beckett, but Stewart died quite young. Marchman had a firm and was involved with other African American CPAs. He was well known for keeping a list of all the black CPAs in the country.

53. Pittman interview, 9 December 1992.

54. Hine, *Black Women in White*, 26–46; Tracy Dell'Angela, "Dr. Elizabeth Webb Hill," *Chicago Tribune*, 17 November 1996, 1; Tracy Dell'Angela, "Laverne Strickland: Black Hospitals Held Out Hope at a Time When White Hospitals Shut the Doors," *Chicago Tribune*, 17 November 1996, 1; "This Week In Black History," *Jet*, 15 July 1996, 19; "Do You Know Them?" *Commercial Appeal*, 16 February 1997, E1; "Along the Color Line," *The Crisis* 40 (August 1933): 183.

55. Pittman interview, 13 August 1996.

56. Ford interview; Pittman interview, 9 December 1992.

57. Pittman interview, 9 December 1992.

58. Letter from Steven Marchman III to Hiram Pittman, 3 September 1952 (copy provided by Hiram Pittman). "It is my opinion that those of us in the accountancy profession do not get together often enough and share our mutual experiences. I further believe that if we should, each of us would be materially benefited. Not that we should form a 'jim crow' club or association, but we should in some informal way sit down and learn to know each other better and share our experiences. To this end, I am wondering if

you would join with me in holding a little luncheon meeting on Wednesday, September 10th, between 6:30 and 8:30 P.M.? Mr. J. B. Blayton, C.P.A. of Atlanta, will be in the City and he told me he would enjoy meeting our members of the profession. Upon the receipt of this letter, will you be kind enough to call me immediately and say what you think about the idea?" None of those interviewed for this book recall a National Society of Accountants, though many recall Jesse B. Blayton himself. Nonetheless, *The Negro Handbook 1946–1947* lists the National Society of Accountants as a "Negro" organization with Blayton and Marchman as officers; Florence Murray, *Negro Handbook*, 219.

59. Fritz Lanham, "The Silent End of Segregation," *Texas Magazine*, 15 June 1997, 8.
60. Pittman interview, 13 August 1996. Pittman did join both societies in the early 1970s, when, after the civil rights movement, he began to seek business with major white-owned organizations and government. See chapter 7.
61. Drake and Cayton, *Black Metropolis*, 314; Sitkoff, *Depression Decade*, 183, 265. See also Delany and Delany with Hearth, *Having Our Say*, 126.
62. Cripps, *Making Movies Black*, 45.
63. *In This Our Life*, John Huston, director, 1942.

CHAPTER FOUR

1. Kurth, *American Cassandra*, 266; Sitkoff, *Depression Decade*, 117, 123, 190–95, 231, 312; Pauli Murray, *Song in a Weary Throat*, 167, 255; "Editorials: Nazis and Negroes," *The Crisis* 48 (May 1941): 151; Sullivan, *Days of Hope*, 136–37; Kluger, *Simple Justice*, 226; Smith, *Killers of the Dream*, 226; Chadakoff, *Eleanor Roosevelt's My Day*, 300; Egerton, *Speak Now Against the Day*, 211; "White House Blesses Jim Crow," *The Crisis* 47 (November 1940): 350–51, 357; "What Negro Youth Expects from National Defense," *The Crisis* 48 (August 1941): 253–54; "Editorials," *The Crisis* 50 (February 1943): 41; "A Declaration by Negro Voters," *The Crisis* 51 (January 1944): 16–17; Merrill, *President Truman's Attempts*, 29–31.
2. Merrill, *President Truman's Attempts*, 104–6; Branch, *Parting the Waters*, 66.
3. Austin interviews.
4. On Cass High School, see Bennett, *When Dreams Came True*, 22.
5. Meier and Rudwick, *Black Detroit*; Louis Emanuel Martin, "The Ford Contract: An Opportunity," *The Crisis* 48 (September 1941): 284–85, 302.
6. In 1957, Austin became the first black member of the board of trustees of the Detroit Institute of Technology; "Detroit College Names First Negro Board Member," *Jet*, 28 November 1957, 56.
7. *The Honorable Richard H. Austin, Michigan Secretary of State, Biographic Information*, n.d. (copy provided by Richard Austin).
8. Whiting interview.
9. Davenport interview.
10. Gloster B. Current, "Let's Get Ten Thousand!" *The Crisis* 49 (September 1942): 292–95, 301; "20,000 Members in 1943," *The Crisis* 50 (May 1943): 140–41, 154; Gloster B. Current, "The Detroit Elections: Problem in Reconversion," *The Crisis* 52 (November 1945): 319–21, 332; Thurgood Marshall, "The Gestapo in Detroit," *The Crisis* 50 (August

1943): 232–33, 246–47; Louis E. Martin, "Detroit—Still Dynamite," *The Crisis* 51 (January 1944): 8–10, 25.

11. Austin interviews.

12. "Notice of Annual Meeting," *The CPA*, July–August 1957, 11.

13. Kim Chatelain, "Falling into Changing Times: End of an Era: Marsalis Inn to Be Razed," *New Orleans Times-Picayune*, 13 March 1993, A1. Institute meetings from 1953–59 were held in Chicago, New York, Washington, D.C., Seattle, New Orleans, Detroit, and San Francisco. It is likely that the hotels for the Washington, D.C., meeting, the Mayflower and the Statler, did not welcome African Americans. See Burt Solomon, "Trading Quality for Quantity: William T. Coleman Jr., Former Transportation Secretary," *National Journal*, 18 March 1989, 662.

14. Moon, *Untold Tales*, 283, 396.

15. "Detroit Next for Black Mayor?" *New York Amsterdam News*, 13 September 1969, 1; "Battle Lines," *New York Amsterdam News*, 18 October 1969, 2; "Black Mayoral Hopeful Unites Detroit's Minority," *Jet*, 25 September 1969, 5; "Stokes Only Black Mayoral: Detroit's Austin Hurt by Too Light Black Turnout," *Jet*, 20 November 1969, 6–8; Lichtenstein, *Walter Reuther*, 413.

16. Sewell and Dwight, *Mississippi Black History Makers*, 147–88; Asa Gordon, *Sketches of Negro Life and History in South Carolina*, 135–55.

17. Saddler interview. She was Blayton's assistant from 1949 until his death in 1977.

18. *History of Black Accountancy*, 8–9; U.S. Department of Commerce, *Statistical Abstract 1960*, 30. For the purposes here, the South includes Delaware, Maryland, the District of Columbia, Virginia, West Virginia, North Carolina, South Carolina, Georgia, Florida, Kentucky, Tennessee, Alabama, Mississippi, Arkansas, Louisiana, Oklahoma, and Texas. If Kentucky and Tennessee are excluded, only three African Americans had earned their CPAs in the South by this time.

19. "Editorial Note."

20. Anderson, *Education of Blacks*, 186–237.

21. "Dangerous Federal School Aid," *The Crisis* 44 (February 1937): 41–42, 50, 60; Kluger, *Simple Justice*, 86–87. In 1908, the U.S. Supreme Court upheld Kentucky's right to forbid Berea College, a private school, from educating African Americans together with whites. See Miller, *Petitioners*, 199–216.

22. Charles H. Houston, "Educational Inequalities Must Go," *The Crisis* 42 (October 1935): 300–301.

23. Tushnet, *NAACP's Legal Strategy*, 36, 87.

24. Some black college administrators strongly discouraged—and sometimes punished—those students who did take part in civil rights activities. See Tushnet, *NAACP's Legal Strategy*, 53, and Maurice Gates, "Negro Students Challenge Social Forces," *The Crisis* 42 (August 1935): 232–33, 251. Many black colleges depended on state funding for their survival, and their administrators were chosen by politicians. Thus, it is not surprising that they were often cautious. See Kluger, *Simple Justice*, 157. In addition, many feared—correctly—that integration at majority schools would result in a loss of jobs for African American educators; Pauli Murray, *Song in a Weary Throat*, 124.

25. Kluger, *Simple Justice*, 137.

26. "Thurgood Marshall Joins NAACP Staff," *The Crisis* 43 (November 1936): 343; Kluger,

Simple Justice, 156, 179, 187; "Court Opens Maryland U. Doors," *The Crisis* 42 (1935): 239; Sitkoff, *Depression Decade*, 240–41.

27. Kluger, *Simple Justice*, 127.

28. Ibid., 213.

29. Charles H. Houston, "Don't Shout Too Soon," *The Crisis* 43 (March 1936): 79, 91; "University of Missouri Case Won," *The Crisis* 46 (January 1939): 10–12, 18; Lucile Bluford, "Missouri 'Shows' the Supreme Court," *The Crisis* 46 (August 1939): 231–32, 242–46; Thurgood Marshall, "Equal Justice Under Law," *The Crisis* 46 (July 1939): 199–201; "Editorial: Equal Opportunity in Education," *The Crisis* 46 (January 1939): 17; "Press Comment on the Gaines Case," *The Crisis* 46 (February 1939): 52–53, 61; Miller, *Petitioners*, 333–34. Despite this decision, Lloyd Gaines never attended the University of Missouri. Shortly before he was to enter the school, he mysteriously disappeared; Pauli Murray, *Song in a Weary Throat*, 127.

30. Kluger, *Simple Justice*, 188–95, 202, 259–60; Miller, *Petitioners*, 336; Tushnet, *NAACP's Legal Strategy*, 71–75; "Virginia Makes a Move toward Graduate Study," *The Crisis* 43 (March 1936): 87; Pauli Murray, *Song in a Weary Throat*, 114–15, 118–19; Charles Thompson, "Editorial Comment"; Egerton, *Speak Now Against the Day*, 132; Walter S. Hallanan, "West Virginia and the Negro," *The Crisis* 38 (January 1931): 10–11, 34; Charles H. Houston, "Cracking Closed University Doors," *The Crisis* 42 (December 1935): 364, 370, 372; "Mr. James Crow: Professional Schools and Negroes," *The Crisis* 40 (June 1933): 136; Charles H. Houston, "A Challenge to Negro College Youth," *The Crisis* 45 (January 1938): 14–15; Glenn Hutchinson, "Jim Crow Challenged in Southern Universities," *The Crisis* 46 (April 1939): 103–5; Sitkoff, *Depression Decade*, 222–23; Sullivan, *Days of Hope*.

   Most of these out-of-state scholarships did not include differentials in tuition, living, or travel expenses. But "Walking to School," *The Crisis* 40 (April 1933): 91, includes an amusing story about one student's reaction when a state did include those expenses: "Herman W. Dennis of Allen, Virginia was granted tuition and traveling fees to Virginia State College by the State of Maryland which does not allow Negroes to matriculate at the University of that state. The lad pocketed his travel money and walked the 250 miles to college." ·

   Some states considered closing their white graduate schools to avoid opening institutions for African Americans: "In early 1942 Missouri took the alternate route to equalization and closed the journalism school at the University of Missouri. [Charles Hamilton] Houston believed that the school was closed because the new course at Lincoln [the African American college in Missouri] . . . was obviously inadequate, but he noted that the draft had severely reduced enrollments at the white school" (Tushnet, *NAACP's Legal Strategy*, 85).

   A few state graduate schools actually argued that the African American students were not qualified to attend their programs because their undergraduate programs—state-funded black colleges—did not prepare students adequately. If anything, this only underscored the fact that the state-sponsored education was unequal. See Pauli Murray, *Song in a Weary Throat*, 122.

31. Mike Bowler, "Gifted, Black—They Were Paid to Study Elsewhere," *Baltimore Sun*, 14 August 1995, A1.

32. Only two schools, New York University and the University of Pennsylvania, had more members of the AIA than did the University of Illinois; Warren W. Nissley, "The Junior Accountant—His Duties and Opportunities," *JoA* 74, no. 3 (1942): 252.

33. *University of Illinois Yearbook* (1947), 234–35, 457; (1948), 83, 281, 394–95, 528, 647; (1949), 610.

34. Ford interview.

35. Kluger, *Simple Justice*, 195.

36. New York University had more members of the AIA than did any other university. See Warren W. Nissley, "The Junior Accountant—His Duties and Opportunities," *JoA* 74, no. 3 (1942): 252. New York University actively recruited southern African American students whose states granted out-of-state tuition. See Mike Bowler, "Gifted, Black— They Were Paid to Study Elsewhere," *Baltimore Sun*, 14 August 1995, A1.

37. "Editorial: Accounting Education," *JoA* 80, no. 3 (1945): 161–63.

38. In 1957, Elvera Taylor, the second African American female CPA in the country, was asked by the *Negro History Bulletin* whether being African American had made her career more difficult. She responded, "As a matter of fact, I think that being a woman in business is more of a barrier" (Marguerite Cartwright, "The Taylors of Milwaukee," *Negro History Bulletin*, October 1957, 8–9).

39. Palen, "Women in Public Accounting," AICPA Library.

40. *History of Black Accountancy*, 45.

41. Gines interview.

42. Tushnet, *NAACP's Legal Strategy*, 123–30; Derrick Bell, "The Freedom of Employment Act," *The Nation*, 23 May 1994, 708–14; Pauli Murray, *Song in a Weary Throat*, 77, 111–13, 266; Miller, *Petitioners*, 342; Smith, *Killers of the Dream*, 241; Sitkoff, *Depression Decade*, 139–68; Egerton, *Speak Now Against the Day*, 11, 167, 172–74.

43. Gines interview; *History of Black Accountancy*.

44. Sitkoff, *Depression Decade*, 76, 331; Hope and Shelton, "Negro in the Federal Government."

45. Pauli Murray, *Song in a Weary Throat*, 182, 200; Kluger, *Simple Justice*, 106–7; "The Secret City: An Impression of Colored Washington," *The Crisis* 39 (June 1932): 185–87.

46. Charles Thompson, "Editorial Comment," 522.

47. Broadus interview.

48. Bennett, *When Dreams Came True*, 21, 251–55, 260–62.

49. Reginald Wilson, "More Than 50 Years Later GI Bill Impact Still Felt," *Philadelphia Tribune*, 10 February 1995, 1.

50. Bennett, *When Dreams Came True*, 26, 29, 150–51, 162–63, 170, 238–40, 260; Charles Thompson, "Editorial Comment"; Derbigny, "Tuskegee Looks at Its Veterans"; Herbold, "Never a Level Playing Field"; Quarles, "Background."

51. Reynolds interview.

52. Ibid.; Lee interview.

53. Callcott, *Maryland and America*, 152; David Folkenflik, "Its Banneker Program Scuttled, UM Puzzles over Racial Remedies," *Baltimore Sun*, 24 May 1995, B1.

54. Lee interview.

55. Ibid.

56. King interview.

57. Lee interview.

58. Reynolds interview.

59. King interview.

60. Letter from Dean George R. Burman to Talmadge Tillman, 21 June 1999 (copy provided by Tillman).

61. Talmadge Tillman, text of presentation given at African American Accounting Doctoral Student Association, Chicago, 13 August 1996 (copy provided by Tillman).

62. Note from Harold Simons to Talmadge Tillman, 1952. The handwritten note reads, "Consistently fine work. Lecture Grade A−. #3 Man in Class. You should make it! Good Luck" (copy provided by Tillman).

63. Notice of Eligibility, United States Civil Service Commission, 3 January 1955: Tillman ranked number 7; Notice of Examination Results, Los Angeles County, 16 September 1952: Tillman ranked number 1; Notice of Eligibility, Utility Accountant, 3 January 1955: Tillman ranked number 5 (copies provided by Tillman). Talmadge Tillman, text of presentation given at African American Accounting Doctoral Student Association, Chicago, 13 August 1996 (copy provided by Tillman).

64. Talmadge Tillman, text of presentation given at African American Accounting Doctoral Student Association, Chicago, 13 August 1996 (copy provided by Tillman); Tillman interview.

65. Collins interview, 3 October 1997.

66. Adams, "Doors Didn't Open Easily"; Reynolds interview.

67. Harold R. Enslow, "A Comparison of Certified and Non-Certified Public Accountants in the State of New York," *JoA* 88, no. 1 (1949): 45.

68. Letter from William D. Collins to Roy V. Johnson, CPA, 2 January 1958 (copy provided by Collins).

69. Rejection letters to William D. Collins from Robert D. Safford, personnel director, Arthur Young & Company, 9 September 1957; Haskins and Sells, 3 September 1957; J. William Oldenkamp, Price Waterhouse & Co., 28 August 1957 (copies provided by Collins).

70. Halberstam, *The Fifties*, 141.

71. Robert N. McMurray, "Study of Personality Traits May Be the Key to Choosing the Valuable Accounting Junior," *JoA* 91, no. 4 (1951): 604–5.

72. Letter from William D. Collins to California State Board of Accountancy, 16 August 1957; letter from Elizabeth Munson, acting secretary, California State Board of Accountancy, to William D. Collins, 22 August 1957; letter from Leslie N. McReynolds, secretary, California State Board of Accountancy, to William D. Collins, 28 January 1958 (copies provided by Collins). Collins reported that McReynolds was very cooperative with him. I said, "He could have ignored you." Collins immediately replied, "I wasn't going to let him do that" (Collins interview, 20 December 1999). From the 1920s through the 1950s, East Los Angeles had the largest Jewish population in the western United States. See Howard Rosenberg, "TV Review: 'Meet Me' A Delightful Bit of History," *Los Angeles Times*, 19 October 1996, F18; Roseanne Keynan, "Southern California File," *Los Angeles Times*, 15 February 1992, F17.

73. Letter from William D. Collins to Safety Savings and Loan Association, 11 December 1957 (copy provided by Collins).

74. Collins interview, 3 October 1997; letter from Bernard S. Jefferson, president, Safety Savings and Loan Association to William D. Collins, 21 August 1959 (copy provided by Collins). An article on early African American attorneys discussed the reluctance of white firms with black clients to hire African American attorneys for fear that they would take their clients. See Christine and LeRoy Clark, "The Black Lawyer," *BE*, February 1973, 14–18.

75. C. S. Nicolas Jr., "A CPA's Successful Experience in Starting a Practice in a Small Community: A Case Study," *JoA* 88, no. 1 (1949): 40.

76. Collins interview, 3 October 1997.

77. *History of Black Accountancy*, 11.

78. "Editorial: Manpower and Selective Service," *JoA* 75, no. 2 (1943): 99–100. "Editorial: The 'Monopoly' Charge against Certified Public Accountants," *JoA* 86, no. 5 (1948): 355.

79. "The Fabulous Gales," *Our World*, August 1951, 32–35; *Negro Year Book*, 140. According to NABA's 1990 publication, *History of Black Accountancy*, there were 27 African American CPAs in 1952. "Milwaukee Woman Elected to Accounting Society," *Jet*, 11 June 1953, 7; "Yesterday in Negro History," *Jet*, 20 October 1955, 7. See also "College Prof becomes Virginia's 1st Negro CPA," *Jet*, 1 March 1956, 48; "Chicagoan Named to U.S. Assay Commission," *Jet*, 21 February 1957, 5; "P.O. Worker Passes CPA Examination," *Los Angeles Sentinel*, 29 August 1957, A7. The most amusing piece indicating the society status of CPAs is the following blurb from "Parnell Drayton, CPA," *Jet*, 6 November 1958, 64: "Harlem society was shocked to learn that prosperous accountant Parnell Drayton and his wife, Barbara, are no longer sharing their breakfast ham and eggs."

80. "Jersey to Certify Negro as a Public Accountant," *NYT*, Schomburg Center Clipping File: Accountants. Parker's achievement was also noted in "1st Negro Public Accountant Certified in New Jersey," *Jet*, 16 December 1954, 27, and "Wilbur Parker," *New York Amsterdam News*, 11 December 1954, 34.

The black newspaper the *New York Age* also recognized Parker's achievement, noting that when Parker completed his master's degree at Cornell in 1950 (where he had been a track and football star), he could have taken many jobs to which the Urban League referred him, but he preferred to pursue his CPA: "Parker's certification on Monday can be attributed to . . . an enlightened attitude to racial hiring shown by the New York firm of Apfel and Englander. Werner E. Regli, personnel manager of the firm to whom Parker was referred by the Urban League and by Dr. Emanuel Saxe of the City College of New York accounting department, states that, to his delight the firm not only received no criticism from their clients when they hired Parker but that their clients congratulated the organization. . . . [Now that Parker has left to open his own firm] Apfel and Englander now has another Negro accountant who has begun his apprenticeship with the firm and states that there will alway [*sic*] be room for Negroes with the firm" ("Swear in First Negro CPA in New Jersey," *New York Age*, 11 December 1954, 22).

Apfel and Englander, a Jewish firm, had a long history of employing African Americans, including Emsar Bradford, who became a CPA in 1960; "Appointed to LIU Faculty," *New York Age*, 27 September 1955, 4, and Briloff interview.

CHAPTER FIVE

1. "Editorial: Many Accounting Practices Have Been Merged in Recent Months," *JoA* 91, no. 1 (1951): 68.

2. "Negroes Filled Over 50% of Year's Federal Jobs," *WSJ*, 3 November 1965, 10; "Negroes Got Top Jobs at Double the Rate of Whites in Decade," *WSJ*, 20 January 1967, 16.

3. Harold Simons was the same professor who helped Talmadge Tillman at UCLA in the 1950s, as discussed in chapter 4. Henry Wilfong, discussed later in this chapter, says that Simons was also instrumental in his persevering in the profession.

4. Hill interview. There was at least one other African American in a Big Eight firm in a different city, but interviews indicate that the firms either did not know that these men were African American or did not openly acknowledge it.

5. Kenneth Young, "Integration in Accounting: A Professional Challenge," *National Public Accountant*, February 1962, 14–15, 28.

6. Ibid., 28. A 1965 article in the *WSJ* indicates that twenty-five African Americans who graduated from Michigan State's business school in 1961 also could not find jobs through campus interviews; "White-Collar Negroes Move Into Better Jobs, Get Friendly Reception," *WSJ*, 17 March 1965, 1.

7. Harrison, "Status of the Negro CPA." See chapter 2.

8. Branch, *Parting the Waters*, 143–205; Lewis with D'Orso, *Walking with the Wind*, 291–320.

9. Branch, *Parting the Waters*, 280, 302, 531; Allison Graham, "The Media and the South," *Arkansas Democrat-Gazette*, 21 September 1997, J1; Kisseloff, *The Box*, 345–46, 381, 389–90, 397–98, 503, 509, 513, 516–21; Beschloss, *Taking Charge*, 457–59.

10. Kisseloff, *The Box*, 403–29; Allison Graham, "The Media and the South," *Arkansas Democrat-Gazette*, 21 September 1997, J1. When Rod Serling wanted to produce a story about the Emmett Till lynching, he was forced to move the setting to New England and make the victim an immigrant, rather than an African American, in order to avoid controversy; Kisseloff, *The Box*, 503. Another writer wanted to do a story about attacks on African Americans who moved into white neighborhoods, and his supervisor insisted that the African American character be changed to an ex-convict; ibid., 516–17.

11. Allison Graham, "The Media and the South," *Arkansas Democrat-Gazette*, 21 September 1997, J1; Diane Wertz, "How Prime Time Defines Us," *Newsday*, 14 June 1992, 18.

12. Kisseloff, *The Box*, 519–20.

13. "Some Important Fiscal Facts about SCLC," King Papers.

14. Saddler interview. She was Blayton's assistant from 1949 until his death in 1977; Branch, *Parting the Waters*, 287.

15. Jesse B. Blayton letter to William R. Ming Jr., King Papers.

16. Branch, *Parting the Waters*, 309–10; "Dr. King to Ask Top Public Panel to Review Taxes," *Jet*, 3 March 1960, 8; John Coombes, "King Cleared of Falsifying Income Tax," *Montgomery Advertiser*, 29 May 1960, 1.

17. Jesse B. Blayton letter to King, 29 April 1960; Jesse B. Blayton invoice to King, 10 June 1959; Jesse B. Blayton invoice to King, 8 June 1960; Jesse B. Blayton letter to William R. Ming Jr. (King attorney), 8 April 1960; letter from Hubert T. Delany (King attorney) to

King, 2 May 1960; all from King Papers; Branch, *Parting the Waters*, 287. CPA billing rates for 1962 (1960 unavailable) from Montagna, *Certified Public Accounting*, 35.

18. Saddler interview.

19. Coulthurst interview.

20. Andrew, *Lyndon Johnson*; Dallek, *Flawed Giant*, 329–34.

21. Dallek, *Flawed Giant*, 208–9.

22. Lee interview.

23. "GS-16 Is Also CPA Firm Partner," *Crystal City (Va.) News*, 10 May 1972, 12; Judy Cook, "C. D. Lee Calls CPA Firm 'Part-Time Job,'" *American University Report*, January/February 1973, 1.

24. Garrett interview; Nathan Garrett resume, May 1999 (copy provided by Garrett); letter from Nathan Garrett to author, 14 July 1999.

25. Loevy, *Civil Rights Act*; Mann, *Walls of Jericho*, 381–432.

26. "What's the Problem?" *NYT*, 1 August 1999, sect. 4, p. 4.

27. The tone of several *WSJ* articles on the subject clearly reveals concern that the new agencies would pressure businesses to change. See "New U.S. Commission Plans Big Push to Open More Posts to Negroes," *WSJ*, 13 October 1965, 1; "A Debate over Racial Records," *WSJ*, 28 October 1965, 16.

28. Perry, "Business—Next Target for Integration?"; Purcell, "Break Down Your Employment Barriers"; Haynes, "Equal Job Opportunity"; Sturdivant, "Limits of Black Capitalism." See also Hammond and Streeter, "Overcoming Barriers."

29. *Proceedings, Council Meetings of the American Institute of Certified Public Accountants*, 3 May 1965, 111–15, AICPA Library.

30. Ibid. The transcript reads "efforts" instead of "evidence."

31. Ibid. The transcript reads "employ" rather than "implore."

32. Ibid.

33. Most speakers at the AICPA council meetings are identified by first and last name and by the state they represent or the office they hold. This information was not available for Mr. Wallace.

34. Haskins & Sells is the firm that rescinded the offer made by its Los Angeles office to Henry Wilfong in 1958; Wilfong interview, 20 December 1999.

35. Lang, "The Education and Recruitment of Ethnic Minority Students for the Accounting Profession," AICPA Library. Lang reported that the client was gratified to learn of his involvement with the AICPA Committee.

36. *Proceedings of Spring Council Meeting American Institute of Certified Public Accountants*, 5–7 May 1969, 109–34, AICPA Library. I base the estimate of attendees on the 95 to 89 vote cited below.

37. Ibid., 112–13.

38. Ibid., 119–20. In an interesting coincidence, one of the leaders of the armed student occupation at Cornell University, Thomas Jones, later worked for Big Eight firm Arthur Young for eleven years; "From Armed College Militant to Philanthropist," *Baltimore Sun*, 14 May 1995, E2.

39. Welsch later added, "I have right in this semester a black student who was elected vice president of the student body of the University of Texas. Thirty-two thousand students selected him as vice president, and he does not want to be classified as someone com-

ing into this profession with a potential. He wants to come as high potential like the rest of the people in that class" (*Proceedings of Spring Council Meeting American Institute of Certified Public Accountants*, 5–7 May 1969, 124–25, AICPA Library).

40. Ibid., 125.

41. Ibid., 120.

42. Ibid., 126–27. Trueblood went on to say, "I invite each of you to vote against the Texas amendment." Welsh, of Texas, responded, "You referred to it as the Texas amendment, and I am surprised you would designate it as that" (ibid., 127).

43. Ibid., 122.

44. Ibid., 123.

45. The other major amendment to the resolution was a change from "minority groups" to "disadvantaged groups." Some council members believed that it should be directed specifically at black students, others argued that it should include Latinos, Native Americans, and Asians. Some argued that "disadvantaged groups" was too broad and could include most of the people in the room.

46. Ibid., 129–31.

47. Ibid., 133–34. The AICPA hosted a few speakers in the late 1960s who discussed economic and employment problems of African Americans. See Bell, "Crisis of Our Times," 11–13, AICPA Library, and Goldsen, "Prospects in Social Development," AICPA Library.

48. Bert Mitchell, "The Black Minority in the CPA Profession," *JoA* 128, no. 4 (1969): 41–48. Mitchell wrote the following letter to African American CPAs across the country in 1968 (copy provided by William Collins): "I am currently engaged in a research study concerning the status of Negroes in the Certified Public Accounting profession in the United States. The Objective of the study is to bring into focus the deplorable sparsity [*sic*] of the participation of Negroes in the CPA profession and to stimulate interest towards the development of meaningful programs to correct the present situation. Being a Negro CPA myself, I am very much aware of our limited number throughout the country, and that there has been to date, no concerted effort, by the profession as a whole, towards increasing the number of minority groups in the profession. This study is intended to be an in-depth research of which the initial phase involved the completion of questionnaires by colleges and universities, all Negro CPAs in the U.S., and major accounting firms throughout the country. The second phase will involve discussions with a number of those completing the questionnaires, as well as professional organizations such as the American Institute of CPAs and the various state societies of CPAs. The third phase will be the development and implementation of programs for increasing the number of Negroes and other minority groups in the CPA profession in the United States. Since many questions included in the questionnaire request information of a confidential nature, it is requested that your name does not appear anywhere on the questionnaire. On the other hand, it is those items which appear to be of confidential nature that will add most significantly to the value of the study. Two self-addressed return envelopes are enclosed for your convenience—one for returning the completed questionnaire and the other to be used for requesting a copy of the completed study and to indicate your interest in further discussions on the research. I am looking forward to your much needed cooperation in this matter."

49. "Editors' Notebook: On Black CPAs," *JoA* 128, no. 4 (1969): 39. In response to Mitchell's article, one letter to the editor from an African American who had been an accountant (though not a CPA) for nine years stated: "It would be interesting to find out how many clients have been lost by white CPA firms because a black accountant has been assigned to an audit. The answer to this question might well show that the fear of adverse client reaction was more imaginary than real even if it did exist." The letter went on to say, "[Underrepresentation] is a direct result of the deliberate and hostile discrimination on the part of white CPA firms, and not, as has been indicated in the Editor's Notebook column, the unthinking, indifferent discrimination that comes about in the absence of the purposeful programs to combat discrimination"; Jimmy Campbell, "Letters to the Journal," *JoA* 128, no. 6 (1969): 24.

50. Emil Michael Aun, "Profession Looks to Negroes, Women as Shortage Looms," *Manpower*, August 1970, 3–7; Hedi Molnar, "Accounting for Blacks," *NYT Magazine*, 8 June 1986, 26; Jane Wollman, "The Two Sides of Being 'the First Black,' " *Newsday Magazine*, 15 April 1990, 8; Mitchell interview.

51. "New York Declares Client Service Bias 'Unprofessional Conduct,' " *JoA* 115, no. 3 (1963): 22; Albert J. Storich, "Letter to the Editor," *JoA* 127, no. 1 (1969): 24, 26; Joe J. Cramer and Robert Strawser, "Recruiting Professional Accountants from Minority Groups," *New York Certified Public Accountant*, October 1970, 797–802; James Nolan, "Black CPA Advances from Beginner to Partner," *JoA* 137, no. 6 (1974): 24–30; Brendan Reilly, "The Time Is Now," *Connecticut CPA*, March 1974, 38–39; John Ashworth, "The Importance of Black Colleges to Accountants," *JoA*, 132, no. 6 (1971): 87–89; Willard Archie and Alford Sweet, "Meeting Our Social Responsibilities," *Arthur Andersen Chronicle*, June 1971, 12–15; *Annual Report*, 36–37; "Black Accountants," *Price Waterhouse Review* 2 (1973): 44–53; "Detroit CPA Enters Political Arena after 25 Years in Practice," *JoA* 129, no. 1 (1970): 20–21; Edward C. Arrendell II, "Attracting Minority Students into Public Accounting," *Pennsylvania CPA Spokesman*, August 1973, 8–12; Lawrence A. Johnson, "Needed: Total Involvement," *Massachusetts CPA Review*, October/November 1968, 62–65; William Campfield, "Needed: That Extra Effort in Recruiting and Developing Staff from Disadvantaged Groups," *Maryland CPA Quarterly*, Spring 1972, 43–52. In 1964, the *New York Certified Public Accountant* published a letter to the editor noting that CPAs complained about the difficulty of finding suitable employees while simultaneously refusing to hire well-qualified African Americans; Seymour Gross, CPA, "Letter to the Editor: Enlarging the Sources for Staff Personnel," *New York Certified Public Accountant*, May 1964, 326.

52. Lang, "The Education and Recruitment of Ethnic Minority Students for the Accounting Profession," AICPA Library.

53. Edwin R. Lang, "Ethnic Minority Students: Their Education and Recruitment for the Accounting Profession," *CPA Review*, January/February 1970, 13.

54. Ibid.

55. Harrison interview, 27 August 1992. The CPA state societies were not alone in this exclusion. In 1966, the NAACP charged that the American Medical Association and the American Dental Association excluded African Americans in southern states; "NAACP Scores Doctors," *NYT*, 14 August 1966, 52.

56. Emil Michael Aun, "Profession Looks to Negroes, Women as Shortage Looms," *Manpower*, August 1970, 3–7.

57. Ross interview. In 1966, Ross became the first African American in the New York office of Peat, Marwick.
58. Marilyn Bender, "Black CPA's a Rare Breed," *NYT*, 18 October 1970, sect. 3, p. 3. A *NYT* article noted the response of two Big Eight firms as follows: "A spokesman for Touche, Ross, Bailey & Smart said that any implication of bias was 'absolutely not true.' Price, Waterhouse & Co. had no comment" ("State Body Accuses 6 Concerns of Bias," *NYT*, 9 May 1968, 51).
59. Marilyn Bender, "Black CPA's a Rare Breed," *NYT*, 18 October 1970, sect. 3, p. 3; Lang, "The Disadvantaged Program: One Year Later," 1–10, AICPA Library. Attention to the issue continued for several years. In 1971 the New York State Society of CPAs began advertising job openings in the *New York Amsterdam News*, a black newspaper; "CPAs Publicizing Its Black Members," *New York Amsterdam News*, 13 February 1971, 40.
60. Anonymous African American former partner in Big Eight firm in New York interview, 20 December 1989; William Gifford, "Black Accountants," *Price Waterhouse Review* 2 (1973): 44–53. In my interviews with several white Big Eight recruiters in 1989— all of whom spoke on condition of anonymity—they repeated the same theme.
61. Anonymous African American Big Eight partner interview, 25 May 1989; anonymous former Big Eight employee interview, 23 May 1989.
62. Anonymous white recruiter for Big Eight firm interview, 24 April 1989.
63. Aiken, *Black Experience*, 4–6.
64. Ibid.; "Black Accounting Firms," *BE*, February 1972, 30–34.
65. Ross interview.
66. See Thomas Bray, "Colleges Race to Open Departments Focusing on Study of Negroes," *WSJ*, 3 February 1969, 1; "Negro Students, Some with Guns, Ended Their Sit-in at Cornell University," *WSJ*, 21 April 1969, 1; Sir Arthur W. Lewis, "Black Studies: A Black Professor's View," *WSJ*, 15 May 1969, 18; Thomas Bray and Urban Lehner, "Enrollment of Negroes Will Jump in the Fall at Many Institutions," *WSJ*, 28 July 1969, 1; "Being Black Can Mean Getting a Job in 1970, College Official Says," *WSJ*, 13 July 1970, 7.
67. Ross interview. As one indication of the loaded nature of the term "black" in mainstream business, the *WSJ* used the term "Negro" to categorize articles about African Americans until 1978, when it switched to "Blacks"; *WSJ Indexes*, 1965–78.
    Aiken interview.
    Wilfong interview, 3 October 1997. Wilfong joined the AICPA in 1974 when he was working with the National Association of Minority CPA Firms; Wilfong interview, 1999; Henry Wilfong e-mail to author, 8 September 1999; Wilfong interview, 20 ber 1999.
    interview, 3 October 1997.
    Wilfong's contemporary African American CPAs, upon reading a draft of this asked to talk to me about this story. Contrary to my expectation, he was not by the precautions Wilfong took—this CPA had also had experiences where rry a gun. He was concerned that readers would think that "we were all a dlums"; anonymous interview, 1999.
    Wire: Racial Policy Jells. Nixon Talks Up Economic, Not Social, Gains for 10 October 1969, 1; "CPA Urges Black Capitalism to Broaden Whole

Outlook," *New York Amsterdam News*, 2 January 1971, 4; "Report Calls OMBE Benefits
for Minorities Only Marginal," *Washington Post*, 29 November 1977, D7; " 'Black Cap-
italism' Doubted by Panel," *NYT*, 12 June 1969, 25; John Herbers, "Small-Business Unit
Faces Inquiry as Criticism Rises," *NYT*, 21 July 1969, 19; James M. Naughton, "Small-
Business Agency Accused of Inaction on Black Capitalism," *NYT*, 24 July 1969, 18;
"Black Capitalism," *NYT*, 24 August 1969, 12; Stephen Cotton, "Capitalist Slow Down,"
New Republic, 27 September 1969, 15–16; Paul Delaney, "Black Capitalism Program
Falling Far Short of Goals," *NYT*, 29 June 1970, 1; Rosenbloom and Shank, "Let's Write
Off the MESBICs"; "G.O.P. Official Sees White House Confidence Gap," *NYT*, 26 June
1971, 11; Thomas Johnson, "More Resources for Blacks Urged," *NYT*, 6 June 1971, 38;
"Shaky Times for Aid to Black Capitalism," *Business Week*, 13 May 1972, 56–58; Paul
Delaney, "Black Supporters of President Under Fire," *NYT*, 17 October 1972, 29; Walter
Rugaber, "Stans to Promote a Minority Business Enterprise," *NYT*, 6 March 1969, 27;
Paul Delaney, "Negro Business Is Assured of Aid," *NYT*, 7 November 1969, 1; Stans,
One of the Presidents' Men, 168; "Black Capitalism: The Crowning Blow," *Newsweek*,
4 October 1971, 68–69. Stans had been president of the AICPA in the mid-1950s and
was later finance chair for Nixon's 1972 reelection campaign. Stans was fined $5,000 for
accepting illegal contributions as part of the Watergate scandal; Martin Weil, "Maurice
Stans Dies; Nixon Fundraiser Tainted by Watergate," *Washington Post*, 15 April 1998,
B7; Carlyle Douglas, "Black Republicans Honor Nixon," *NYT*, 18 October 1985, A27.

73. Wilfong reports that he had some difficulty persuading other African American CPAs
to participate in Nixon administration programs because they did not like Nixon.
Wilfong responded, "Do you like money?" (Wilfong interview, 3 October 1997).

74. Boyer, "Aid to Minority Business Enterprise: A Challenge to the Profession," 1–11,
AICPA Library; Rocco Siciliano, "Helping Them Get a Piece of the Action," *Nation's
Business*, March 1970, 56–59; Ralph Estes, "The Accountant's Social Responsibility," *JoA*
129, no. 1 (1970): 40–43.

75. Wilfong interview, 3 October 1997.

76. Garrett interview. For a discussion of the question of whether black business owners
had a "vested interest" in segregation, see Young, "Negro Participation."

77. Johnson and Bennett, *Succeeding Against the Odds*, 133.

78. Saddler interview.

79. Untitled document on suggested merger of various black-owned CPA firms, circa 1972
(copy provided by Carroll D. Lee).

CHAPTER SIX

1. For simplicity, "HBCU" is used throughout this chapter despite the fact that during
the early years covered herein the schools were de jure segregated; thus, the use of "historically" is incorrect. These schools were also known as the "1890 schools" because
they developed as a result of the second Morrill Act in 1890. The acronym HBCU tech-
nically applies only to these seventeen institutions, but it is often used to refer to any
predominantly African American college. During most of the twentieth century there
were over one hundred such schools, including Howard University, which was started
immediately after the Civil War and is thus not one of the 1890 schools. Tuskegee Uni-

versity had been a private institution before 1890, but it also benefited from the Morrill Act. See "N.C. Lucky to Have Two Land-Grant Institutions," *Greensboro News & Record*, 28 June 1998, R4; Jerry Hagstrom, "The Last Plantation," *Government Executive*, May 1997, 29; Christy and Williamson, *Century of Service*; William V. Muse, "One Man's Concept Produced Colossal Educational Benefits," *Montgomery Advertiser*, 9 August 1998, A13; Arthur Davis, "The Negro Professor," *The Crisis* 43 (April 1936): 103–4; Jencks and Riesman, *Academic Revolution*, 407–79. Throughout the rest of the chapter HBCU is used to refer to all colleges with a majority of African American students.

2. Fred G. Wale, "Chosen for Ability," *Atlantic Monthly*, July 1947, 81–85; Walter H. Waggoner, "Allison Davis, Psychologist, Dies; Wrote about Blacks in America," *NYT*, 22 November 1983, B8; Allen B. Ballard, "Academia's Record of Benign Neglect," *Change* 26, no. 4 (1994): 39; Moss, "Negro Teachers," 451. *The Crisis* reports that there were 107 African American Ph.D.'s in 1935, "107 Negroes Have Ph.D.," *The Crisis* 42 (February 1935): 52. Two African Americans worked as researchers in white universities but none as full-fledged teaching and research faculty; David Moberg, "Scholar's Life Bears Stamp of Greatness," *Chicago Tribune*, 16 February 1994, C1.

3. Fred G. Wale, "Chosen for Ability," *Atlantic Monthly* 180 (July 1947): 81–85. Adelaide Cromwell became a professor of sociology at Boston University.

4. Allen B. Ballard, "Academia's Record of Benign Neglect," *Change* 26, no. 4 (1994): 39.

5. Basalla, "African Americans," 82. George Owens had an interview with an accounting firm in New York, and the interviewer told him, "Yes, I have an opening. I would very much like to hire you, but it just wouldn't be good for my business. . . . [Being an auditor already causes conflict because we review the accounting records of the client and] your being a Negro would just exacerbate the situation" (ibid., 82).

6. Harrison interview, 27 August 1992. Harrison laughed when he said this.

7. See Brown, "Graduate and Professional Education," 239.

8. Brenda Birkett, former student and colleague of Lincoln Harrison at Southern University, presentation on Harrison at the African American Accounting Doctoral Students Association Meeting, Chicago, 16 August 1996.

9. "Marsalis Inn Denied New Lease on Life," *Atlanta Journal and Constitution*, 11 April 1993, M3.

10. Pierson et al., *Education of American Business*, 361.

11. Harrison had met his experience requirement partly through his advanced degrees—he now had master's degrees from both Atlanta University and the University of Illinois—and partly through experience provided by Jesse B. Blayton. Harrison interview, 27 August 1992.

12. Ohio State awarded its first doctoral degree in accounting in 1950. Louisiana State University has one of the oldest Ph.D. programs in the country, but Harrison did not have the option of attending. For age of doctoral programs, see Hasselback, *Accounting Faculty Directory*, 73.

13. *American Accounting Association 1948 Annual Meeting Program*, Memphis, 9, 10 September 1948 (copy provided by American Accounting Association).

14. A 1960 study found that professors at HBCUs had high social status within the African American community and that they were satisfied with having chosen teaching given the limited job opportunities available to them. Nevertheless, like Lincoln Harrison at

Southern University, faculty often felt cut off from professional development because they had no contact with faculty at other local colleges—almost invariably white colleges—and they often could not attend professional meetings in their field. See Daniel Thompson, "Problems of Faculty Morale."

15. See Moss, "Negro Teachers," 461.

16. "The American Negro in College," *The Crisis* 65 (August–September 1958): 391–406.

17. Brenda Birkett, presentation on Harrison at the African American Accounting Doctoral Students Association Meeting, Chicago, 16 August 1996.

18. Harrison's wife did join the society a few years later.

19. An early study of the business education of African Americans reveals that many business faculty in the HBCUs held membership in the American Accounting Association in the early 1940s. No faculty were listed as holding memberships in either the AICPA or any state society of CPAs, though Jesse B. Blayton was a professor at an HBCU and was a CPA. See Pierce and Butler, *Negro Business*, 261. As noted in chapter 3, Theodore Jones became the first African American member of the AICPA (then the AIA) in 1942.

20. Harrison interviews, 27 August 1992 and 28 January 1993; Lincoln Harrison resume, undated (copy provided by Harrison). Some of the pain may also have been ameliorated by the establishment of the Harrison-Rochon CPAs Educational Foundation in 1997, which honored Harrison as well as the second African American CPA in Louisiana, Reynard Rochon; Robert Miller, "Foundation Supports Black CPAs' Education," *New Orleans Times-Picayune*, 28 September 1997, C1.

21. Heman Sweat was the nephew of Heman Perry, Jesse Blayton's first employer in Atlanta. See chapter 2.

22. Barr and Calvert, *Black Leaders*, 167, 170; Terry, *Origin and Development*, 56. Despite the fact that the NAACP had recommended it, Heman Sweatt was disappointed by the establishment of Texas State University for Negroes because it made his demand to enter the University of Texas more difficult. He wrote to Walter White, head of the NAACP, "If my alliance with the NAACP in the current educational problem wasn't rooted in very firm soil, the present sight of Negro Ph.D.s flocking here madly for the self-fattening dollars being invested in Jim Crow education would make me toss in the towel of disgust" (Barr and Calvert, *Black Leaders*, 177). Sweatt's role as plaintiff involved intense personal sacrifice, including withstanding death threats, one of which came from a police officer. See Jacqueline Trescott, "Reflections on a Milestone Past: Black Activists Review 25 Years Since the Brown Decision," *Washington Post*, 17 May 1979, D1.

23. See Jencks and Riesman, *Academic Revolution*, 470–71; Milton Wilson interview, 2 May 1999.

24. Milton Wilson interview, 16 November 1991.

25. Hale interview.

26. Ibid. In 1984, Hale became president of the American Womens' Society of CPAs, and she thanked this woman for extending her that courtesy.

27. Ibid.

28. Records developed by author. The seven were William Campfield, Illinois, 1951; Milton Wilson, Indiana, 1951; Lincoln Harrison, Ohio State, 1953; Broadus Sawyer, New York University, 1955; Larzette Hale, Wisconsin, 1955; Joseph Cramer, Indiana, 1963; and

Sybil Mobley, Illinois, 1964. According to e-mail from James Hasselback to author, 24 June 1999, there were 573 people with Ph.D.'s in accounting at the end of 1965. Hasselback is the author of the annual *Accounting Faculty Directory*.

29. Moody, *Coming of Age in Mississippi*; Lewis with D'Orso, *Walking with the Wind*; Nelson and Bass, *Orangeburg Massacre*; Rhodes, *Jackson State University*, 177; "Two Blacks Were Killed as Police Re-took a Louisiana College Building," *WSJ*, 17 November 1972, 1.

30. Jaffe, Adams, and Meyers, *Negro Higher Education*, 3; Milton Gordon, "Analysis of Enrollment Data."

31. Ware and Determan, "Federal Dollar"; Plaut, "Plans for Assisting Negro Students"; Spearman, "Federal Roles and Responsibilities"; *Carnegie Commission*, 51. See also Brazziel, *Quality Education*, 149.

32. Ware and Determan, "Federal Dollar." See Sims, "Guest Editorial."

33. Neil Maxwell, "Negro Campuses: Colleges in South Seek to Improve Facilities, Lift Academic Levels," *WSJ*, 4 May 1964, 1.

34. Agnew, "Foundation Support of Education for Black Americans in the South"; "Ford Foundation to Boost Minority Student Grants," *WSJ*, 11 October 1971, 12; Glickstein, "Federal Education Programs and Minority Groups"; "Business Group Visits Negro Colleges to See Where Aid Is Needed," *WSJ*, 11 January 1968, 1; Willie, "Philanthropic and Foundation Support for Blacks."

35. Edwin R. Lang, "Creating Opportunities for Members of Minority Groups," *Pennsylvania CPA Spokesman*, October 1969, 10–11. The committee is discussed in chapter 5. Marilyn Bender, "Black CPAs a Rare Breed," *NYT*, 18 October 1970, sect. 3, p. 3; "CPAs to Aid Black Students," *BE*, July 1971, 11; "Negro Businessmen to Aid 2 Colleges," *NYT*, 18 January 1969, 29; "Black CPAs Take On Teaching Assignments at Black Campuses for BEEP," *The CPA*, March 1971, 9.

36. Plaut, "Plans for Assisting Negro Students to Enter and to Remain in College"; Hale interview.

37. Fichter, "Career Preparation"; Fichter, *Special Report*, 160–64; "Industry Rushes for Negro Grads," *Business Week*, 25 April 1964, 78–82; Harrison, "Role of the Negro Business School"; "Negro Recruiters Increase as Firms Seek More Minority-Group Employees," *WSJ*, 13 August 1968, 1; W. W. Ecton, "Letter to the Journal," *JoA* 129, no. 4 (1970): 28.

38. "Recruiting Negroes for Corporate Openings Approaches Fever-Pitch," *WSJ*, 9 February 1965, 1; "Negro Recruiters Increase as Firms Seek More Minority-Group Employees," *WSJ*, 13 August 1968, 1; "Negro Executives Increase as Firms Try Harder to Integrate Management," *WSJ*, 26 November 1968, 1; "Labor Letter," *WSJ*, 10 August 1971, 1; "Being Black Can Mean Getting a Job in 1970, College Official Says," *WSJ*, 13 July 1970, 7.

39. Bert Mitchell, "The Black Minority in the CPA Profession," *JoA* 128, no. 4 (1969): 42.

40. Harris interview.

41. Ibid.; Clark interview. Both Harris and Johnnie Clark, a professor at the Atlanta University complex, reported that their female students had difficulty obtaining positions. Ruth Harris became the first African American female CPA in Virginia in 1963. She earned her Ed.D. because there were no doctoral programs in business available to her

in Virginia. She is the sister of Bernadine Coles Gines, the first African American female CPA in New York in 1954, discussed in chapter 4. Harris was honored by a scholarship in her name at the Virginia Union University Business School and in 1998 was chosen for the "Strong Men & Women: Excellence in Leadership" series sponsored by Virginia Power; Michael Paul Williams, "Leadership Series Honors 9 Blacks in Various Fields," *Richmond Times-Dispatch*, 28 January 1998, B7. See also "Professor Broke Barriers: Harris Retiring after 48 Years at VUU," *Richmond Times-Dispatch*, 29 April 1997, C1, C8.

42. Bowles and DeCosta, *Between Two Worlds*, 143. See also John Burton, "The Importance of Black Colleges to Accountants," *JoA* 132, no. 6 (1971): 87–89.

43. Paul Martin, "Interracial U.: Northern Colleges Seek to Draw More Negroes from Schools in the South," *WSJ*, 23 September 1965, 1; Dan Rottenberg, "Colleges' Bid to Enroll 'Disadvantaged' Brings Problems and Protests," *WSJ*, 24 January 1969, 1; "Business Schools Try Harder to Recruit Negro Students," *WSJ*, 21 December 1967, 1; "Future Black Executives: Business Schools Recruit More Negro Students," *WSJ*, 10 February 1970, 1; "Black Business Students Form Professional Group," *WSJ*, 27 July 1970, 17.

44. Pamela G. Hollie, "Black College Finds the Social Changes It Sought Hurt It," *WSJ*, 5 May 1975, 1; Jonathan Spivak, "U.S. to Seek to Integrate State Colleges By Use of Aid Cuts Under '64 Rights Act," *WSJ*, 8 August 1968, 6; Mohr, *Black Colleges*; Sims, "Guest Editorial."

45. "Michigan State University Names Negro President," *WSJ*, 20 October 1969, 25; Thomas J. Bray, "Black Studies Boom: Colleges Race to Open Departments Focusing on Study of Negroes," *WSJ*, 3 February 1969, 1; Thomas J. Bray and Urban C. Lehner, "Black Collegians: Enrollment of Negroes Will Jump in the Fall at Many Institutions," *WSJ*, 28 July 1969, 1; "Negro Colleges Lose More Professors and Administrators to Big-Name Schools," *WSJ*, 21 October 1969, 1.

46. "The Unfinished Business of Negro Jobs," *Business Week*, 12 June 1965, 82–106; Marilyn Bender, "Black CPAs a Rare Breed," *NYT*, 18 October 1970, sect. 3, p. 3.

47. Meeth, "Breaking Racial Barriers."

48. "Negro Professors Get More Job Offers from 'White' Colleges and Government," *WSJ*, 12 September 1967, 1; "Negro Colleges Lose More Professors and Administrators to Big-Name Schools," *WSJ*, 21 October 1969, 1; "Colleges Hire More Negro Faculty as Black Students Increase," *WSJ*, 22 October 1968, 1.

49. *University of San Francisco Catalogue*, 16–39.

50. Heck and Bremser, "Six Decades"; Campfield's publications in the *Accounting Review* include "An Approach to Formulation of Professional Standards for Internal Auditors"; "A Blueprint for Appraising and Guiding Audit Staff"; "A Broad-Gauge Course in Governmental Accounting"; "Critical Paths for Professional Accountants during the New Management Revolution"; "Experiences in Extension of Staff Training to In-Charge Auditors"; "Good Judgment and Public Accounting Practice"; "A Governmental Agency's Program for Developing Its Professional Accountants"; "Professional Status for Internal Auditors"; "Re-Examination of Bases and Opportunities for Applying Accounting Judgment"; "Toward Making Accounting Education Adaptive and Normative"; and "Training for Law and for Public Accounting." In 1971, twenty years after

earning his Ph.D., Campfield became vice president of the American Accounting Association and a contributing editor of the "Educational and Professional Training" section of the *JoA*. Carol Cox, presentation on William Campfield at African American Doctoral Student Association meeting, Chicago, 16 August 1996; Philip E. Fess, "Educational Opportunities for Disadvantaged Groups," *JoA* 130, no. 4 (1970): 102–3.

51. Carol Cox, presentation on William Campfield at African American Doctoral Student Association meeting, Chicago, 16 August 1996; Craig interview; Gary Previts, e-mail to author, 15 August 1999; Previts interview.

52. In 1996, Harvard University had no African American accounting doctoral students, had no African American accounting faculty, and had never awarded an accounting doctorate to an African American (out of a total of ninety-seven graduates); survey conducted by author; Harvard results verified via e-mail by Robert S. Kaplan of the Harvard Business School. Thirty-four of the eighty-seven accounting doctoral-granting programs extant in 1996 had similar records: no students, no faculty, no graduates.

53. Milton Wilson interview, 24 June 1999.

54. Records compiled by author. E-mail from George Gamble, professor of accounting at the University of Houston, 23 June 1999; Milton Wilson interview, 24 June 1999.

55. Hale also became president of the National Beta Alpha Psi fraternity and a member of council at both the American Accounting Association and the AICPA. In 1993, Hale became the first African American member of the Utah Board of Regents, which governs public universities in that state; Hale interview; *Biography, Larzette G. Hale*, program of KPMG PhD Project Meeting, Chicago, Ill., November 1996; Lili Wright, "A Brief History of Blacks in Utah," *Salt Lake Tribune*, 27 March 1994, A13.

56. Porter, "Negro Publicly-Supported Higher Institutions in Florida"; Young, "Negro Participation"; V. V. Oak, "Our Aimless Business Education," *The Crisis* 44 (September 1937): 264–65, 277; Jenkins, "Significant Programs," 311. See also V. V. Oak, "Business Education in Negro Colleges," *The Crisis* 45 (June 1938): 175–76, 190, and Pierce, *Negro Business*.

57. Petrof, "Business Administration Curricula"; Bert Mitchell, "The Black Minority in the CPA Profession," *JoA* 128, no. 4 (1969): 42; "Equal Opportunity in Education," *JoA* 132, no. 6 (1971): 37; William Gifford, "Black Accountants," *Price Waterhouse Review* 18, no. 2 (1973): 49; Bayer, *Black College Freshman*, 40–42.

58. Bert Mitchell, "The Black Minority in the CPA Profession," *JoA* 128, no. 4 (1969): 42.

59. By 1973, a total of 1,525 Ph.D.'s had been granted in accounting; Hasselback, *Accounting Faculty Directory*, 73. The eleven African Americans were those listed in note 28 plus Talmadge Tillman, Southern California, 1968; Herbert Watkins, Wisconsin, 1970; Quiester Craig, Missouri, 1971; and Johnnie Clark, Georgia, 1973.

60. Terry, *Origin and Development*, 60.

61. Asgill, "Importance of Accreditation"; Howard Simmons, "Accreditation Process."

62. *American Association of Collegiate Schools of Business*, 98–145; Gordon and Howell, *Higher Education for Business*, 446; Le Breton, *Dynamic World*, 229–39; Pierson et al., *Education of American Business*, 50–52, 355–91. In later years the requirements became more stringent.

63. Terry, *Origin and Development*, 87, 89, 95.

64. Basalla, "African Americans," 82. A 1966 study identified eight "Negro" colleges as "elite": Xavier, Howard, Lincoln (Pennsylvania), Fisk, Morehouse, Hampton, Lincoln (Missouri), and Central State (Ohio); Jaffe, Adams, and Meyers, *Negro Higher Education*, 242; advertisement for Howard University, *The Crisis* 42 (February 1955): 118; Monroe W. Karmin, "Black Capitalism: Nixon's Plan to Assist Minority Entrepreneurs Makes Faltering Start," *WSJ*, 10 July 1969, 1; Milton Wilson interview, 2 May 1999; Brian W. Mosley, "Howard's Business School Accredited," *Washington Post*, 7 July 1980, 14; "Howard Business Students Move to New $13 Million Facility," *Washington Post*, 24 September 1984, 9.

65. Craig interview.

66. Bowles and DeCosta, *Between Two Worlds*, 295; Branch, *Parting the Waters*, 271–75.

67. In 1959, the A&T College had been accredited by the Southern Association of Colleges and Schools; in 1969, the School of Engineering was accredited by the Engineers' Council for Professional Development; and in 1971 the School of Nursing was accredited by the National League for Nursing; "Historical Milestones," *North Carolina A&T University Founders' Day Convocation Program*, 22 October 1997 (copy provided by Ida Robinson Backmon).

68. Ibid.; Roscoe, *Accreditation*, 45–47; *Policies, Procedures and Standards*.

69. Harris, "Publicly-Supported Negro Higher Institutions of Learning in North Carolina"; Spruill, *Great Recollections for Aggieland*, 113–14.

70. A 1999 A&T brochure indicates that twelve of thirteen faculty members in the accounting department are CPAs and the thirteenth is a certified management accountant; *Building a Foundation for a Successful Accounting Career*, pamphlet, Department of Accounting, School of Business and Economics, N.C. A&T State University, 1999 (copy provided by Ida Robinson Backmon).

71. William Aiken, "Progress Report, 1971–1973," *Spectrum* (Winter 1974): 2; *Historical Milestones, North Carolina A&T University Founders' Day Convocation Program*, 22 October 1997 (copy provided by Ida Robinson Backmon); Craig interview; Bert Mitchell and Virginia Flintall, "The Status of the Black CPA: Twenty-Year Update," *JoA* 170, no. 2 (1990): 59–69. Five percent is a conservative estimate based on the number of A&T graduates who are CPAs, Mitchell and Flintall's estimate of 2,500 black CPAs in 1989, and data from the AICPA's annual *Report on Minority Accounting Graduates, Enrollment and Public Accounting Professionals*, AICPA Library. This report indicates stagnation in new African American hires by major public accounting firms in the 1990s, though it does not attempt to estimate the total number of African American CPAs.

CHAPTER SEVEN

1. "Big Board Admits a Black," *WSJ*, 13 February 1970, 6; "General Motors Names a Negro to Board, First Such Appointment in Auto Industry," *WSJ*, 5 January 1971, 6; "Black-Controlled Firm Is Formally Admitted as Big Board Member," *WSJ*, 25 January 1971, 20. See also Freeman, *Black Elite*.

2. Bert Mitchell's column, called "Bottom Line," included the following articles: "The Operational Budget," *BE*, July 1972, 48; "The Profit Break-Even Point," *BE*, August 1972, 53; "Financial Management of Non-Profit Organizations," *BE*, September 1972,

52; "Estate Planning," *BE*, October 1972, 21–22; "Credit Management," *BE*, October 1972, 22–23; "Tax Planning," *BE*, October 1972, 62; "Computerized Accounting for the Small Business," *BE*, November 1972, 53; "Filing for an SBA Loan," *BE*, January 1973, 44; "Financing a Business," *BE*, February 1973, 47; "Equity Financing," *BE*, March 1973, 70; "Short Term Financing," *BE*, May 1973, 50; "Cost Accounting," *BE*, June 1973, 124; "Going into a New Business—Many Pitfalls," *BE*, July 1973, 54; "Financial Statements as a Management Tool," *BE*, August 1973, 43; "How to Avoid Corporate Income Tax," *BE*, September 1973, 61; "Profits, Costs, and Sale Pricing," *BE*, November 1973, 66; "How to Read a Balance Sheet," *BE*, February 1974, 52; "Bigger Profits through Better Merchandise Management," *BE*, March 1974, 70; "Should a Professional Incorporate?" *BE*, May 1974, 50; "A Way to Cut Your Taxes," *BE*, June 1974, 150.

Frank Ross's Personal Finance column included "Starting Now on '73 Taxes," *BE*, April 1973, 56; "The Family Budget," *BE*, May 1973, 51; "Buying on Credit," *BE*, June 1973, 21; "Investing in Stocks," *BE*, July 1973, 56; "Planning Your Estate," *BE*, August 1973, 44; "What Makes You a Good Credit Risk?" *BE*, October 1973, 14; "Year-End Tax Planning," *BE*, November 1973, 14; "How to Stretch Your Health Insurance Dollar," *BE*, February 1974, 54; "Three Ways of Saving," *BE*, March 1974, 12; "The Smart Shopper's Guide," *BE*, May 1974, 49; "You and the Social Security Act," *BE*, June 1974, 149; "Buying a House," *BE*, July 1974, 33. The centrality of the African American CPA to black business was further underscored by articles such as "It's Up to You How Much Your Accountant Helps Your Business," *BE*, October 1976, 41–45.

3. Most of these employees were not yet CPAs; they were earning the experience requirement in order to *become* CPAs; William Gifford, "Accounting's Aim," *Journal of College Placement*, Winter 1975, 40–45.

4. Schneider, *Availability of Minorities and Women*, 80; William Aiken, "Reflections of NABA: The Formative Years," *Spectrum*, Fall/Winter 1992, 12–14; Bert Mitchell, "The Status of the Black CPA—An Update," *JoA* 41, no. 5 (1976): 52–58; Lisa Chapman, "College Recruitment '73: Economy Lift and Affirmative Action Lend New Hope to Grads," *BE*, March 1973, 37. Most members of NABA, which is open to all financial professionals, are not CPAs.

5. *Proceedings, Eighty-Ninth Annual Meeting of the AICPA*, 23 October 1976, 32–54, AICPA Library; "Minority Groups Join in Accounting Seminar," *JoA* 138, no. 1 (1974): 14.

6. "Mitchell/Titus Partner Named to State Board," *PR Newswire*, 9 May 1983; "Bert N. Mitchell," *New York Daily Challenge*, 7 November 1975, 4; "Bert N. Mitchell on Governing Council of CPA Institute," *New York Amsterdam News*, 7 October 1972, A2.

7. *NABA Second Annual Awards Dinner*, program, 16 February 1973, New York (copy provided by Talmadge Tillman). "Panelists Discuss the Black Accountant," *JoA* 131, no. 2 (1971): 20; *Conceptual Framework for Financial Accounting and Reporting: Present and Future*, pamphlet, 26–30 April 1976, Pennsylvania State University (copy provided by George Gamble).

8. *Black Enterprise*, other African American periodicals, and the mainstream press also noted the changes: "Mitchell/Titus Partner Named to State Board," *PR Newswire*, 9 May 1983; "Bert N. Mitchell," *New York Daily Challenge*, 7 November 1975, 4; "Bert N.

Mitchell on Governing Council of CPA Institute," *New York Amsterdam News*, 7 October 1972, A2; "Names in the News," *BE*, August 1974, 8; "Names in the News," *BE*, January 1976, 15; "Names in the News," *BE*, October 1975, 13; "Names in the News," *BE*, November 1976, 10; "Names in the News," *BE*, February 1977, 15; "Names in the News," *BE*, July 1977, 6; "Names in the News," *BE*, September 1977, 12; "Names in the News," *BE*, December 1977, 9; "CPA Urges Black Capitalism to Broaden Whole Outlook," *New York Amsterdam News*, 2 January 1971, 4; "Black Accounting Firm Opens New Offices," *New York Amsterdam News*, 11 December 1971, D12; Stephen Collins, "Blacks in the Profession," *JoA* 165, no. 2 (1988): 38–44; *Who's Who in Finance and Industry*; Richard Rogin, "John Henry Howell Makes It (into the Middle Class)," *NYT Magazine*, 24 June 1973, Schomburg Center Clipping File: Accountants.

9. James Nolan, "Black CPA Advances from Beginner to Partner," *JoA* 137, no. 6 (1974): 24–30. Ernst & Ernst admitted the first black partner in the Big Eight when it purchased Elmer Whiting's firm in Cleveland. Goodall, however, is different from Whiting in that he started with Lester Witte when he graduated from college.

10. Ibid., 24.

11. Ibid., 28.

12. Ibid.

13. Goodall interview. Goodall left the firm in the 1980s and in 1997 opened his own CPA firm, Goodall, Jefferson & Kenner. One of his clients was his former employer, the Chicago Transit Authority.

14. "Accounting Firms Cited in Complaint on Trust Violations," *WSJ*, 26 July 1979, 28.

15. Smigel, *Wall Street Lawyer*, 45. This would have been virtually impossible in a large CPA firm.

16. William Aiken, "The Black Experience in Large Public Accounting Firms," *JoA* 134, no. 2 (1972): 60–63. Responding to the survey were 128 men and 18 women; James Nolan, "Black Accounting Firm Faces Future," *JoA* 131, no. 3 (1971): 22–26. The survey was sent to 314 black accountants in large firms.

17. Anonymous interviews with four white male recruiting managers for Big Eight firms, May 1989.

18. David Satterfield, "Black CPAs: A Shrinking Minority," *Miami Herald*, 10 June 1984, F1.

19. Booker interview.

20. McFadden interview; "BEEP: Black Executive Exchange Program Brings Corporate Reality to Campus," *BE*, March 1972, 67–70.

21. Allan Gold, "Miami Company Is One of the Country's Few Black Accounting Firms," *Miami Herald*, 20 October 1980, sect. 6, p. 7; *Career Development Seminar Report, 1978*, AICPA Library.

22. There are several national firms that are not Big Eight firms.

23. The authors surveyed every office of the national firms, so, for example, these twenty-six "firms" may include a few offices from a single Big Eight firm; David Dennis and William Stephens, "Recruitment and Utilization of Minority-Group Members," *JoA* 141 no. 5 (1976): 64–73.

24. In regards to assigning women to jobs, 26 percent "always" or "frequently" considered client reaction, and 30 percent "never" considered client reaction. Nine of twenty-four

firms said they "infrequently" encountered negative client reaction and fifteen of twenty-four "never" encountered such reaction. Because only one local firm employed an African American, questions about job assignments were not tallied for this group.

25. David Dennis and William Stephens, "Recruitment and Utilization of Minority-Group Members," *JoA* 141, no. 5 (1976): 64–73.When asked the same question about a (presumably white) woman, all firms replied that they would hire the candidate.

26. Montagna, *Certified Public Accounting*, 15–89.

27. "Black Accounting Firms," *BE*, February 1972, 30–34; "Miami Company Is One of the Country's Few Black Accounting Firms," *Miami Herald*, 20 October 1980, B7; Dolores Barclay, "Up Against the Big Eight," *BE*, October 1981, 47–52; "Limits for Blacks in Business Seen: Chances for Professionals to Advance Said to Be Poor," *NYT*, 11 September 1973, 21; "CPA Aims for $1 Million," *BE*, September 1973, 14. Frank Ross, one of the founders of NABA, was one of the prominent African American CPAs who left Big Eight firms to start their own firms; *Profile: Frank K. Ross, Community Leader*, pamphlet, KPMG Peat Marwick, ca. 1990 (copy provided by Frank Ross).

28. Bert Mitchell, "The Status of the Black CPA—An Update," *JoA* 141, no. 5 (1976): 52–58.

29. Mitchell interview.

30. Bert Mitchell, "Financial Management of Non-Profit Organizations," *BE* , September 1972, 52.

31. James Nolan, "Black Accounting Firm Faces Future," *JoA* 131, no. 3 (1971): 22–26.

32. Alix Freedman, "Polyglot among Accountants," *NYT*, 17 August 1980, sect. 3, p. 9; *1995 Distinguished Service and Alumni Achievement Awards*, Harvard Business School, 1995 (copy provided by Bert Mitchell); "Hearing of the Senate Governmental Affairs Committee: Financial Management of the Federal Government," *Federal News Service*, 15 December 1995; "Firm Gets $4 Million Contract," *New York Amsterdam News*, 22 March 1986, 4; "NYC Agency Audits go to Minority Firms," *JoA* 166, no. 3 (1988): 142, 144; Gail Collins, "Successful Black CPA Encourages Minority Entrants in His Field," *United Press International*, 7 April 1981; Bert Mitchell, "How to Revive Black Business," *Newsday*, 7 September 1988, 56; Matthew Scott, "2 Decades in the Black," *BE*, October 1994, 150–55; "Names in the News," *BE*, June 1973, 14. All this work—120 to 140 hours a week—took a toll on Bert Mitchell, who had a heart attack in 1978 when he was only 36; Errol Louis, "An Accountant and His Finances," *BE*, October 1986, 42–48. In 1986, when its revenues topped $5 million, Mitchell's firm became too large to qualify for special status under the Small Business Administration's programs.

33. Francis Ward, "Black CPAs in America," *PUSH Magazine*, Fall 1991, 16–21, 56. It was when he became involved with Chicago United that Pittman joined the Illinois Society of CPAs and the AICPA. See chapter 3.

34. Steven Roberts, "New Negro Mayors Make 'Black Power' Daily Reality," *NYT*, 23 May 1969, 49; Francis Ward, "Black CPAs in America," *PUSH Magazine*, Fall 1991, 16–21, 56; Chinta Strausberg, "New Team to Audit City's Books," *Chicago Defender*, 26 November 1986, 3; McKeever interview; "Washington, Pittman & McKeever CPAs," brochure, 1992 (copy provided by Lester McKeever). David Wilkins has found a similar connection between black lawyers and black politicians; Richard Zitrin and Carol M. Langford, "Waving the Flag," *San Francisco Recorder*, 15 March 2000, 6. See also Wilkins and Gulati, "Why Are There So Few," and Wilkins, "Identities and Roles."

35. Russell Grantham, "An 'Ordinary Man' Can Get Extraordinary Things Done; Banks Made Dreams Come True for African Americans," *Commercial Appeal*, 4 April 1999, C1; Diane Weathers, "The Fast Rise of Banks, Finley, Thomas and White," *BE*, January 1978, 46–50. When Harold Ford Sr. was elected the first African American congressman from Tennessee in 1974, Banks's firm oversaw the voting process for Ford. When Banks's records did not match those of the television stations, who were declaring Ford's opponent, a white Republican, the winner, he and his colleagues went to the election commission building to reconcile the vote discrepancy. It was determined that the votes for one of the black precincts had not been counted.

36. A contemporaneous *NYT* article pointed out that private enterprises that had government contracts were more likely to hire African Americans than those that did not have such contracts; "For a Negro, a Place in Private Enterprise," *NYT*, 19 October 1967, 67.

37. Marvel Turner, e-mail to author, 19 March 2001.

38. Thomas Watkins, "New CPA Head," *New York Daily Challenge*, 3 May 1978, 4.

39. Bruno interview; Greg M. Thibadoux, Raymond Jeffords, and Ira Greenberg, "Plugging into Minority Markets," *JoA* 178, no. 3 (1994): 50–56. In 1993, Bruno was instrumental in founding the Harrison-Rochon Educational Foundation, named for the first two African American CPAs in Louisiana, to provide scholarships to African Americans pursuing accounting majors; documents of the Harrison-Rochon Educational Foundation (copies provided by Michael Bruno).

40. Brian Dickerson, "The Numbers Game Adds Up for Accounting Firms," *Miami Herald*, 28 December 1981, 1.

41. U.S. Senate, Committee on Government Operations, *The Accounting Establishment*, 845–75: Arthur Andersen responded that its first two African American partners *would be* admitted later in the year of the request and offered the following analysis: "Prior to the mid-sixties there were only a limited number of women and blacks graduating from universities with appropriate qualifications for employment in the public accounting profession. . . . Considering the relatively recent entry of women and blacks into the public accounting profession, the development period required to achieve partnership status and our personnel retention experience, we only now are reaching the point in time when there should be an increasing number of women and blacks available for partnership consideration." Haskins & Sells reported that it had no black partners. Like Arthur Andersen and Ernst & Ernst, it stressed the timing of the question: "The partners admitted in the United States this year averaged 12 years of experience with Haskins & Sells. . . . We have found that minority group members who have earned their CPA certificates are particularly attractive to the business and professional community. In spite of our efforts to retain and promote these individuals, many are attracted by different responsibilities or by higher salaries, and so choose to leave public accounting. . . . We hope that you recognize the challenges we face and the commitments we have made to emphasize equal opportunity. We believe that many of the minority group members we have hired and whom we now are training and helping to develop will choose to remain with Haskins & Sells, and that they will demonstrate the abilities and judgment we require for admission as partners." Coopers & Lybrand stated: "Your other request with respect to the numbers of women and black partners

raises grave questions since it is hard for us to recognize any plausible nexus between the requested information and the jurisdiction of your Subcommittee, or to understand the omission of reference to other minorities. Nevertheless, we are willing to report that we are an equal opportunity employer with a strong affirmative action program and a record of subsidizing minority scholarships and related educational assistance in the accounting field. Accordingly, our organization includes minorities at all levels. [Coopers & Lybrand provides a table indicating that, of 611 partners, 2 were women, 1 was black, 7 were "Oriental," and 8 were "Spanish Surname."] Since discrimination for creed no longer seems to be, no relevant statistics are given. However we have large numbers of Jewish and Roman Catholic people at all levels. It should also be recognized that membership in the management group reflects the impact of educational realities of the past few decades." Peat, Marwick, Mitchell & Company provided a copy of the report it was required to file with the Equal Employment Opportunity Commission, which identified 14 "Negro" "Officials and Managers." By combining managers and partners together, the firm avoided the question of whether any of its *partners* were African American. Peat, Marwick, Mitchell stated: "Each of the offices has an Affirmative Action Program meeting the requirements of the EEO regulations. The Firm is rather proud of the progress made over the past few years. For example, you will notice from the enclosed statistics that women and minority group persons are represented at all staff levels within the Firm."

42. William Aiken, "The Black Experience in Large Public Accounting Firms," *JoA* 134, no. 2 (1972): 60–63.

43. *Career Development Seminar Report 1978*, AICPA Library.

44. Whiting interview.

45. Ibid.; "From an Ideal to a Fact," *E&E*, Summer 1971, 25–28; Joe Cramer and Robert Strawser, "Perception of Selected Job Related Factors by Black CPAs," *CPA Journal*, February 1972, 129. Although within a few years women made up a substantial portion of CPA firm hires, in the very early 1970s it was still unusual for the Big Eight to hire women. On different experiences for male and female African Americans in this period, see "BEEP: Black Executive Exchange Program Brings Corporate Reality to Campus," *BE*, March 1972, 67–70.

46. Anthony Lewis, "A White Enclave?" *NYT*, 17 February 1977, 39; Tom Goldstein, "Minority Admissions Defended by Report," *NYT*, 24 July 1977, 27; Edward B. Fiske, "Report Backs Colleges on Use of Race as Entry Criterion," *NYT*, 12 October 1977, sect. 2, p. 12; Steven Roberts, "Educators Fear a Ruling for Bakke Would Undo Minorities' Vast Gains," *NYT*, 25 October 1977, 1; Schwartz, *Behind Bakke*; "U.S. Aid Suggests Business Rethink Affirmative Action," *WSJ*, 30 June 1978, 4.

47. Glazer, *Affirmative Discrimination*; Duker and Grinnell, "Accountancy"; Joel Dreyfuss, "The New Racism," *BE*, January 1978, 41–54.

48. Stevens, *The Big Eight*, 47.

49. Bound and Freeman, "What Went Wrong?"; Scott Jaschik, "College Outlook Grim for Blacks 25 Years after Barriers Fell," *Chronicle of Higher Education*, 2 September 1987, A88; Carolyn Mooney, "Only 4 Black Americans Said to Have Earned Math Ph.D.s in 1987–88," *Chronicle of Higher Education*, 2 August 1989, A11; Howard French, "Business Schools Warned on Decline in Minorities," *NYT*, 13 December 1987, sect. 1, p. 35; Bil-

lingsley, "Building Strong Faculties in Black Colleges"; Allen, "Mobility of Black Collegiate Faculty Revisited"; Claudia Deutsch, "The Ax Falls on Equal Opportunity," *NYT*, 4 January 1987, sect. 3, p. 1. For a discussion of moving women and African Americans to support positions, see Kanter, *Men and Women of the Corporation*, 55, 233. Things were also dismal in the mid-1980s for African Americans graduating from law school: "[A]t NYU . . . Forty-two second- and third-year black law students had a total of 1,132 on-campus job interviews [in fall 1982]; only nine of these interviews led to offers"; David Margolick, "The Blue-Chip Firms Remain Mostly White," *NYT*, 13 February 1983, sect. 4, p. 18.

50. Ronald Roel, "Will Rulings Make It Harder to Move Up?: High Court Decisions Seen as Possible Threat to Affirmative Action," *Newsday*, 26 June 1989, 1; Earl Graves, "The Erosion of Civil Rights by the Supreme Court," *BE*, September 1984, 9; Hasty, "Minority Business Enterprise Development"; Rogers, "When Logic and Reality Collide"; Mitchell interview; Bruce Holbrook and Marilynn Moschel, "Joint Ventures—A Profitable Relationship," *Practicing CPA*, December 1985, 1, 3.

51. Christopher C. Williams, "Promising Prospects Despite Recent Setbacks," *NYT*, 12 November 1989, sect. 3, p. 5; Bert Mitchell, "How to Revive Black Business," *Newsday*, 7 September 1988, 56.

52. One exception to this 1980s erosion came in 1984 when Dade County, Florida, limited its accounting contracts to firms that had black managers or partners or firms that joint ventured with black-owned CPA firms; David Satterfield, "Black CPAs: A Shrinking Minority," *Miami Herald*, 10 June 1984, F1.

53. Hedi Molnar, "Accounting for Blacks," *NYT*, 8 June 1986, sect. 6, p. 26; *Report on the Status of Blacks*; Bert Mitchell, "How to Revive Black Business," *Newsday*, 7 September 1988, 56. In 1985, Bert Mitchell and others started a new organization, the Association of Black CPA Firms (ABCPAF); "Association of Black CPA Firms," *CPA Journal*, October 1985, 10.

54. Bert N. Mitchell and Virginia L. Flintall, "The Status of the Black CPA: Twenty-Year Update," *JoA* 170, no. 2 (1990): 59–69.

55. There were four African American partners at Arthur Andersen, two at Coopers & Lybrand, and one each at Peat, Marwick and Mitchell; Arthur Young; and Ernst & Whinney (formerly Ernst & Ernst). Price Waterhouse, Haskins & Sells, and Touche, Ross had no African American partners; Chris Benson, "Blacks in Accounting," *Ebony*, March 1981, 86–92; David Satterfield, "Black CPAs: A Shrinking Minority," *Miami Herald*, 10 June 1984, F1.

56. *Report on Minority Accounting Graduates, Enrollment and Public Accounting Professionals* (1976–89), AICPA Library; Linda C. Bowen, "Social Responsiveness of the Accounting Profession," *CPA Journal*, June 1978, 29–35; "AICPA Report Shows the Profession Hasn't Integrated," *Public Accounting Report*, May 1983, 5–6; Celia Herron, "How Can We Interest These People in Accounting?" *Outlook* 49, no. 2 (1981): 31–36; Hammond, "From Complete Exclusion to Minimal Inclusion," 42.

57. Francis Ward, "Black CPAs in America," *PUSH Magazine*, Fall 1991, 16–21, 56; Marya Ostrowski, "Minorities in Accounting," *New Accountant*, February 1986, 7–12, 41; David Dennis and William Stephens, "Recruitment and Utilization of Minority-Group Members," *JoA* 141, no. 5 (1976): 64–73; *Upward Mobility of Women Special Committee*

Report to the AICPA Board of Directors 1988, AICPA Library; William Aiken and Helen Brown, "Are Black Accountants Mainstreaming?" *New Accountant*, February 1989, 18–24, 48; Celia Herron, "How Can We Interest These People in Accounting?" *Outlook* 49, no. 2 (1981): 31–36; *Report on Minority Accounting Graduates, Enrollment and Public Accounting Professionals* (1976–89), AICPA Library; Mitchell, "Ethics, the Black Minority, and the CPA Profession," 7–8. By the end of the period, women constituted 32 percent of all professionals in the firms. Native American underrepresentation, however, is more abysmal than any other group.

58. *Report on Minority Accounting Graduates, Enrollment and Public Accounting Professionals* (1976–89), AICPA Library. Data on total turnover rates is unavailable. See also Alvin Lieberman and R. Penny Marquette, "Student Attitudes toward Careers in Accounting: The Problem of Minority Recruitment," *Ohio CPA Journal*, Summer 1986, 27–30, 51–53; "AICPA Report Shows the Profession Hasn't Integrated," *Public Accounting Report*, May 1983, 5–6; David Satterfield, "Black CPAs: A Shrinking Minority," *Miami Herald*, 10 June 1984, F1.

59. William Aiken and Helen Brown, "Are Black Accountants Mainstreaming?" *New Accountant*, February 1989, 18–24, 48; Hammond, "From Complete Exclusion to Minimal Inclusion"; interviews with six African American partners in the largest New York firms, May 1989. All interviewees were willing to speak only on condition of anonymity. From 1920 through 1968 there were a total of five articles on African Americans listed in the *Accountants Indexes*; in the 1970s, the *Indexes* listed fifty-six articles; in the 1980s the *Indexes* listed forty-two such articles. This decline is despite an almost 50 percent increase in the number of articles indexed—approximately 600,000 in the 1970s and approximately 900,000 in the 1980s.

60. "Minority Scholarship Amount Sets Record," *JoA* 167, no. 5 (1989): 31; Stephen Collins, "Blacks in the Profession," *JoA* 165, no. 2 (1988): 38–44; Frank Ross, "Reflections on NABA's First Twenty Years and a Challenge for Its Future," *Spectrum*, Spring 1990, 16–17.

61. Marya Ostrowski, "Minority Networking," *New Accountant*, February 1987, 12–16.

62. Jenkins interview; Tracy Herman, "Overcoming Barriers," *New Accountant*, February 1988, 8–12, 48; Ronald Leverett and Thaddeus Spratlen, "Accounting Career Awareness Programs: The First Ten Years," *Spectrum*, Spring 1991, 40–45; Rhoda Gilinsky, "Accounting Opportunities," *NYT*, 26 June 1988, sect. 12WC, p. 3; Mitchell, "Ethics, the Black Minority, and the CPA Profession," 7–8; Marya Ostrowski, "Minority Networking," *New Accountant*, February 1987, 12–16.

63. Frank Ross, "Reflections on NABA's First Twenty Years and a Challenge for Its Future," *Spectrum*, Spring 1990, 16–17.

64. Stephen Collins, "Blacks in the Profession," *JoA* 165, no. 2 (1988): 38, 40–44; "Mitchell/Titus Partner Named to State Board," *PR Newswire*, 9 May 1983; "Mitchell Heads New York Accountants," *World Accounting Report*, May 1987, 8. Not all the coverage on Moultrie was positive; he had disputes over fees with the Jackson Five during its "Victory Tour"; Dennis McDougal, "The Thriller of 'Victory,'" *Los Angeles Times*, 6 January 1985, 3.

65. Bert N. Mitchell and Virginia L. Flintall, "The Status of the Black CPA: Twenty Year Update," *JoA* 170, no. 2 (1990): 59–69; Julia Lawlor, "Blacks Counted Out of Accounting, Study Says," *USA Today*, 9 August 1990, B1.

CHAPTER EIGHT

1. In the interest of full disclosure, I have been involved with several of the initiatives described in this chapter. I have been a member of NABA since 1988. I served on the AICPA's Minority Initiatives Committee from 1995–98. I was a cofounder of the African American Accounting Doctoral Student Association, now part of the PhD Project, and I was the co-coordinator of the PhD Project's first annual meeting of African American Doctoral Students in accounting. I have not received research funding from any of these organizations. Since 1996 my research has been supported by Big Five firm Ernst & Young.

2. *Report on Minority Accounting Graduates, Enrollment and Public Accounting Professionals* (1997), AICPA Library. Until 2001, when a white woman was appointed, the Financial Accounting Standards Board maintained its composition of seven white men. A 1990 article discussed the possibility of appointing a woman or a minority to the FASB; "Practitioner's Update," *Practical Accountant*, September 1990, 14, 16. For current composition of the FASB, see www.FASB.org.

3. "United to Pay $1.7 Million in Pilot Hiring Discrimination Settlement," *Aviation Daily*, 23 May 1994, 293; "USAir Agrees to $1.8 Million Settlement in Piedmont Case," *Aviation Daily*, 8 May 1992, 238; "Northwest Is Closing Gap in Hiring of Women, Minorities," *Minneapolis Star Tribune*, 6 July 1998, A1.

4. Twice the percentage of black men as black women perceived this bias.

5. *Report on the Status of Blacks.*

6. Ibid.; data provided for 1994 by the Equal Employment Opportunity Commission. At 11 percent female in 1965, there was a higher proportion of women among African American CPAs than among white CPAs at the time. In the late 1990s that phenomenon was even more marked: 70 percent of the African Americans hired by major CPA firms were women; "Minority Women Tend to Dominate," *International Accounting Bulletin*, 14 February 1997, 2.

7. Forrest Thompson, "Performance of CPA Candidates from Historically Black Colleges and Universities," *Spectrum*, Fall/Winter 1991, 36–40.

8. Judy Anne Ramage and Howard Lawrence, "The 150-Hour Education Requirement," *New Accountant*, April 1994, 16–17, 26; "Jackson Rips 150-Hour Law," *Accounting Today*, 8 June 1992, 1; Virginia Flintall, "The 150-Hour Requirement," *JoA* 176, no. 4 (1993) 95–101; "NABA Chief Demands More Roles for Blacks," *Accounting Today*, 7 September 1992, 2; Forrest Thompson, "Performance of CPA Candidates from Historically Black Colleges and Universities," *Spectrum*, Fall/Winter 1991, 36–40; Nathan Garrett, "Bringing Minorities into Public Accounting," *New Accountant*, February 1990, 16–18, 34; "Special Issue on the 150-Hour Requirement," *Spectrum*, 1998.

9. Virginia Flintall, "The 150-Hour Requirement," *JoA* 176, no. 4 (1993): 95–101.

10. Ibid.; *Report on the Status of Blacks.*

11. Virginia Flintall, "The 150-Hour Requirement," *JoA* 176, no. 4 (1993): 101; emphasis added.

12. Ibid., 96.

13. "News and Views," *CPA Journal*, May 1995, 10; "AICPA Testified before Labor Depart-

ment," *Public Accounting Report*, 28 February 1994, 2; "Briefings," *Public Accounting Report*, 15 October 1993, 8.

14. Philip Chenok, "AICPA Strategic Thrusts for the Future," *JoA* 173, no. 1 (1992), 75–83. Minority recruitment was one of the AICPA's "high-priority thrusts."

15. See chapter 5.

16. See Greg Thibadoux, Raymond Jeffords, and Ira Greenberg, "Plugging into Minority Markets," *JoA* 178, no. 3 (1994): 50–56; Theresa Hammond and Kenneth Paige, "Still Seeking the Ideal," *JoA* 188, no. 3 (1999): 75–79; Catherine L. Carlozzi, "Diversity Is Good for Business," *JoA* 188, no. 3 (1999): 81–86. The use of this justification is not confined to accounting. See Weems, *Desegregating the Dollar*, 101–31.

17. www.ey.com; www.kpmgcampus.com; www.deloitte.com; www.pwcglobal.com; www.andersen.com.

18. James Emerson, "KPMG Peat Marwick," *Professional Services Review*, July/August 1994, 1; "Peat Marwick commits over $1 Million for Black Doctoral Candidates," *Accounting Today*, 15 November 1993, 8.

19. "D&T Employees Charge Race Discrimination," *Public Accounting Report*, 15 June 1995, 3; "Women in the Profession—1995," *Public Accounting Report*, 15 June 1995, 5; Elaine Song, "Appleton v. Deloitte & Touche," *Connecticut Law Tribune*, 7 August 1995, 14; "5 Blacks File Class-Action Discrimination Lawsuit against Deloitte & Touche," *Chattanooga Free Press*, 14 May 1995, 1. The judge denied class-action certification for this lawsuit; *Rose Appleton et al. v. Deloitte & Touche L.L.P.*, 168 FRD 221 (1996).

20. "The Changing Demographics of Accounting Firms," *Practical Accountant*, March 1996, 10; Allen Boston and Warren Rappleyea, "Ernst & Young Congratulates NABA on its Silver Anniversary," *Spectrum*, Spring/Summer 1995, 13–16; Betty Maple, "How to Succeed in the Corporate World," *Spectrum*, 1996, 15–19.

21. Graham, *Best Companies for Minorities*, 158–63; "Briefings," *Public Accounting Report*, 15 January 1994, 5.

22. Other ads feature athletes with CPAs of other minority groups; "Star Ads Promote the Profession," *JoA* 187, no. 2 (1999): 69.

23. Hammond, "Some Considerations"; Blackwell, *Mainstreaming Outsiders*.

24. "The Ph.D. Project Accounting Doctoral Students Association Records," KPMG Foundation, Montvale, N.J. (copy provided by Tara Perino); *Summary Report*.

25. Hammond, "Some Considerations." In 1992, 197 people earned Ph.D.'s in accounting in the United States; in 1998, 124 people did so; Hasselback, *Accounting Faculty Directory*, 73.

26. Hammond, "Some Considerations."

27. "The Ph.D. Project Accounting Doctoral Students Association Records," KPMG Foundation, Montvale, N.J. (copy provided by Tara Perino). The five HBCUs that had accreditation when KPMG launched its program were Clark Atlanta University, Howard University, Norfolk State, North Carolina A&T, and Tennessee State. The six that received accreditation with support from the KPMG foundation are Jackson State, Morehouse College, Morgan State, Southern University at Baton Rouge, Tuskegee, and Winston-Salem State.

28. "KPMG Named among Top 15 for Support of Minority Education," *Infotrack*, 7 Septem-

ber 1999, 1; "Organizations That Made (and Are Making) a Difference," *Black Issues in Higher Education*, 19 August 1999, 102.

29. Richard Morin, "Poll Shows a Divided America," *Washington Post*, 19 July 1995, A1; Jonathan Kaufman, "White Men Shake Off That Losing Feeling on Affirmative Action," *WSJ*, 5 September 1996, 1; "Poll: Whites Increasingly Accept Blacks," *USA Today*, 11 June 1997, A1; "In Poll, Americans Reject Means but Not Ends of Racial Diversity," *NYT*, 14 December 1997, sect. 1, p. 1; Patterson, *Ordeal of Integration*. The biggest setback to affirmative action in higher education, the Supreme Court's 1996 *Hopwood v. Texas* decision, was brought by Cheryl Hopwood against the University of Texas law school. Hopwood is a CPA; Stephen Chapman, "Diversity Can Foster Racial Bias," *Charleston Post and Courier*, 2 April 1996, A11.

30. Studies indicate that preference for hiring and mentoring whites over equally qualified African Americans continued into the 1990s; Khan, Chawla, and Devine, "Impact of Gender, Race, and Dress"; Viator, "An Examination." In *JoA* 188, no. 3 (1999) there are two articles on diversity in the profession: Theresa Hammond and Kenneth Paige, "Still Seeking the Ideal," 75–79, and Catherine L. Carlozzi, "Diversity Is Good for Business," 81–86. The only two letters to the editor *JoA* published in response to these articles criticized race-based recruiting efforts; William N. McNairn, "Letters to the Journal: Human Diversity More Than Skin Color," *JoA* 188, no. 6 (1999): 104; Keith Frazier, "Letters to the Journal: Diversity or Discrimination," *JoA* 188, no. 6 (1999): 103.

31. In 1998, the *Wall Street Journal* reported on the strong connection between Jewish chief executive officers of major corporations and the promotion of black executives; Jonathan Kaufman, "As Blacks Rise High in the Executive Suite, CEO Is Often Jewish," *WSJ*, 22 April 1998, 1. For an excellent analysis of other factors in the promotion of African American executives, see Thomas and Gabarro, *Breaking Through*.

32. Bradford Smith, "Making a Difference," *Accounting Today*, 1 February 1993, 1, 24.

33. Betty Maple, "How to Succeed in the Corporate World," *Spectrum* 1996, 15–19.

34. Maynard, *Jobs People Do*, 20.

Bibliography

ARCHIVES AND COLLECTIONS

American Institute of Certified Public Accountants (AICPA) Library, Jersey City, N.J.

Bell, Daniel. "Crisis of Our Times." *American Institute of Certified Public Accountants Plenary Session*. Washington, D.C., 15 October 1968.

Boyer, Robert. "Aid to Minority Business Enterprise: A Challenge to the Profession." In *Proceedings of Council of the American Institute of Certified Public Accountants*. Detroit, 9 October 1971.

Career Development Seminar Report, 1978. New York: American Institute of Certified Public Accountants Minority Recruitment and Equal Opportunity Committee, 1978.

Certified Public Accountants Laws, Rules, and Information Handbook 14. New York: The University of the State of New York, 1921.

Goldsen, Joseph M. "Prospects in Social Development." In *Eightieth Annual Meeting of the American Institute of Certified Public Accountants*. Portland, Ore., 24–27 September 1967.

Lang, Edwin R. "The Disadvantaged Program: One Year Later." *Annual Spring Meeting of Council of the American Institute of Certified Public Accountants*. Boca Raton, Fla., 4–6 May 1970.

———. "The Education and Recruitment of Ethnic Minority Students for the Accounting Profession." *American Institute of Certified Public Accountants Meeting of Council*. Colorado Springs, 5 May 1969.

Minutes, 54th Annual Meeting, American Institute of Accountants General Sessions. Detroit, 15, 18 September 1941.

Palen, Jennie M. "Women in Public Accounting." Pamphlet, ca. 1951.

Proceedings, Council Meetings, American Institute of Accountants. New York, 11–12 May 1942.

Proceedings, Council Meetings of the American Institute of Certified Public Accountants. Colorado Springs, 3 May 1965.

Proceedings, Eighty-ninth Annual Meeting of the AICPA. Philadelphia, 23 October 1976.

Proceedings of Spring Council Meeting, American Institute of Certified Public Accountants. Colorado Springs, 5–7 May 1969.

Report on Minority Accounting Graduates, Enrollment, and Public Accounting Professionals. New York: American Institute of Certified Public Accountants, 1976–89, 1994–97.

Upward Mobility of Women Special Committee Report to the AICPA Board of Directors. New York: American Institute of Certified Public Accountants, 1988.

Atlanta University, Atlanta, Ga., Clipping File: Jesse B. Blayton

"Blayton to Speak for 'Guide Right' This Sunday." *Atlanta Daily World*, 24 April 1936, no page number.

"Get Blayton as Chief Speaker." *Atlanta Daily World*, 15 December 1936, no page number.

"Negro Banks Fill Real Economic Need, Declares J. B. Blayton." *Atlanta Daily World*, 22 December 1936, no page number.

Boston University, Boston, Mass., Martin Luther King Jr. Papers
Jesse B. Blayton invoice to Martin Luther King Jr., 10 June 1959, Box 1, Folder 24.
Jesse B. Blayton invoice to Martin Luther King Jr., 8 June 1960, Box 1, Folder 24.
Jesse B. Blayton letter to Martin Luther King Jr., 29 April 1960, Box 1, Folder 24.
Jesse B. Blayton letter to William R. Ming Jr. (King attorney), 8 April 1960, Box 1, Folder 24.
Hubert T. Delany (King attorney) letter to Martin Luther King Jr., 2 May 1960, Box 1, Folder 24.
"Some Important Fiscal Facts about SCLC," ca. 1958, Box 1, Folder 18.

Schomburg Center for Research in Black Culture, New York Public Library, New York, N.Y., Clipping Files: Accountants
"Jersey to Certify Negro as a Public Accountant." *New York Times*, 5 December 1954, no page number.
Richard Rogin, "John Henry Howell Makes It (into the Middle Class)." *NYT Magazine*, 24 June 1973, no page number.

Schomburg Center for Research in Black Culture, New York Public Library, New York, N.Y., Clipping Files: John W. Cromwell Sr.
"John W. Cromwell, Noted Historian, Dead in Capital." *New York Age*, 23 April 1927, no page number.
"Notes," *Journal of Negro History* (1927): 564–66.

INTERVIEWS

Aiken, William. New York, N.Y., 22 May 1989.
Anderson, William. Chicago, Ill., 10 December 1992.
Anonymous African American partners and white recruiters in Big Eight accounting firms, April, May, and December 1989.
Austin, Richard H. Telephone, 17 September 1992, 24 February 1993.
Banks, Frank. Telephone, 6 June 2001.
Beckett, Charles, and Jean Chambliss. Chicago, Ill., 8 December 1992.
Booker, Quinton. Jackson, Miss., 13 August 1998.
Briloff, Abraham. New York, N.Y., 1 November 1996.
Broadus, Jerome. Washington, D.C., 10 January 1992.
Bruno, Michael. New Orleans, La., 15 August 1998.
Christian, Chauncey, Jr. Framingham, Mass., 18 June 1992, 31 May 2001.
Clark, Johnnie. Atlanta, Ga., 30 June 1993.
Collins, William D. Los Angeles, Calif., 3 October 1997, 20 December 1999.
Cooke, Calvin. Telephone, 13 January 1992.
Coulthurst, Audley. New York, N.Y., 11 March 1992.
Craig, Quiester. Dallas, Tex., 16 August 1997.
Crockett, Benjamin. Chicago, Ill., 4 December 1992.
Davenport, Ernest. Silver Spring, Md., 11 January 1992.
Fambro, Edmond. Chicago, Ill., 9 December 1992.

Ford, Frederick. Chicago, Ill., 4 December 1992.
Garrett, Nathan. Durham, N.C., 29 May 1997.
Gines, Bernadine C. New York, N.Y., 11 March 1992.
Goodall, William. Telephone, 1 October 1999.
Hale, Larzette. Dallas, Tex., 17 August 1997.
Harris, Ruth C. E-mail, 16 November 1998.
Harrison, Lincoln. Telephone, 27 August 1992, 28 January 1993.
Hill, Robert E. Silver Spring, Md., 22 May 1989.
Jenkins, Edwin. New York, N.Y., 22 May 1989.
Jones, Theodore. Chicago, Ill., 7 December 1992.
Kelly, David. Chicago, Ill., 9 December 1992.
King, Benjamin, Sr. Baltimore, Md., 1 November 1997.
Lee, Carroll. Lanham, Md., 11 January 1992.
Little, Isaac. Chicago, Ill., 8 December 1992.
Lucas, Wilmer F., Jr. Telephone, 13 December 1997.
McFadden, Gwendolyn. Greensboro, N.C., 30 May 1998.
McKeever, Lester. Chicago, Ill., 7 December 1992.
Mitchell, Bert N. New York, N.Y., 17 November 1997.
Pittman, Hiram. Chicago, Ill., 9 December 1992, 13 August 1996.
Previts, Gary. Chestnut Hill, Mass., 2 October 1999.
Reynolds, Arthur. Washington, D.C., 10 January 1992.
Ross, Frank. Washington, D.C., 16 August 1997.
Rutherford, Theodora. Telephone, 11 June 1992.
Saddler, Willie B. Atlanta, Ga., 17 June 1997.
Tillman, Talmadge, Jr. Chicago, Ill., 13 August 1996.
Tinius, David. Telephone, 18 September 1998.
Whiting, Elmer. Telephone, 15 September 1992.
Wilfong, Henry. Los Angeles, Calif., 3 October 1997, 8 July 1999, 20 December 1999.
Williams, Edward. Chicago, Ill., 8 December 1992.
Wilson, John. Chicago, Ill., 8 December 1992.
Wilson, Milton. Silver Spring, Md., 16 November 1991, 2 May 1999, 24 June 1999.

GOVERNMENT PUBLICATIONS

U.S. Bureau of the Census. *Fifteenth U.S. Census, 1930.* Washington, D.C.: Government Printing Office, 1930.
——. *Eighteenth U.S. Census, 1960.* Washington, D.C.: Government Printing Office, 1960.
——. *Statistical Abstract of the United States, 1998.* Washington, D.C.: Government Printing Office, 1998.
U.S. Department of Commerce. *Statistical Abstract of the United States, 1940.* Washington, D.C.: Government Printing Office, 1940.
——. *Statistical Abstract of the United States, 1960.* Washington, D.C.: Government Printing Office, 1960.
U.S. Senate. Committee on Government Operations. *The Accounting Establishment: A Staff Study Prepared by the Subcommittee on Reports, Accounting and Management.* 95th Cong., 1st sess., 1977. Washington, D.C.: Government Printing Office, 1977.

PERIODICALS

Accounting Today, 1992–93, 1998
American University Report, 1973
Arkansas Democrat-Gazette, 1997
Arthur Andersen Chronicle, 1971
Atlanta Daily World, 1936, 1977
Atlanta Historical Bulletin, 1977
Atlanta Journal and Constitution, 1993
Atlantic Monthly, 1947
Aviation Daily, 1992, 1994
Baltimore Sun, 1995
Black Enterprise, 1972–94
Black Issues in Higher Education, 1999
Business Week, 1964–65, 1972
Change, 1994
Charleston Post and Courier, 1996
Chattanooga Free Press, 1995
Chicago Daily Tribune, 1927
Chicago Defender, 1986
Chicago Sun-Times, 1993
Chicago Tribune, 1987, 1994, 1996, 1998
Chronicle of Higher Education, 1987, 1989
Color, 1951
Commercial Appeal (Memphis, Tenn.),
   1997, 1999
Connecticut CPA, 1974
Connecticut Law Tribune, 1995
The CPA, 1957, 1971
CPA Journal, 1971–72, 1978, 1985, 1995
CPA Review, 1970
The Crisis (NAACP), 1929–45, 1958
Crystal City (Va.) News, 1972
Dallas Morning News, 1994
E&E (Ernst & Ernst), 1971
Ebony, 1981
Federal News Service, 1995
Government Executive, 1997
Greensboro (N.C.) News & Record, 1998
Inc., 1999
Infotrack (KPMG), 1999
International Accounting Bulletin, 1997
Jet, 1953–57, 1960, 1969, 1972, 1977–78, 1996
Journal of Accountancy, 1915–99
Journal of College Placement, 1975
Los Angeles Times, 1985, 1990, 1992, 1996
Louisville Courier-Journal, 1991, 1997

Manpower (U.S. Department of Labor), 1970
Maryland CPA Quarterly, 1972
Massachusetts CPA Review, 1968
*The Messenger: New Opinion of the New
   Negro*, 1922–28
Miami Herald, 1980–81, 1984
Minneapolis Star Tribune, 1998
Montgomery Advertiser, 1960, 1998
The Nation, 1994
National Journal, 1989
National Public Accountant, 1962
Nation's Business, 1970
Negro History Bulletin, 1957
New Accountant, 1986–90, 1994
New Orleans Times-Picayune, 1993, 1997
New Republic, 1969
Newsday, 1988–89, 1992
Newsday Magazine, 1990
Newsweek, 1971
New York Age, 1927, 1954–55
New York Amsterdam News, 1969, 1971–73,
   1980, 1986
New York Certified Public Accountant, 1964,
   1970
New York Daily Challenge, 1975, 1978
New York Times, 1954–98
New York Times Magazine, 1973, 1986
Ohio CPA Journal, 1986
Our World, 1951
Outlook (California Society of CPAs), 1981,
   1999
Pennsylvania CPA Spokesman, 1969, 1973
Philadelphia Tribune, 1995
Practical Accountant, 1990, 1996
Practicing CPA, 1985
Price Waterhouse & Co. Review, 1973
PR Newswire, 1983, 1988
Professional Services Review, 1994
Public Accounting Report, 1983, 1993–95
PUSH Magazine, 1991
Richmond Times-Dispatch, 1997–98
Salt Lake Tribune, 1994
San Francisco Recorder, 2000
Spectrum (National Association of Black
   Accountants), 1974, 1990–98

Technology Review, 1991
Texas Magazine, 1997
The Times (London), 1996
United Press International, 1981
USA Today, 1990, 1997

Wall Street Journal, 1964–98
Washington Post, 1977, 1979–80, 1983–84,
    1995
World Accounting Report, 1987

BOOKS AND ARTICLES

Abbot, Andrew. *The System of Professions: An Essay on the Division of Expert Labor.*
    Chicago: University of Chicago Press, 1988.
Accountants' Indexes. New York: American Institute of Accountants, 1920–60.
Adams, Edwards A. "Doors Didn't Open Easily for Howard's Class of '57." *National Law
    Journal*, 29 December 1986, 24–37.
Agnew, Donald C. "Foundation Support of Education for Black Americans in the South."
    Journal of Negro Education 40, no. 3 (1971): 240–47.
Aiken, William. *The Black Experience in Large Public Accounting Firms.* New York: National
    Association of Black Accountants, 1971.
Alkire, Durwood L. *The Accounting Profession in Washington State: One Hundred Years of
    Progress.* Dubuque, Iowa: Kendall/Hunt Publishing, 1989.
Allen, David Grayson, and Kathleen McDermott. *Accounting for Success: A History of Price
    Waterhouse in America.* Boston: Harvard Business School Press, 1993.
Allen, Henry Lee. "The Mobility of Black Collegiate Faculty Revisited: Whatever
    Happened to the 'Brain Drain'?" *Journal of Negro Education* 60, no. 1 (1991): 97–109.
The American Association of Collegiate Schools of Business, 1916–1966. Homewood, Ill.:
    Richard D. Irwin, 1966.
Anderson, James D. *The Education of Blacks in the South, 1860–1935.* Chapel Hill:
    University of North Carolina Press, 1988.
Andrew, John A. *Lyndon Johnson and the Great Society.* Chicago: Ivan R. Dee, 1998.
Annual Catalogue of Howard University, 1920. Washington, D.C.: Howard University,
    1920.
Annual Catalogue of Howard University, 1924. Washington, D.C.: Howard University, 1940.
Annual Report of the United States Firm, Price Waterhouse & Company. New York: Price
    Waterhouse & Company, 30 June 1973.
Aptheker, Herbert. *A Documentary History of the Negro People in the United States.* New
    York: Citadel Press, 1964.
Asgill, Amanda. "The Importance of Accreditation: Perceptions of Black and White
    College Presidents." *Journal of Negro Education* 45, no. 3 (1976): 284–94.
Barlow, William. *Voice Over: The Making of Black Radio.* Philadelphia: Temple University
    Press, 1999.
Barr, Alwyn, and Robert Calvert. *Black Leaders, Texans for Their Times.* Austin: Texas State
    Historical Association, 1981.
Basalla, Susan. "African Americans Who Broke the Color Barrier at America's Leading
    Business Schools." *Journal of Blacks in Higher Education* 6 (Winter 1994–95): 81–86.
Bayer, Alan E. *The Black College Freshman: Characteristics and Recent Trends.* Washington,
    D.C.: Office of Research, American Council on Education, 1972.
Bennett, Michael J. *When Dreams Came True: The GI Bill and the Making of Modern
    America.* Washington, D.C.: Brassey's, 1996.

Beschloss, Michael. *Taking Charge: The Johnson White House Tapes, 1963–1964*. New York: Simon and Schuster, 1997.

Billingsley, Andrew. "Building Strong Faculties in Black Colleges." *Journal of Negro Education* 51, no. 1 (1982): 4–15.

The Bison, Class of 1923. Washington, D.C.: Howard University, 1923.

Blackwell, James. *Mainstreaming Outsiders: The Production of Black Professionals*. Dix Hills, N.Y.: General Hall, 1987.

Blayton, Jesse B. *The Need for Better Records in Negro Business: An Opportunity for Negro Accountants*. Bulletin 11. Atlanta: National Youth Administration of Georgia, Colored Division, 1939.

Bound, John, and Richard Freeman. "What Went Wrong?: The Erosion of Relative Earnings and Employment among Young Black Men in the 1980s." *Quarterly Journal of Economics* 107, no. 2 (1992): 201–32.

Bowles, Frank, and Frank DeCosta. *Between Two Worlds: A Profile of Negro Higher Education*. New York: McGraw-Hill, 1971.

Branch, Taylor. *Parting the Waters: America in the King Years, 1954–1963*. New York: Simon and Schuster, 1988.

Brazziel, William F. *Quality Education for All Americans*. Washington, D.C.: Howard University Press, 1974.

Brown, Aaron. "Graduate and Professional Education in Negro Institutions." *Journal of Negro Education* 27, no. 3 (1958): 233–42.

Callcott, George. *Maryland and America, 1940 to 1980*. Baltimore: Johns Hopkins University Press, 1985.

Campfield, William. "An Approach to Formulation of Professional Standards for Internal Auditors." *Accounting Review* 35, no. 3 (1960): 521–27.

———. "A Blueprint for Appraising and Guiding Audit Staff." *Accounting Review* 32, no. 4 (1957): 625–29.

———. "A Broad-Gauge Course in Governmental Accounting." *Accounting Review* 33, no. 4 (1958): 669–75.

———. "Critical Paths for Professional Accountants during the New Management Revolution." *Accounting Review* 38, no. 3 (1963): 521–27.

———. "Experiences in Extension of Staff Training to In-Charge Auditors." *Accounting Review* 30, no. 2 (1955): 293–97.

———. "Good Judgement and Public Accounting Practice." *Accounting Review* 27, no. 1 (1952): 73–78.

———. "A Governmental Agency's Program for Developing Its Professional Accountants." *Accounting Review* 37, no. 2 (1962): 295–99.

———. "Professional Status for Internal Auditors." *Accounting Review* 40, no. 3 (1965): 594–98.

———. "Re-Examination of Basis and Opportunities for Applying Accounting Judgment." *Accounting Review* 34, no. 4 (1959): 555–63.

———. "Toward Making Accounting Education Adaptive and Normative." *Accounting Review* 45, no. 4 (1970): 683–89.

———. "Training for Law and for Public Accounting." *Accounting Review* 28, no. 3 (1953): 401–11.

Carey, John L. *The Rise of the Accounting Profession: From Technician to Professional, 1896–1936*. New York: American Institute of Certified Public Accountants, 1969.

———. *The Rise of the Accounting Profession: To Responsibility and Authority, 1937–1969*. New York: American Institute of Certified Public Accountants, 1970.

The Carnegie Commission on Higher Education, from Isolation to Mainstream: Problems of the Colleges Founded for Negroes. New York: McGraw-Hill, 1971.

Chadakoff, Rochelle, ed. *Eleanor Roosevelt's "My Day": Her Acclaimed Columns, 1936–1945*. New York: Pharos Books, 1989.

Christy, Ralph D., and Lionel Williamson, eds. *A Century of Service: Land Grant Colleges and Universities, 1890–1990*. New Brunswick, N.J.: Transaction Publishers, 1992.

Crawford, George Williamson. *The Talladega Manual of Vocational Guidance*. Talladega, Ala.: Board of Trustees, Talladega College, 1937.

Cripps, Thomas. *Making Movies Black: The Hollywood Message Movie from World War II to the Civil Rights Era*. New York: Oxford University Press, 1993.

Dallek, Robert. *Flawed Giant: Lyndon Johnson and His Times, 1961–1973*. New York: Oxford University Press, 1998.

Delany, Sarah, and A. Elizabeth Delany, with Amy Hill Hearth. *Having Our Say: The Delany Sisters' First 100 Years*. New York: Kondansha International, 1993.

Derbigny, I. A. "Tuskegee Looks at Its Veterans." *Quarterly Review of Higher Education among Negroes* 14, no. 1 (1946): 11–18.

Derrick, Noah E. *The South Carolina Society of Certified Public Accountants, 1915–1965*. Columbia, S.C.: South Carolina Association of Certified Public Accountants, 1965.

Drake, St. Clair, and Horace R. Cayton. *Black Metropolis: A Study of Negro Life in a Northern City*. 1945. Reprint, Chicago: University of Chicago Press, 1993.

Du Bois, W. E. B. *The Souls of Black Folk*. New York: Penguin Books, 1969.

——, ed. *The College-Bred Negro: Report of a Social Study Made under the Direction of Atlanta University*. Atlanta: Atlanta University Press, 1900.

——. *The Negro in Business: Report of a Social Study Made under the Direction of Atlanta University*. Atlanta: Atlanta University, 1899.

Duker, Jacob, and Jacque D. Grinnell. "Accountancy: Opportunity for Black Economic Penetration." *Review of Black Political Economy* 7, no. 1 (1977): 373–82.

Dulaney, W. Marvin. *Black Police in America*. Bloomington: Indiana University Press, 1996.

Duncan, Otis Dudley, and Beverly Duncan. *The Negro Population of Chicago: A Study of Residential Succession*. Chicago: University of Chicago Press, 1957.

"Editorial Comment: The Vocational Guidance of Negroes." *Journal of Negro Education* 4, no. 1 (1935): 1–4.

"Editorial Note." *Journal of Negro Education* 4, no. 3 (1935): 289–92.

Edwards, James Don. *History of Public Accounting in the United States*. Tuscaloosa: University of Alabama Press, 1978.

Egerton, John. *Speak Now against the Day: The Generation before the Civil Rights Movement in the South*. Chapel Hill: University of North Carolina Press, 1994.

Fichter, Joseph. "Career Preparation and Expectations of Negro College Seniors." *Journal of Negro Education* 35, no. 4 (1966): 322–35.

——. *Special Report on Graduates of Predominantly Negro Colleges, Class of 1964*. Washington, D.C.: U.S. Department of Health, Education and Welfare, undated.

Freeman, Richard. *Black Elite: The New Market for Highly Educated Black Americans*. New York: McGraw-Hill, 1976.

Gates, Henry Louis, Jr. *Colored People*. New York: Vintage, 1994.

Gatewood, Willard B. *Aristocrats of Color: The Black Elite, 1880–1920*. Bloomington: Indiana University Press, 1990.

Gibson, Mary. *The Dunbar Story (1870–1950)*. New York: Vantage Press, 1965.

Gifford, William. "Accounting's Aim." *Journal of College Placement* 35, no. 2 (1975): 40–45.

Glazer, Nathan. *Affirmative Discrimination: Ethnic Inequality and Public Policy.* New York: Basic Books, 1975.

Glickstein, Howard. "Federal Education Programs and Minority Groups." *Journal of Negro Education* 38, no. 3 (1969): 303–14.

Goodwin, Doris Kearns. *No Ordinary Time: Franklin and Eleanor Roosevelt: The Home Front in World War II.* New York: Simon and Schuster, 1994.

Gordon, Asa H. *Sketches of Negro Life and History in South Carolina.* Columbia: University of South Carolina Press, 1971.

Gordon, Milton A. "An Analysis of Enrollment Data for Black Students in Institutions of Higher Education from 1940–1972." *Journal of Negro Education* 45, no. 2 (1976): 117–21.

Gordon, Robert Aaron, and James Edwin Howell. *Higher Education for Business.* New York: Columbia University Press, 1959.

Graham, Lawrence Otis. *The Best Companies for Minorities.* New York: Plume, 1993.

Grant, Julia, ed. *The New York State Society of Certified Public Accountants: Foundation for a Profession.* New York: Garland Publishing, 1995.

Greene, Harry Washington. *Holders of Doctorates among American Negroes.* Boston: Meador Publishing Company, 1946.

Grossman, James R. *Land of Hope: Chicago, Black Southerners, and the Great Migration.* Chicago: University of Chicago Press, 1989.

Halberstam, David. *The Fifties.* New York: Fawcett Columbine, 1993.

Hamilton, Diane Slaughter, ed. *History of the West Virginia Society of Certified Public Accountants.* Charleston: West Virginia Society of Certified Public Accountants, 1990.

Hammond, Theresa. "African-American Certified Public Accountants." In *African Americans and Business: The Path toward Empowerment.* Washington, D.C.: Association for the Study of Afro-American Life and History, 1998.

——. "African-American Female Accountants: The Stories and the Statistics." *Advances in Accountability: Regulation, Research, Gender and Justice* 8 (2001): 275–77.

——. "Culture and Gender in Accounting Research: Going beyond Mynatt, et al." *Critical Perspectives on Accounting* 8 (1997): 685–92.

——. "From Complete Exclusion to Minimal Inclusion: African Americans and the Public Accounting Industry, 1965–1988." *Accounting, Organizations and Society* 22, no. 1 (1997): 29–53.

——. "Histories Outside the Mainstream: Women and African Americans in the Accounting Profession." In *Methodologies in Accounting History Research.* Stamford: JAI Inc., 2002.

——. "Some Considerations in Attracting and Retaining African-American Doctoral Candidates in Accounting." *Issues in Accounting Education* (1995): 143–58.

——. "Témoignage et Histoire des Comptables Noirs-Americains: L'histoire de Theodora Rutherford." Translated by Yvone Pesqueux. *Comptabilité, Contrôle, Audit* (September 1998): 109–20.

Hammond, Theresa, and Denise Streeter. "Overcoming Barriers: Early African-American Certified Public Accountants." *Accounting Organizations and Society* 19, no. 3 (1994): 271–88.

Harris, Abraham L. *The Negro as Capitalist: A Study of Banking and Business among American Negroes.* Chicago: Urban Research Press, 1992.

Harris, Nelson H. "Publicly-Supported Negro Higher Institutions of Learning in North Carolina." *Journal of Negro Education* 31, no. 3 (1962): 284–91.

Harrison, Lincoln J. "The Role of the Negro Business School in Promoting Black Capitalism." *Journal of Negro Education* 40, no. 1 (1971): 45–47.

———. "The Status of the Negro CPA in the United States." *Journal of Negro Education* 31, no. 4 (1962): 503–6.

Hasselback, James R. *Accounting Faculty Directory, 2000–01.* Upper Saddle River, N.J.: Prentice Hall, 2000.

Hasty, Thomas Jefferson, III. "Minority Business Enterprise Development and the Small Business Administration's 8 (a) Program: Past, Present, and (Is There a) Future?" *Military Law Review* 145 (Summer 1994): 1–112.

Haynes, Uric, Jr. "Equal Job Opportunity: The Credibility Gap." *Harvard Business Review* 46, no. 3 (1968): 113–20.

Heck, J. Louis, and Wayne G. Bremser. "Six Decades of *The Accounting Review*: A Summary of Author and Institutional Contributors." *Accounting Review* 61, no. 4 (1986): 735–44.

Herbold, Hilary. "Never a Level Playing Field: Blacks and the GI Bill." *Journal of Blacks in Higher Education* 6 (Winter 1994/1995): 104–8.

Hine, Darlene Clark. *Black Women in White: Racial Conflict and Cooperation in the Nursing Profession.* Bloomington: Indiana University Press, 1989.

The History of Black Accountancy: The First 100 Black CPAs. Washington, D.C.: National Association of Black Accountants, 1990.

History of Florida Institute of Certified Public Accountants, 1905–1963. N.p.: Florida Institute of Certified Public Accountants, 1963.

A History of the CPA Profession in Missouri. St. Louis: Missouri Society of Certified Public Accountants, 1983.

History of the Oklahoma Society of Certified Public Accountants, 1918–1968. Oklahoma City: Oklahoma Society of Certified Public Accountants, 1967.

Hope, John, II, and Edward E. Shelton. "The Negro in the Federal Government." *Journal of Negro Education* 32, no. 4 (1963): 367–74.

Horton, James. "Black Education at Oberlin College: A Controversial Commitment." *Journal of Negro Education* 54, no. 4 (1985): 477–99.

Houston, Charles H. "The Need for Negro Lawyers." *Journal of Negro Education* 4, no. 1 (1935): 49–52.

Ingham, John N., and Lynne B. Feldman. *African-American Business Leaders: A Biographical Dictionary.* Westport, Conn.: Greenwood Press, 1994.

Jaffe, A. J., Walter Adams, and Sandra G. Meyers. *Negro Higher Education in the 1960s.* New York: Praeger, 1968.

Jencks, Christopher, and David Riesman. *The Academic Revolution.* Chicago: University of Chicago Press, 1977.

Jenkins, Martin D. "Significant Programs in Institutions of Higher Education of Negroes." *Educational Record* 26, no. 1 (1945): 301–11.

Johnson, Charles S. *The Negro College Graduate.* College Park, Md.: McGrath Publishing Company, 1969.

Johnson, John H., with Lerone Bennett. *Succeeding against the Odds.* New York: Amistad Press, 1989.

Kanter, Rosabeth Moss. *Men and Women of the Corporation.* New York: Basic Books, 1977.

Khan, Zafar, Sudhir Chawla, and Elton Devine. "Impact of Gender, Race, and Dress on Choice of CPA." *Journal of Applied Business Research* 13, no. 1 (1996–97): 53–68.

Kisseloff, Jeff. *The Box: An Oral History of Television, 1920–1961*. New York: Penguin, 1995.

Kluger, Richard. *Simple Justice: The History of Brown v. Board of Education and Black America's Struggle for Equality*. New York: Random House, 1975.

Krause, Elliott. *Death of the Guilds: Professions, States, and the Advance of Capitalism, 1930 to the Present*. New Haven: Yale University Press, 1996.

Kurth, Peter. *American Cassandra: The Life of Dorothy Thompson*. Boston: Little, Brown and Company, 1990.

Larson, Magali Sarfatti. *The Rise of Professionalism: A Sociological Analysis*. Berkeley: University of California Press, 1977.

Le Breton, Preston, ed. *The Dynamic World of Education for Business: Issues, Trends, Forecasts*. Chicago: Southwestern Publishing, 1969.

Lemann, Nicholas. *The Promised Land: The Great Black Migration and How It Changed America*. New York: Knopf, 1991.

Lewis, John, with Michael D'Orso. *Walking with the Wind: A Memoir of the Movement*. New York: Simon and Schuster, 1998.

Lichtenstein, Nelson. *Walter Reuther: The Most Dangerous Man in Detroit*. Urbana: University of Illinois Press, 1995.

Littlejohn, E. J., and D. L. Hobson. "Black Lawyers, Law Practice, and Bar Associations, 1844 to 1970: A Michigan History." *Wayne State Law Review* 33, no. 1605 (1987): 1625–91.

Loevy, Robert D. *The Civil Rights Act of 1964: The Passage of the Law That Ended Racial Segregation*. Albany: State University of New York Press, 1997.

Logan, Rayford W. *Howard University: The First Hundred Years, 1867–1967*. New York: New York University Press, 1969.

Mabee, Carleton. *Black Education in New York State: From Colonial to Modern Times*. Syracuse, N.Y.: Syracuse University Press, 1979.

Mann, Robert. *The Walls of Jericho: Lyndon Johnson, Hubert Humphrey, Richard Russell, and the Struggle for Civil Rights*. New York: Harcourt Brace, 1996.

Mason, Herman, Jr. *Going against the Wind: A Pictorial History of African Americans in Atlanta*. Atlanta: Longstreet Press, 1992.

Maynard, Christopher. *Jobs People Do*. New York: DK Publishing, 1997.

Meeth, L. Richard. "Breaking Racial Barriers, Part I: Interracial Student Exchange Programs." *Journal of Higher Education* 37, no. 3 (1966): 137–43.

Meier, August. *Negro Thought in America, 1880–1915*. Ann Arbor: University of Michigan Press, 1963.

Meier, August, and Elliot Rudwick. *Black Detroit and the Rise of the UAW*. Oxford: Oxford University Press, 1979.

Merrill, Dennis, ed. *President Truman's Attempts to Put the Principles of Racial Justice into Law, 1948–1950*. Vol. 12 of *Documentary History of the Truman Presidency*. N.p.: University Publications of America, 1996.

Miles to Go: Progress of Minorities in the Legal Profession. New York: American Bar Association, Commission on Opportunities for Minorities in the Profession, 1998.

Miller, Loren. *The Petitioners: The Story of the Supreme Court of the United States and the Negro*. Cleveland: World Publishing, 1966.

Miranti, Paul J., Jr. *Accountancy Comes of Age: The Development of an American Profession, 1886–1940*. Chapel Hill: University of North Carolina Press, 1990.

Mitchell, Bert. "Ethics, the Black Minority, and the CPA Profession." In *Abraham J. Briloff Lecture Series on Accounting and Society, 1987, 1988, 1989*. Binghamton, N.Y.: School of Management, State University of New York at Binghamton, 1989.

Mohr, Paul, ed. *Black Colleges and Equal Opportunity in Higher Education*. Lincoln, Neb.: Chicago–Southern Network Study Commission on Undergraduate Education and the Education of Teachers, 1975.

Montagna, Paul. *Certified Public Accounting: A Sociological View of a Profession in Change*. Houston: Scholars Book Company, 1974.

Moody, Anne. *Coming of Age in Mississippi*. New York: Dell Publishing, 1968.

Moon, Elaine Latzman. *Untold Tales, Unsung Heroes: An Oral History of Detroit's African-American Community, 1918–1967*. Detroit: Wayne State University Press, 1994.

Moss, James Allen. "Negro Teachers in Predominantly White Colleges." *Journal of Negro Education* 27, no. 4 (1958): 451–62.

Murray, Florence. *The Negro Handbook, 1946–1947*. New York: Current Books, 1947.

Murray, Pauli. *Song in a Weary Throat: An American Pilgrimage*. New York: Harper and Row, 1987.

Negro Year Book, 1952. New York: William H. Wise, 1952.

Nelson, Jack, and Jack Bass. *The Orangeburg Massacre*. New York: World Publishers, 1970.

Organ, Claude H., Jr., and Margaret M. Kosiba, *A Century of Black Surgeons: The USA Experience*. Norman, Okla.: Transcript Press, 1987.

Patterson, Orlando. *The Ordeal of Integration: Progress and Resentment in America's "Racial" Crisis*. Washington, D.C.: Civitas/Counterpoint, 1997.

Perry, John. "Business—Next Target for Integration?" *Harvard Business Review* 4, no. 2 (1963): 104–15.

Petrof, John V. "Business Administration Curricula in Predominantly Negro Colleges." *Journal of Negro Education* 35, no. 3 (1966): 276–79.

Pierce, Joseph A. *Negro Business and Business Education: Their Present and Prospective Development*. New York: Plenum, 1995.

Pierson, Frank C., et al. *The Education of American Business: A Study of University-College Programs in Business Administration*. New York: McGraw-Hill, 1959.

Plaut, Richard L. "Plans for Assisting Negro Students to Enter and to Remain in College." *Journal of Negro Education* 35, no. 4 (1966): 393–99.

Policies, Procedures and Standards. St. Louis: American Association of Collegiate Schools of Business Accreditation Council, 1976–77.

Porter, Gilbert L. "Negro Publicly-Supported Higher Institutions in Florida." *Journal of Negro Education* 31, no. 3 (1962): 293–98.

Previts, Gary John, and Barabara Dubis Merino. *A History of Accounting in America: An Historical Interpretation of the Cultural Significance of Accounting*. New York: Wiley, 1979.

Purcell, Theodore V. "Break Down Your Employment Barriers." *Harvard Business Review* 46, no. 4 (1968): 65–76.

Quarles, Benjamin. "The Background of the 1947 College Student." *Quarterly Review of Higher Education among Negroes* 15, no. 1 (1947): 87–90.

Reed, Christopher Robert. *The Chicago NAACP and the Rise of Black Professional Leadership, 1910–1966*. Bloomington: Indiana University Press, 1997.

Report on the Status of Blacks in the CPA Profession. New York: New York State Society of Certified Public Accountants, 1990.

Rhodes, Lelia Gaston. *Jackson State University, The First Hundred Years, 1877–1977*. Jackson: University Press of Mississippi, 1979.

Rogers, Edward D. "When Logic and Reality Collide: The Supreme Court and Minority Business Set-Asides." *Columbia Journal of Law and Social Problems* 24 (1990): 117–68.

Roscoe, Wilma J., ed. *Accreditation of Historically and Predominantly Black Colleges and Universities*. New York: University Press of America, 1989.

Rosenbloom, Richard S., and John K. Shank. "Let's Write Off the MESBICs." *Harvard Business Review* 48, no. 5 (1970): 90–97.

Schneider, Stephen. *The Availability of Minorities and Women for Professional and Managerial Positions, 1970–1985*. Philadelphia: Industrial Research Unit, Wharton School, University of Pennsylvania, 1977.

Schwartz, Bernard. *Behind Bakke: Affirmative Action and the Supreme Court*. New York: New York University Press, 1988.

Seder, John, and Berkeley Burrell. *Getting It Together: Black Businessmen in America*. New York: Harcourt, 1971.

Sewell, George A., and Margaret L. Dwight. *Mississippi Black History Makers*. Jackson: University Press of Mississippi, 1984.

Sheldahl, Terry K. *Beta Alpha Psi, from Alpha to Omega: Pursuing a Vision of Professional Education for Accountants, 1919–1945*. New York: Garland Press, 1982.

Simmons, Howard. "The Accreditation Process as a Factor in the Improvement of Traditionally Black Institutions." *Journal of Negro Education* 53, no. 4 (1984): 400–405.

Simmons, William J. *Men of Mark: Eminent, Progressive and Rising*. Cleveland: G. M. Rewell, 1887.

Sims, William. "Guest Editorial: Black Colleges—Bicentennial Offers Little Hope." *Journal of Negro Education* 45, no. 3 (1976): 219–24.

Sinclair, Andrew. *The Available Man: The Life behind the Masks of Warren Gamaliel Harding*. New York: Macmillan, 1967.

Sitkoff, Harvard. *The Depression Decade*. Vol. 1 of *A New Deal for Blacks: The Emergence of Civil Rights as a National Issue*. New York: Oxford University Press, 1978.

——. *The Struggle for Black Equality, 1954–1992*. New York: Hill and Wang, 1993.

Smigel, Erwin. *The Wall Street Lawyer*. Bloomington: Indiana University Press, 1969.

Smith, Lillian. *Killers of the Dream*. New York: W. W. Norton, 1994.

Spacek, Leonard. *The Growth of Arthur Andersen & Co., 1928–1973: An Oral History*. New York: Garland, 1989.

Spearman, Leonard. "Federal Roles and Responsibilities Relative to the Higher Education of Blacks since 1967." *Journal of Negro Education* 50, no. 3 (1981): 285–98.

Spruill, Albert W. *Great Recollections for Aggieland: A Human Interest Account of the Development of the Agricultural and Technical College of North Carolina from 1893–1960*. Wilmington, N.C.: Whitehead Printing Company, 1964.

Stans, Maurice H. *One of the Presidents' Men: Twenty Years with Eisenhower and Nixon*. Washington, D.C.: Brassey's, 1995.

Stevens, Mark. *The Big Eight*. New York: Macmillan, 1981.

Sturdivant, Frederick. "The Limits of Black Capitalism." *Harvard Business Review* 47, no. 1 (1969): 122–28.

Sullivan, Patricia. *Days of Hope: Race and Democracy in the New Deal Era*. Chapel Hill: University of North Carolina Press, 1996.

Summary Report: Doctorate Recipients from United States Universities. Washington, D.C.: National Academy Press, 1983–98.

Terry, William E. *Origin and Development of Texas Southern University*. Houston: William Terry, 1978.

Thomas, David A., and John J. Gabarro. *Breaking Through: The Making of Minority Executives in Corporate America*. Boston: Harvard Business School Press, 1999.

Thompson, Charles H. "Editorial Comment: Some Critical Aspects of the Problem of the Higher and Professional Education for Negroes." *Journal of Negro Education* 14, no. 4 (1945): 509–26.

Thompson, Daniel C. "Problems of Faculty Morale." *Journal of Negro Education* 29, no. 1 (1960): 37–46.

Tinsley, James A. *History of the Texas State Board of Public Accountancy, 1915–1981*. Austin: Texas State Board of Public Accountancy, 1983.

———. *Texas Society of Certified Public Accountants: A History, 1915–1981*. College Station: Texas A&M University Press, 1983.

Travis, D. J. *An Autobiography of Black Politics*. Chicago: Urban Research Press, 1987.

Tushnet, Mark V. *The NAACP's Legal Strategy against Segregated Education, 1925–1950*. Chapel Hill: University of North Carolina Press, 1987.

University of Illinois Yearbook. Urbana: University of Illinois, 1947–49.

University of San Francisco Catalogue for 96th Year, 1951–1952. San Francisco: University of San Francisco, 1952.

Viator, Ralph. "An Examination of African Americans' Access to Public Accounting Mentors: Perceived Barriers and Intentions to Leave." *Accounting Organizations and Society* 26, no. 6 (2001): 541–62.

Walker, Juliet E. K. *The History of Black Business in America: Capitalism, Race, Entrepreneurship*. New York: Macmillan, 1998.

Wall Street Journal Indexes, 1965–1978. Ann Arbor: University of Michigan Press, 1965–78.

Ware, Gilbert, and Dean Determan. "The Federal Dollar, the Negro College, and the Negro Student." *Journal of Negro Education* 35, no. 4 (1966): 459–68.

Washington, Booker T. *The Negro in Business*. 1907. Reprint, New York: Johnson Reprint Corporation, 1970.

Weems, Robert E., Jr. *Desegregating the Dollar: African American Consumerism in the Twentieth Century*. New York: New York University Press, 1998.

Wescott, Shari H., and Robert E. Seiler. *Women in the Accounting Profession*. New York: Markus Wiener Publishing, 1986.

Who's Who in Finance and Industry. Chicago: Marquis Who's Who, 1984.

Wilkins, David B. "Identities and Roles: Race, Recognition, and Professional Responsibility." *Maryland Law Review* 57, no. 4 (1998): 1502–94.

Wilkins, David B., and G. Mitu Gulati. "Why Are There So Few Black Lawyers in Corporate Law Firms?: An Institutional Analysis." *California Law Review* 84, no. 3 (1996): 493–625.

Willie, Charles. "Philanthropic and Foundation Support for Blacks: A Case Study from the 1960s." *Journal of Negro Education* 50, no. 3 (1981): 270–84.

Yenser, Thomas, ed. *Who's Who in Colored America: A Biographical Dictionary of Notable Living Persons of African Descent in America*. Brooklyn: Yenser, 1940.

Young, Harding B. "Negro Participation in American Business." *Journal of Negro Education* 32, no. 4 (1963): 390–401.

Index